# READINGS

IN

# ANCIENT HISTORY

BY

HUTTON WEBSTER, Ph.D.

PROFESSOR IN THE UNIVERSITY OF NEBRASKA

*Nec historia debet egredi veritatem,
et honeste factis veritas sufficit.*

Pliny the Younger, Epistolæ, vii, 33.

D. C. HEATH & CO., PUBLISHERS

BOSTON          NEW YORK          CHICAGO

930
W

930

930

# PREFACE

THIS volume includes selections from the *Iliad* and the *Odyssey*, and from the writings of Hesiod, Herodotus, Thucydides, Xenophon, Plato, Demosthenes, Arrian, Plutarch, Livy, Cicero, Cæsar, Suetonius, Tacitus, Pliny the Younger, and Martial. Of the twenty-three chapters into which the work is divided, two are devoted to the Oriental period (Herodotus) and one to the Germans (Tacitus). The other chapters deal with Greek and Roman history as seen through the eyes of the classical historians themselves.

The arrangement of the volume follows, in general, that of my *Ancient History*, published simultaneously with it. Each chapter contains the work of a single author and relates to a single definite period or personality. Sufficient editorial matter, in the shape of introductions, notes, and connections between passages, has been supplied to make the book useful to the beginner in ancient history.

The translations quoted have been carefully revised with a view to uniformity and accuracy. All omissions, save those of a trivial character, have been indicated by the usual signs.

Some parts of the book, for instance, the opening chapter on the Oriental peoples and the closing chapter on the Germans, lend themselves to intensive study and may serve to provide an elementary training in historical criticism. The use of the table of contents and of the full index should also suggest helpful topics for essays and reports. Thus, the student may be asked to describe the civilization of the Homeric Age as revealed in the accounts of the Shield of Achilles and the Palace of Alcinous (secs. 13, 16), to set forth the old Roman character as illustrated by the stories of Brutus, Mucius Scævola, and Cincinnatus (secs. 68, 70, 73), to contrast Cæsar's statements about the Germans with the later statements by Tacitus (secs. 94, 119–124), to make a comparative study of the Egyptian, Persian, and Gallic priesthoods (secs. 1, 3, 93). Similar subjects, involving some discipline of the critical faculty, some exercise of the mental powers in discrimination and judgment, should readily occur to the teacher.

My book, however, is not so much a classroom manual as a volume for supplementary reading. In choosing the selections, I have been influenced mainly by the desire to provide immature pupils with a variety of extended, unified, and interesting extracts on matters which a textbook treats with necessary, though none the less deplorable, condensation. Particular emphasis, therefore, has been placed on biography and entertaining narrative. If the work shall help to arouse in the student's mind an attitude of sympathetic appreciation for the great characters and the great deeds of classical antiquity, it will have fulfilled its purpose.

I wish to acknowledge here with hearty thanks the permission graciously granted to me by the Delegates of the Clarendon Press and by Prof. A. W. Mair of Edinburgh University, to use the extracts from Hesiod, by Messrs. G. Bell and Sons, to reproduce certain passages from Mr. E. J. Chinnock's version of Arrian, and by the Walter Scott Publishing Company, to insert various letters of Pliny the Younger, as rendered by Mr. J. B. Firth. The selections from Xenophon, translated by the late H. G. Dakyns, and from Cæsar, translated by Mr. T. Rice Holmes, are used through an agreement with the publishers, Macmillan and Company, London.

HUTTON WEBSTER

LINCOLN, NEBRASKA
*March, 1913*

# CONTENTS

# CONTENTS

# READINGS IN ANCIENT HISTORY

## CHAPTER I

### THREE ORIENTAL PEOPLES AS DESCRIBED BY HERODOTUS[1]

ABOUT the middle of the fifth century before Christ, an enterprising Greek, named Herodotus, set forth upon a series of travels which led him to all parts of the civilized world. By dint of sharp questioning and close observation, Herodotus gained a rich fund of information about lands and peoples, the very existence of which was unknown to many of his countrymen. His impressions are those of an intelligent tourist who, ignorant of any language except his own, spends a few months in a foreign land, busily occupied with sight-seeing. What Herodotus tells us is always interesting, often true, seldom very profound. But we must accept our author for what he is — the first and the most charming of story-tellers.

#### 1. The Egyptians[2]

Concerning Egypt itself I shall extend my remarks to a great length, because there is no country that possesses so many wonders, or any that has such a number of works which defy description. Not only is the climate different from that of the rest of the world, and the rivers unlike any other rivers,

[1] Herodotus. The translation of George Rawlinson, edited by A. J. Grant. 2 vols. London, 1897. John Murray.

[2] Herodotus, ii, 35-37, 65-67, 78, 80, 84-86, 123.

but the people also, in most of their manners and customs, exactly reverse the common practice of mankind. The women attend the markets and trade, while the men sit at home at the loom. While the rest of the world works the woof up the warp, the Egyptians work it down. The women likewise carry burdens upon their shoulders, while the men carry them upon their heads . . . . A woman cannot serve in the priestly office, either for god or goddess, but men are priests to both. Sons need not support their parents unless they choose, but daughters must, whether they wish to do so or not.

In other countries the priests have long hair; in Egypt their heads are shaven. Elsewhere it is customary, in mourning, for near relatives to cut their hair close. The Egyptians, however, who wear no hair at any other time, when they lose a relative, let their beards and the hair of their heads grow long. All other men pass their lives separate from animals; the Egyptians have animals always living with them. Others make barley and wheat their food; it is a disgrace to do so in Egypt, where the grain they live on is spelt.[1] . . . Dough they knead with their feet; but they mix mud, and even take up dirt, with their hands. . . . Their men wear two garments apiece, their women but one. They put on the rings and fasten the ropes to sails inside; others put them outside. When they write or calculate, instead of going, like the Greeks, from left to right, they move the hand from right to left. They insist, notwithstanding, that it is they who go to the right, and the Greeks who go to the left. They have two quite different kinds of writing, one of which is called sacred, the other common.[2]

They are religious to excess, far beyond any other race of men, and use the following ceremonies. They drink out of

[1] One of the most ancient of the varieties of wheat. It is still raised in parts of Europe.

[2] A reference to the so-called hieratic writing, and to the demotic or popular script of the Egyptians in the time of Herodotus. Hieratic writing was a simpler form of the earlier hieroglyphics. Demotic writing, derived from hieratic, came into use about 700 B. C.

brazen cups, which they scour every day. To this practice there is no exception. They wear linen garments, which they are specially careful to have always fresh washed. . . . The priests shave the whole body every other day, that no impure thing may adhere to them when they are engaged in the service of the gods. Their dress is entirely of linen, and their shoes of the papyrus plant. It is not lawful for them to wear either dress or shoes of any other material. They bathe twice every day in cold water, and twice each night; besides which they observe, so to speak, thousands of ceremonies. They enjoy, however, not a few advantages. They consume none of their own property, and are at no expense for anything. Every day bread is baked for them of the sacred corn, and a plentiful supply of beef and of goose flesh is assigned to each, and also a portion of wine made from the grape. Fish they are not allowed to eat. . . . The priests will not even look at beans, which are considered unclean. Instead of a single priest, each god has the attendance of a college, at the head of which is a chief priest. When one of these dies, his son is appointed in his place. . . .

Egypt, though it borders upon Libya,[1] is not a region abounding in wild animals. The animals that do exist in the country, whether domesticated or otherwise, are all regarded as sacred. If I were to explain why they are consecrated to the several gods, I should be led to speak of religious matters, which I particularly shrink from mentioning. . . . The inhabitants of the various cities, when they have made a vow to any god, pay it to his animals in the way which I will now explain. At the time of making the vow they shave the head of the child, cutting off all the hair, or else half, or sometimes a third part. This they then weigh in a balance against a sum of silver. Whatever sum the hair weighs is presented to the guardian of the animals, who thereupon cuts up some fish, and gives it to them for food. . . . When a man has killed one of the sacred animals, if he did it with intentional malice, he is punished

[1] The ancient name for the continent of Africa exclusive of Egypt.

with death; if unwittingly, he has to pay such a fine as the priests choose to impose. When, however, an ibis or a hawk is killed, whether by accident or on purpose, the man must needs die.

The number of domestic animals in Egypt is very great. . . . On every occasion of a fire in Egypt the strangest prodigy occurs with the cats. The inhabitants allow the fire to rage as it pleases, while they stand about at intervals and watch these animals, which, slipping by the men or else leaping over them, rush headlong into the flames. When this happens, the Egyptians are in deep affliction. If a cat dies in a private house by a natural death, all the inmates of the house shave their eyebrows; on the death of a dog they shave the head and the whole of the body. The cats on their decease are taken to the city of Bubastis,[1] where they are embalmed, after which they are buried in sacred repositories. The dogs are interred in the cities to which they belong, likewise in sacred burial places. . . . The bears, which are scarce in Egypt, and the wolves, which are not much bigger than foxes, they bury wherever they happen to find them lying. . . .

In social meetings among the rich, when the banquet is ended, a servant carries round to the several guests a coffin. In it there is a wooden image of a corpse, carved and painted to resemble nature as nearly as possible, about a cubit or two cubits in length. As he shows it to each guest in turn, the servant says, "Gaze here, and drink and be merry; for when you die, such will you be." . . .

There is custom in which the Egyptians resemble a particular Greek people, namely the Spartans. Their young men, when they meet their elders in the streets, give way to them and step aside; and if an elder comes in where youths are present, the latter rise from their seats. In another respect they differ entirely from all the peoples of Greece. Instead of speaking to each other when they meet in the streets, they make an obeisance, sinking the hand to the knee. . . .

[1] In the Delta.

Each physician treats a single disorder, and no more. The country, therefore, swarms with medical practitioners. Some undertake to cure diseases of the eye, others of the head, others again of the teeth . . . and some treat diseases which are not local.

The following is the way in which they conduct their mournings and their funerals. On the death of a man of consequence, the women of his family at once plaster their heads, and sometimes even their faces, with mud. Then, leaving the body indoors, they sally forth and wander through the city, with their dress fastened by a band, and their bosoms bare, beating themselves as they walk. All the female relations join them and do the same. The men, too, similarly begirt, beat their breasts in like manner. When these ceremonies are over, the body is carried away to be embalmed.

There are a set of men in Egypt who practice the art of embalming and make it their proper business. These persons, when a body is brought to them, show the bearers various models of corpses, made in wood, and painted so as to resemble nature. The most perfect is said to be after the manner of him whom I do not think it religious to name in connection with such a matter.[1] The second sort is inferior to the first, and less costly; the third is the cheapest of all. All this the embalmers explain, and then ask in which way it is wished that the corpse should be prepared. The bearers tell them, and having concluded their bargain, take their departure, while the embalmers, left to themselves, proceed with their task. . . .

The Egyptians were the first to broach the opinion that the soul of man is immortal. They believe that, when the body dies, it enters into the form of an animal which is born at the moment. Thence it passes on from one animal into another, until it has circled through the forms of all the creatures which tenant the earth, the water, and the air, after which it enters again into a human frame and is born anew. The whole period of the transmigration is (they say) three thousand years. . . .

[1] A reference to the Egyptian divinity Osiris.

## 2. Babylon and the Babylonians[1]

. . . Babylonia possesses a vast number of great cities, of which the most renowned and strongest is Babylon. . . . The city stands on a broad plain, and is an exact square, a hundred and twenty furlongs[2] in length each way, so that the entire circuit is four hundred and eighty furlongs. In magnificence there is no other city that compares with Babylon. It is surrounded, in the first place, by a broad and deep moat, full of water, behind which rises a wall fifty royal cubits in width and two hundred in height.[3] . . .

And here I must not omit to tell the use to which the earth dug out of the great moat was turned, and the way the wall was made. As fast as they dug the moat, the soil obtained from the cutting was formed into bricks. When a sufficient number were completed they baked the bricks in kilns. Then they set to building, and began with bricking in the borders of the moat. Afterwards they proceeded to construct the wall itself, using throughout for their cement hot bitumen,[4] and interposing a layer of wattled reeds at every thirtieth course of the bricks. On the top, along the edges of the wall, they constructed buildings of a single chamber facing one another, leaving between them room for a four-horse chariot to turn. In the circuit of the wall are a hundred gates, all of brass, with brazen lintels and side-posts. . . .

The city is divided into two portions by the river which runs through the midst of it. This river is the Euphrates, a broad,

[1] Herodotus, i, 178–181, 193–195, 197.

[2] A furlong is one-eighth of a mile.

[3] According to this exaggerated statement, the wall would be nearly 400 feet high. The ideas of the enormous dimensions and magnificence of Babylon, conveyed by Herodotus, have not been borne out by recent excavations upon the site of the city. Explorations conducted by the German Oriental Society have shown that in its most prosperous days Babylon covered little over one square mile of territory. Its famous wall was only about thirty feet high and four miles long. Instead of the hundred gates described by Herodotus, it had but four.

[4] Bitumen is a kind of pitch.

deep, swift stream, which rises in Armenia, and empties itself into the Erythræan Sea.[1] The city wall is brought down on both sides to the edge of the stream. From the corners of the wall, a fence of burnt bricks is carried along each bank of the river. The houses are mostly three and four stories high. The streets all run in straight lines, not only those parallel to the river, but also the cross streets which lead down to the water-side. At the river end of these cross streets are low gates in the fence that skirts the stream. They are of brass, as are the great gates in the outer wall, and open on the water.

The outer wall is the main defense of the city. There is, however, a second inner wall, of less thickness than the first, but very little inferior to it in strength. The center of each division of the town was occupied by a fortress. In the one stood the palace of the kings, surrounded by a wall of great strength and size. In the other was the sacred precinct of Zeus Belus,[2] a square enclosure two furlongs each way, with gates of solid brass. . . . In the middle of the precinct there was a tower of solid masonry, a furlong in length and breadth, upon which was raised a second tower, and on that a third, and so on up to eight. The ascent to the top is on the outside, by a path which winds round all the towers. When one is about half-way up, one finds seats on which persons are wont to rest during their climb to the summit. On the topmost tower there is a spacious temple, and inside the temple stands a couch of unusual size, richly adorned, with a golden table by its side. There is no statue of any kind set up in the place. . . .

Very little rain falls in Babylonia. It is enough, however, to make the corn begin to sprout, after which the plant is nourished by means of irrigation from the river. For the river does not, as in Egypt, overflow the corn-lands of its own accord, but is spread over them by the hand, or by the help of engines. The whole of Babylonia is, like Egypt, intersected with canals. The largest of them all . . . is carried from the

[1] The Indian Ocean.
[2] The Babylonian god, Bel-Merodach.

Euphrates into another stream, called the Tigris, the river upon which the town of Nineveh formerly stood.

Of all the countries that we know there is no other so fruitful in grain. It makes no pretension, indeed, of growing the fig, the olive, the vine, or any other tree of the kind. But in grain it is so fruitful as to yield commonly two hundred-fold, and when the production is greatest, even three hundred-fold.[1] The blade of the wheat-plant and barley-plant is often four fingers in breadth. As for the millet and the sesame, I shall not say to what height they grow, though within my own knowledge; for I am not ignorant that what I have already written concerning the fruitfulness of Babylonia must seem incredible to those who have never visited the country. . . . Palm-trees grow in great numbers over the whole of the flat country, mostly of the kind which bears fruit, and this fruit supplies them with bread, wine, and honey. . . . The natives tie the fruit of the male palms, as they are called by the Greeks, to the branches of the date-bearing palm, to let the gall-fly enter the dates and ripen them. . . . The male palms, like the wild fig-trees, have usually the gall-fly in their fruit.

But that which surprises me most in the land, after the city itself, I will now proceed to mention. The boats which come down the river to Babylon are circular, and made of skins.[2] The frames, which are of willow, are cut in the country of the Armenians above Assyria. A covering of skins is stretched outside the frames, and thus the boats are made, without either stem or stern, quite round like a shield. They are then entirely filled with straw, and their cargo is put on board, after which they are suffered to float down the stream. Their chief freight is wine, stored in casks made of the wood of the palm-tree. They are managed by two men who stand upright in them,

[1] Very probably an exaggerated statement. At present, the yield is only some thirty or forty-fold.

[2] Boats such as Herodotus describes, made usually of wicker work covered with native asphalt, are still used in this region. The boatmen scull their craft with a broad, single-bladed paddle.

each plying an oar, one pulling and the other pushing. The boats are of various sizes. . . . Each vessel has a live ass on board; those of larger size have more than one. When they reach Babylon, the cargo is landed and offered for sale. After this the men break up their boats, sell the straw and the frames, and loading their asses with the skins, set off on their way back to Armenia. The current is too strong to allow a boat to return up-stream, for which reason they make their boats of skins rather than wood. On their return to Armenia they build fresh boats for the next voyage.

The dress of the Babylonians is a linen tunic reaching to the feet, and above it another tunic made of wool. Besides these garments they wear a short white cloak and shoes of a peculiar fashion, not unlike those worn by the Bœotians.[1] They have long hair, wear turbans on their heads, and anoint the whole body with perfumes. Every one carries a seal and a walking-stick. The latter is carved at the top into the form of an apple, a rose, a lily, an eagle, or something similar. It is not their habit to use a stick without an ornament. . . .

The following practice seems to me to be very wise. They have no physicians, but when a man is ill, they lay him in the public square, and the passers-by come up to him. If they have ever had his disease themselves, or have known anyone who has suffered from it, they give him advice, recommending him to do whatever they found good in their own case, or in the case known to them. No one is allowed to pass the sick man in silence without asking him what his ailment is..

### 3. The Persians [2]

The customs which I know the Persians to observe are the following. They have no images of the gods, no temples or altars, and consider the use of them a sign of folly. This comes, I think, from their not believing the gods to have the same nature with men as the Greeks imagine. The Persians, however,

---

[1] Natives of Bœotia, one of the states of Greece.

[2] Herodotus, i, 131–140.

ascend the summits of the loftiest mountains, and there offer sacrifice to Zeus,[1] which is the name they give to the whole circuit of the firmament. They likewise sacrifice to the sun and moon, to the earth, to fire, to water, and to the winds. These are the only gods whose worship has come down to them from ancient times. . . .

The Persians offer sacrifice in the following manner. They raise no altar, light no fire, pour no libations. There is no sound of the flute, no putting on of chaplets, no consecrated barley-cake. The man who wishes to sacrifice simply brings his victim to a spot of ground which is pure from pollution, and there calls upon the name of the god to whom he intends to offer. It is usual to have the turban encircled with a wreath, most commonly of myrtle. The sacrificer is not allowed to pray for blessings on himself alone, but he prays for the welfare of the king, and of the whole Persian people, among whom he is of necessity included. He cuts the victim in pieces, and having boiled the flesh, he lays it out upon the tenderest herbage that he can find. . . . When all is ready, one of the Magi[2] comes forward and chants a hymn, which, they say, recounts the origin of the gods. It is not lawful to offer sacrifice unless there is a Magus present. After waiting a short time the sacrificer carries the flesh of the victim away with him, and makes whatever use of it he may please.

Of all the days in the year, the one which they celebrate most is their birthday. It is customary to have the table furnished on that day with an ampler supply than common. The richer Persians cause an ox, a horse, a camel, and an ass to be baked whole and so served up to them; the poorer classes use the smaller kinds of cattle. They eat little solid food but abundance of dessert, which is set on the table a few dishes at a time. It is this custom which makes them say that " the Greeks, when they eat, leave off hungry, having nothing worth

[1] A reference to the Persian supreme god, Ahura-Mazda, whom Herodotus identifies with the Greek Zeus.

[2] The Magi (singular, Magus) were the priests of the Persians.

mention served up to them after the meats; whereas, if they had more put before them, they would not stop eating." . . .

The Persians are very fond of wine. It is their practice to deliberate upon affairs of weight when they are drunk. On the morrow, when they are sober, the decision they reached on the preceding night is put before them by the master of the house in which it was made. If the decision is then approved, they act on it; if not, they set it aside. Sometimes, however, they are sober at their first deliberation, but in this case they always reconsider the matter under the influence of wine.

When they meet each other in the streets, you may know that the persons meeting are of equal rank . . . if, instead of speaking, they kiss each other on the lips. In the case where one is a little inferior to the other, the kiss is given on the cheek. Where the difference of rank is great, the inferior prostrates himself upon the ground. . . .

There is no nation which so readily adopts foreign customs as the Persians. Thus, they have taken the dress of the Medes, considering it superior to their own; and in war they wear the Egyptian breastplate. As soon as they hear of any luxury, they instantly make it their own. . . .

Next to bravery in battle, it is regarded as the greatest proof of manly excellence to be the father of many sons. Every year the king sends rich gifts to the man who can show the largest number; for they hold that number is strength. Their sons are carefully instructed from their fifth to their twentieth year, in three things alone: to ride, to draw the bow, and to speak the truth. Until their fifth year they are not allowed to come into the sight of their father, but pass their lives with the women. This is done that, if the child dies young, the father may not be afflicted by its loss.

To my mind the following are wise rules — that the king shall not put anyone to death for a single fault, and that none of the Persians shall visit a single fault in a slave with any extreme penalty. In every case the services of the offender must be set against his misdoings. If the latter are found to outweigh the former, the aggrieved party only then shall proceed to punishment. . . .

The most disgraceful thing in the world, they think, is to tell a lie; the next worst, to owe a debt; because, among other reasons, the debtor is obliged to tell lies. If a Persian has the leprosy, he is not allowed to enter into a city or to have any dealings with the other Persians. He must, they say, have sinned against the sun. Foreigners attacked by this disorder are forced to leave the country: even white pigeons are often driven away, as guilty of the same offense. . . . There is another peculiarity, which the Persians themselves have never noticed, but which has not escaped my observation. Their names, which are expressive of some bodily or mental excellence, all end with the same letter — the letter which is called San by the Dorians and Sigma by the Ionians.[1] Anyone who examines will find that the Persian names, one and all without exception, end with this letter.[2]

Thus much I can declare of the Persians with entire certainty, from my own actual knowledge. There is another custom which is spoken of with reserve, and not openly, concerning their dead. It is said that the body of a male Persian is never buried, until it has been torn either by a dog or a bird of prey. That the Magi have this custom is beyond a doubt, for they practice it without any concealment. The dead bodies are covered with wax and are then buried in the ground.

The Magi are a very peculiar race, differing entirely from the Egyptian priests, and indeed from all other men whatsoever. The Egyptian priests make it a point of religion not to kill any live animals except those which they offer in sacrifice. The Magi, on the contrary, kill animals of all kinds with their own hands, excepting dogs and men. They think they do a meritorious act to destroy ants, snakes, and other flying or creeping things. However, since this has always been their custom, let them keep it. . . .

---

[1] Dorians and Ionians were two divisions of the Greek race.
[2] Herodotus is mistaken in this statement.

# CHAPTER II

## THE FOUNDERS OF THE PERSIAN EMPIRE: CYRUS, CAMBYSES, AND DARIUS [1]

AROUND the personalities of the first three Persian kings there soon gathered a great mass of legendary material, for all of which Herodotus finds a place in his history. Until the ancient records of the Orient had been deciphered, the stories which Herodotus tells were generally accepted by historians. Now, however, we are able to check his statements by reference to the monuments and inscriptions. These give a far more prosaic account of Oriental history than that which we find in the fascinating pages of Herodotus. The student who reads his chapters on the Orient must never forget that he is learning what the Greeks of antiquity thought about their eastern neighbors rather than what modern historians know concerning them.

### 4. Crœsus and Solon [2]

The foundations of the mighty Persian Empire were laid by Cyrus the Great. A successful revolt against his brother-in-law, the Median monarch Astyages, enabled Cyrus to unite the Medes and Persians under his single sway. Encouraged by this success he now entered on a career of wider conquests. In the west his most formidable rival was the famous Crœsus, king of Lydia

---

[1] Herodotus. The translation of George Rawlinson, edited by A. J. Grant. 2 vols. London, 1897. John Murray.

[2] Herodotus, i, 29–33.

(560–546 B.C.), who had built up an empire that included the larger part of Asia Minor.

When all these dominions had been added to the Lydian Empire and the prosperity of Sardis [1] was at its height, there came thither, one after another, all the wise men of Greece, living at the time. Among them was Solon the Athenian. He was on his travels, having left Athens to be absent ten years, under the pretense of wishing to see the world. Really it was to avoid being forced to repeal any of the laws which, at the request of the Athenians, he had made for them. Without his sanction the Athenians could not repeal them, as they had bound themselves under a heavy curse to be governed for ten years by the laws which should be imposed on them by Solon.

On this account, as well as to see the world, Solon set out upon his travels. In the course of these he went to Egypt to the court of Amasis,[2] and also came on a visit to Crœsus at Sardis. Crœsus received him as his guest and lodged him in the royal palace. On the third or fourth day after, he bade his servants conduct Solon over his treasuries, and show him all their greatness and magnificence. When he had seen them all, and as far as time allowed, inspected them, Crœsus addressed this question to him, "Stranger of Athens, we have heard much of thy wisdom and of thy travels through many lands, from love of knowledge and a wish to see the world. I am curious, therefore, to inquire of thee, whom, of all the men that thou hast seen, thou deemest the most happy." This Crœsus asked because he thought himself the happiest of mortals. But Solon answered him without flattery, "Tellus of Athens." Full of astonishment at what he heard, Crœsus demanded sharply, "And wherefore dost thou deem Tellus happiest?" The other replied, "First, because his country was flourishing in his lifetime, and he himself had sons both beautiful and good,

---

[1] The capital of Lydia.     [2] Amasis II (570–525 B.C.).

and he lived to see children born to each of them, and these children all grew up. Further, because, after a life spent in what our people look upon as comfort, his end was surpassingly glorious. In a battle between the Athenians and their neighbors he came to the assistance of his countrymen, routed the foe, and died upon the field most gallantly. The Athenians gave him a public funeral on the spot where he fell, and paid him the highest honors." . . .

When Solon had ended, Croesus inquired a second time, who after Tellus seemed to him the happiest, expecting that, at any rate, he would be given the second place. "Cleobis and Bito," Solon answered. "They were of Argive [1] race; their fortune was enough for their wants; and they were endowed with such bodily strength that they both gained prizes at the Olympic games. Of these two men this tale is told: — There was a great festival in honor of the goddess Hera at Argos, to which their mother must needs be taken in a car. Since the oxen did not come home from the field in time, the youths, fearful of being too late, put the yoke on their own necks, and themselves pulled the car in which their mother rode. Five and forty furlongs did they draw her, and then stopped before the temple. This deed of theirs was witnessed by the whole assembly of worshipers, and then their life closed in the best possible way. Herein, too, God showed forth most evidently, how much better a thing for man death is than life. For the Argive men who stood around the car, extolled the vast strength of the youths; and the Argive women extolled the mother who was blessed with such a pair of sons. And the mother herself, overjoyed at the deed and at the praises it had won . . . besought the goddess to bestow on Cleobis and Bito, the sons who had so mightily honored her, the highest blessing to which mortals can attain. Her prayer ended, they offered sacrifice and partook of the holy banquet. After this the two youths fell asleep in the temple. They never woke again, but so passed from earth. The Argives, looking on them as among

[1] Natives of Argos, a famous Peloponnesian city.

the best of men, caused statues of them to be made, which they gave to the shrine at Delphi." [1]

When Solon had thus assigned these youths the second place, Crœsus broke in angrily, "Stranger of Athens, is my happiness, then, so utterly set at naught by thee, that thou dost not even put me on a level with private men?"

"O Crœsus," replied the other, "thou askest a question concerning the condition of man, of one who knows that the power above us is full of jealousy, and fond of troubling our lot. A long life gives one to witness much and experience much oneself, that one would not willingly suffer. . . . For thyself, O Crœsus, I see that thou art wonderfully rich, and art the lord of many nations, but with respect to that about which thou questionest me, I have no answer to give, until I hear that thou hast closed thy life happily. . . . In every matter it behooves us to mark well the end: for oftentimes God gives men a gleam of happiness, and then plunges them into ruin."

Such was the speech which Solon addressed to Crœsus, a speech which brought him neither gifts nor honor. The king saw him depart with much indifference, since he thought that a man must be an arrant fool who made no account of present good, but bade men always wait and mark the end.[2]

### 5. Crœsus and Cyrus [3]

Solon's warning soon came true. Uneasy at the rising power of Cyrus, his eastern neighbor, Crœsus resolved to make war on the Persian king. First he consulted the oracle of Apollo at Delphi and learned that the war would end in the destruction of a great empire. This ambiguous response encouraged Crœsus to begin the conflict with Cyrus. It resulted, however, in disaster for the Lydian monarch.

[1] The celebrated oracle of Apollo.

[2] This famous tale of Solon's interview with Crœsus cannot be reconciled with the received chronology, which places the reforms of Solon at Athens and his subsequent travels nearly half a century earlier, 594–593 B. C.

[3] Herodotus, i, 86–87.

Sardis was taken by the Persians, and Crœsus himself fell into their hands, after having reigned fourteen years. . . . Thus, too, did Crœsus fulfill the oracle, which said that he should destroy a mighty empire — by destroying his own. Then the Persians who had made Crœsus prisoner brought him before Cyrus. Now a vast pile had been raised by his orders, and Crœsus, laden with fetters, was placed upon it, and with him twice seven of the sons of the Lydians. I know not whether Cyrus was minded to make an offering to some god or other, or whether he had vowed a vow and was performing it. Perhaps, as may well be, he had heard that Crœsus was a holy man, and so wished to see if any of the heavenly powers would appear to save him from being burnt alive.[1] . . .

Crœsus was already on the pile, when it entered his mind in the depth of his woe that there was a divine warning in the words which had come to him from the lips of Solon. . . . When this thought smote him he fetched a long breath, and breaking his deep silence, groaned out aloud, thrice uttering the name of Solon. Cyrus caught the sounds, and bade the interpreters inquire of Crœsus on whom it was he called. They drew near and asked him, but he held his peace, and for a long time made no answer to their questionings. At length, forced to say something, he exclaimed, "One I would like much to see converse with every monarch." Not knowing what he meant by this reply, the interpreters begged him to explain himself. As they pressed for an answer . . . he told them how, a long time before, Solon, an Athenian, had come and seen all his splendor, and made light of it; and how whatever he had said to him had fallen out exactly as he foreshowed. . . .

Meanwhile, as Crœsus thus spoke, the pile was kindled, and the outer portion began to blaze. Then Cyrus, hearing from

---

[1] Another and more probable story of the burning of Crœsus describes it as a voluntary act, not as a punishment inflicted on him by his Persian conqueror. Oriental history contains several references to defeated monarchs who, unable to endure the thought of slavery, consigned themselves and their families to the flames.

the interpreters what Crœsus had said, relented. For Cyrus considered that he too was a man, and that it was a fellow-man, and one who had once been as blessed by fortune as himself, that he was burning alive. . . . So he bade them quench the blazing fire as quickly as they could, and take down Crœsus and the other Lydians, which they tried to do, but the flames were not to be mastered.

Then . . . Crœsus, perceiving by the efforts made to quench the fire that Cyrus had relented, and seeing also that all was in vain, and that the men could not put out the fire, called with a loud voice upon the god Apollo. He besought Apollo, if he had ever received at his hands any acceptable gift,[1] to come to his aid, and deliver him from his present danger. As thus with tears he cried to the god, suddenly . . . dark clouds gathered, and a storm burst over their heads with rain of such violence, that the flames were speedily extinguished. Cyrus, convinced by this that Crœsus was a good man and a favorite of heaven, asked him after he was taken off the pile, "who it was that had persuaded him to lead an army into his country, and so become his foe rather than continue his friend?" To this inquiry Crœsus made answer as follows: "What I did, O king, was to thy advantage and to my own loss. If there is blame, it rests with the god of the Greeks, who encouraged me to begin the war. No one is so foolish as to prefer to peace, war, in which, instead of sons burying their fathers, fathers bury their sons. But the gods willed it so."

### 6. The Death of Cyrus [2]

The conquest of Lydia was soon followed by the addition of Babylonia to the Persian dominions. Cyrus now determined to annex the country of the wild Scythians to his empire. Crossing the Araxes River, he led his army

---

[1] In the days of his prosperity Crœsus had enriched the oracle of Apollo at Delphi with many presents.

[2] Herodotus, i, 211–214.

against the Massagetæ, a Scythian tribe living east of the Caspian under the rule of their queen Tomyris.

Cyrus, having advanced a day's march from the Araxes, adopted a stratagem proposed by Crœsus. Leaving the worthless portion of his army in the camp, the Persian king drew off with his good troops toward the river. Soon afterwards a detachment of the Massagetæ, led by Spargapises, son of the queen Tomyris, attacked the soldiers who had been left behind by Cyrus. On their resistance the Massagetæ put them to the sword. Then, seeing a banquet prepared, they sat down and began to feast. When they had eaten and drunk their fill, and were now sunk in sleep, the Persians under Cyrus arrived, slaughtered a great multitude, and made even a larger number prisoners. Among these last was Spargapises himself.

When Tomyris heard what had befallen her son and her army, she sent a herald to Cyrus, who thus addressed the conqueror: "Thou bloodthirsty Cyrus, pride not thyself on this poor success. It was the grape-juice — which, when ye drink it, makes you so mad, and as ye swallow it down brings up to your lips such bold and wicked words — it was this poison wherewith thou didst ensnare my child, and so overcamest him, not in fair, open fight. Now hearken to what I advise, and be sure I advise thee for thy good. Restore my son to me and get thee from the land unharmed, triumphant over a third part of the host of the Massagetæ. Refuse, and I swear by the sun, the sovereign lord of the Massagetæ, bloodthirsty as thou art, I will give thee thy fill of blood."

To the words of this message Cyrus paid no manner of regard. As for Spargapises, the son of the queen, when his drunkenness went off, and he saw the extent of his calamity, he requested Cyrus to release him from his bonds. When his prayer was granted, and the fetters were taken from his limbs, as soon as his hands were free, he destroyed himself.

Tomyris, when she found that Cyrus paid no heed to her

advice, collected all the forces of her kingdom and gave him battle. Of all the combats in which the barbarians have engaged among themselves, I consider this to have been the fiercest. . . . At length the Massagetæ prevailed. The greater part of the army of the Persians was destroyed, and Cyrus himself fell, after reigning nine and twenty years. Search was made among the slain by order of the queen for the body of Cyrus. When it was found, she took a skin, and filling it full of human blood, she dipped the head of Cyrus in the gore, saying, as she thus insulted the corpse, "I live and have conquered thee in fight, and yet by thee am I ruined, for thou tookest my son with guile; but thus I make good my threat, and give thee thy fill of blood." [1] . . .

### 7. The Madness of Cambyses [2]

Cambyses, son of Cyrus, on attaining the throne, determined to add Egypt to the Persian Empire. He easily defeated the Egyptian troops and took their king captive.

After this Cambyses left Memphis, and went to Saïs,[3] wishing to do that which he actually did on his arrival there. He entered the palace of Amasis,[4] and straightway ordered that the body of the king should be brought forth from the sepulcher. When the attendants did according to his commandment, he further bade them scourge the body, and prick it with goads, and pluck the hair from it, and heap upon it all manner of insults. The body, however, having been embalmed, resisted, and refused to come apart, do what they would to it. . . . Whereupon Cambyses bade them take the corpse and burn it. This was truly an impious command to give, for the Persians hold fire to be a god, and never by any chance burn their dead.[5] . . .

---

[1] With charming simplicity Herodotus remarks, "Of the many different accounts which are given of the death of Cyrus, this which I have followed appears to me most worthy of credit."

[2] Herodotus, iii, 16, 30, 34–35.

[3] A city in the Delta.

[4] Amasis II.   See page 14.

[5] See page 12.

Cambyses now entered upon a career marked by misfortune, impiety, and cruelty. Against the Ethiopians he sent an army so ill supplied with provisions that the soldiers turned cannibals and devoured one another. A second Persian army directed against the Ammonians, who lived in an oasis west of Egypt, perished in a desert sand storm. Cambyses, moreover, deeply offended the Egyptians by stabbing the sacred bull or Apis — an act of the greatest sacrilege.

And now Cambyses, who even before had not been quite in his right mind, was forthwith, as the Egyptians say, smitten with madness for this crime. The first of his outrages was the slaying of Smerdis, his full brother. . . .

He was mad, also, with others besides his kindred; among the rest, with Prexaspes, the man whom he esteemed beyond all other Persians. He it was who carried his messages, and whose son held the office — an honor of no small account in Persia — of his cupbearer. Him Cambyses is said to have once addressed as follows: "What sort of man, Prexaspes, do the Persians think me?" Prexaspes answered, "Oh! sir, they praise thee greatly in all things but one — they say thou art too much given to love of wine." . . . Cambyses, full of rage, made answer, "What! they say now that I drink too much wine, and so have lost my senses, and am gone out of my mind! Then their former speeches about me were untrue." For once, when the Persians were sitting with him, and Crœsus was by, he had asked them, "What sort of man they thought him compared to his father Cyrus?" To this they had answered, "That he surpassed his father, for he was lord of all that his father ever ruled, and further had made himself master of Egypt and the sea." Then Crœsus, who was standing near, and disliked the comparison, spoke thus to Cambyses: "In my judgment, O son of Cyrus, thou art not equal to thy father, for thou hast not yet left behind thee such a son as he."

Cambyses was delighted when he heard this reply, and praised the judgment of Crœsus.

Recollecting these answers, Cambyses spoke fiercely to Prexaspes, saying, "Judge now thyself, Prexaspes, whether the Persians tell the truth, or whether it is not they who are mad for speaking as they do. Look there now at thy son standing in the vestibule — if I shoot and hit him right in the middle of the heart, it will be plain the Persians have no grounds for what they say: if I miss him, then I admit that the Persians are right, and that I am out of my mind." So speaking he drew his bow to the full, and struck the boy, who straightway fell down dead. Then Cambyses ordered the body to be opened, and the wound examined. When the arrow was found to have entered the heart, the king was quite overjoyed, and said to the father with a laugh, "Now thou seest plainly, Prexaspes, that it is not I who am mad, but the Persians who have lost their senses. I pray thee tell me, sawest thou ever mortal man send an arrow with a better aim?" Prexaspes, seeing that the king was not in his right mind, and fearing for himself, replied, "Oh! my lord, I do not think that God Himself could shoot so dexterously." Such was the outrage which Cambyses committed at this time. . . .

### 8. Accession of Darius [1]

While Cambyses still lingered in Egypt, he learned that one of the Magi, who resembled the murdered Smerdis, had personated him and had actually seized the throne. According to Herodotus, Cambyses set out at once for Persia, meaning to punish the impostor, but died suddenly in Syria. However the false Smerdis did not rule long. In the eighth month of his reign he was killed by some of the leading Persian nobles (521 B.C.). One of these men, Darius by name, is said to have attained the kingship in the following singular fashion.

[1] Herodotus, iii, 84–86.

After the death of the false Smerdis the conspirators took counsel together, as to the fairest way of setting up a king. . . . The resolve to which they came was the following: they would ride together next morning to the outskirts of the city, and he whose steed first neighed after the sun was up should have the kingdom.

Now Darius had a groom, a sharp-witted fellow, called Œbares. After the meeting had broken up, Darius sent for him, and said, "Œbares, this is the way in which the king is to be chosen — we are to mount our horses, and the man whose horse first neighs after the sun is up is to have the kingdom. If then you have any cleverness, contrive a plan whereby the prize may fall to us, and not go to another." "Truly, master," Œbares answered, "if it depends on this whether thou shalt be king or not, set thine heart at ease, and fear nothing. I have a charm which is sure not to fail." "If thou hast really anything of the kind," said Darius, "hasten to get it ready. The matter does not allow delay, for the trial is to be to-morrow." So Œbares . . . when night came, took one of the mares, the chief favorite of the horse which Darius rode, and tethering it in the suburb, brought his master's horse to the place. Then, after leading him round and round the mare several times, and nearer at each circuit, he ended by bringing them close together.

When morning broke, the six Persians, according to agreement, met together on horseback and rode out to the suburb. As they went along, they neared the spot where the mare was tethered the night before, whereupon the horse of Darius sprang forward and neighed. Just at the same time, though the sky was clear and bright, there was a flash of lightning, followed by a thunder-clap. It seemed as if the heavens conspired with Darius, and thereby inaugurated him king. So the five other nobles leaped with one accord from their steeds, and bowed down before him and owned him for their king.[1]

[1] It is hardly necessary to point out that this story has no basis in fact. It is one of those quaint legends which make the pages of Herodotus entertaining, if not always trustworthy.

## 9. Darius in Scythia [1]

Cyrus had conquered Asia; Cambyses, Africa. Darius determined to add Europe to the Persian dominions. With a vast army he crossed the Bosporus and quickly subdued the inhabitants of Thrace (about 512 B.C.). Having bridged the Danube, he next invaded the territory of some Scythian tribes which lived beyond that river. But the barbarians refused a battle, and as Darius advanced, ever retreated before him into their northern wilderness.

The Scythians, when they perceived signs that the Persians were becoming alarmed, took steps to induce them not to quit Scythia. They hoped, if the Persians stayed, to inflict on them the greater injury, when their supplies should altogether fail. To effect this the Scythians would leave some of their cattle exposed with the herdsmen, while they themselves moved away to a distance. The Persians would make a foray, and take the beasts, whereupon they would be highly elated.

This they did several times, until at last Darius was at his wit's end. Hereupon the Scythian princes, understanding how matters stood, dispatched a herald to the Persian camp with presents for the king. These were a bird, a mouse, a frog, and five arrows. The Persians asked the bearer to tell them what the gifts might mean, but he made answer that he had no orders except to deliver them, and return again with all speed. If the Persians were wise, he added, they would find out the meaning for themselves. So when the Persians heard this, they held a council to consider the matter.

Darius gave it as his opinion, that the Scythians intended to surrender themselves and their country, both land and water, into his hands. This he conceived to be the meaning of the gifts, because the mouse is an inhabitant of the earth, and eats the same food as man, while the frog passes his life in the water;

[1] Herodotus, iv, 130–132.

the bird bears a great resemblance to the horse; and the arrows might signify the surrender of all their power. To the explanation of Darius, Gobryas, one of the conspirators against the false Smerdis, opposed another, which was as follows: "Unless, Persians, ye can turn into birds and fly up into the sky, or become mice and burrow under the ground, or make yourselves frogs and take refuge in the fens, ye will never get away from this land, but die pierced by our arrows." Such were the meanings which the Persians assigned to the presents.

Understanding at length the true significance of the Scythian gifts, Darius reluctantly ordered a retreat. He recrossed the Danube and the Bosporus and brought back into Asia the remnant of his great host. With this first invasion of Europe by the army of an Asiatic king, there begins the story of those relations between Persia and Greece which form the subject of a later chapter.[1]

[1] Modern historians believe that this European expedition of Darius was by no means so fruitless as Herodotus pictures it. The enterprise added Thrace to the Persian Empire and restrained the Scythian tribes in their wild maraudings. Hence it seems to have been both a reasonable and a successful undertaking.

# CHAPTER III

## EARLY GREEK SOCIETY AS PICTURED IN THE HOMERIC POEMS [1]

THE *Iliad* and the *Odyssey* are not simply the noblest examples of epic poetry which have come down to us from antiquity. To the historian these two poems are the chief source of information for the life and culture of the early Greeks before the dawn of history. It is true that the poet of the *Iliad* and the *Odyssey* professes to relate events that in his own time were already ancient; events which we may well believe never happened. But if the stories he has to tell are pure fictions, the manners and customs he describes are not imaginary. The civilization pictured by the poet is mainly that with which he is himself familiar. Homer paints the past in the colors of his own day.

### 10. A Popular Assembly [2]

The *Iliad* deals with the events of only a few days during the tenth and last year of the siege of Troy (or Ilium). From other poems we learn how Paris, son of Priam the Trojan king, carried off to Troy the beautiful Helen, wife of Menelaus, king of Sparta; and how the Greek chieftains gathered from far and near to avenge the wrong. Under Agamemnon of Mycenæ for nine long years the Greeks besieged the city. But the Trojans kept behind

---

[1] *The Iliad of Homer*, translated by Lang, Leaf, and Myers. 2d edition. London, 1892. Macmillan and Co. *The Odyssey of Homer*, translated by S. H. Butcher and Andrew Lang. London, 1879. Macmillan and Co.

[2] *Iliad*, ii, 84–154.

their walls and refused a battle, for they feared the deadly might of Achilles, greatest of the Greek heroes. And now in the tenth year, from King Agamemnon Achilles suffered a grievous insult. Then Achilles withdrew to his hut by the seashore and vowed never again to fight for Agamemnon. To the Greeks, thereby, came woes innumerable, for Zeus the cloud-gatherer had given his pledge that the wrong of Achilles should be avenged on Agamemnon and all his host. So Zeus sent a deceitful dream to Agamemnon beguiling the king with the hope he might take the city of the Trojans. Then Agamemnon called a council of the elders and chieftains telling them of his vision and bidding them call an assembly of the host. "But first I will speak to make trial of them as is fitting, and will bid them flee with their benched ships; only do ye from this side and from that speak to hold them back."

So spake he, and led the way forth from the council, and all the other sceptered chiefs rose with him and obeyed the shepherd of the host; and the people hastened to them. . . . And the place of assemblage was in an uproar, and the earth echoed again as the hosts sate them down, and there was turmoil. Nine heralds restrained them with shouting, if perchance they might refrain from clamor, and hearken to their kings, the fosterlings of Zeus. And hardly at the last would the people sit, and keep them to their benches and cease from noise. Then stood up Lord Agamemnon bearing his scepter, that Hephæstus [1] had wrought curiously. . . . Thereon he leaned and spake his saying to the Argives.[2]

"My friends, Danaan warriors, men of Ares' [3] company, Zeus hath bound me with might in grievous blindness of soul.

---

[1] The divine smith.

[2] The Greeks at Troy are spoken of by the poet as Argives, Danaans, and Achæans.

[3] God of war.

Hard of heart is he, for that erewhile he promised me and pledged his nod that not till I had wasted well-walled Ilium should I return. Now see I that he planned a cruel wile and biddeth me return to Argos dishonored, with the loss of many of my folk. So meseems it pleaseth most mighty Zeus, who hath laid low the head of many a city, yea, and shall lay low; for his is highest power. Shame is this even for them that come after to hear; how so goodly and great a folk of the Achæans thus vainly warred a bootless war, and fought scantier enemies, and no end thereof is yet seen. . . . Already have nine years passed away, and our ships' timbers have rotted and the tackling is loosed; while there our wives and little children sit in our halls awaiting us; yet is our task utterly unaccomplished wherefor we came hither. So come, even as I shall bid, let us all obey. Let us flee with our ships to our dear native land; for now shall we never take wide-wayed Troy."

So spake he, and stirred the spirit in the breasts of all throughout the multitude, as many as had not heard the counsel. And the assembly swayed like high sea-waves . . . that east wind and south wind raise, rushing upon them from the clouds of Father Zeus. And even as when the west wind cometh to stir a deep cornfield with violent blast, and the ears bow down, so was all the assembly stirred. And they with shouting hasted toward the ships; and the dust from beneath their feet rose and stood on high. Then each man bade his neighbor to seize the ships and drag them into the bright salt sea. . . .

### 11. Odysseus and Thersites [1]

Then would the Achæans have accomplished their return against the will of fate, but that the goddess Hera spake a word to Athena, bidding her refrain the soldiers from their mad design. And Athena darted down from the peaks of Olympus and came with speed to the ships of the Achæans. And finding there the wise Odysseus

[1] *Iliad*, ii, 212–277.

she sent him up and down the host to carry out the orders of the goddess Hera. Then Odysseus straightway bade the warriors sit down and keep their places upon the benches.

Only Thersites still chattered on, the uncontrolled of speech, whose mind was full of words many and disorderly, wherewith to strive against the chiefs idly and in no good order, but even as he deemed that he should make the Argives laugh. And he was ill-favored beyond all men that came to Ilium. Bandy-legged was he, and lame of one foot, and his two shoulders rounded, arched down upon his chest; and over them his head was warped, and a scanty stubble sprouted on it. Hateful was he to Achilles above all and to Odysseus, for them he was wont to revile.

But now with shrill shout he poured forth his upbraidings upon goodly Agamemnon. . . . "Son of Atreus, for what art thou now ill content and lacking? Surely thy huts are full of bronze and many women are in thy huts, the chosen spoils that we Achæans give thee first of all, whene'er we take a town. Can it be that thou yet wantest gold as well, such as some one of the horse-taming Trojans may bring from Ilium to ransom his son, whom I perchance or some other Achæan have led captive; or else some young girl whom thou mayest keep apart to thyself? But it is not seemly for one that is their captain to bring the sons of the Achæans to ill. Soft fools, base things of shame, ye women of Achæa and men no more, let us depart home with our ships, and leave this fellow here in Troy-land to gorge him with meeds of honor." . . .

So spake Thersites, reviling Agamemnon, shepherd of the host. But goodly Odysseus came straight to his side, and looking sternly at him with hard words rebuked him: "Thersites, reckless in words, shrill orator though thou art, refrain thyself, nor aim to strive singly against kings. . . . But I will tell thee plain, and that I say shall even be brought to pass: if I find thee again raving as now thou art, then may Odysseus' head no longer abide upon his shoulders. Nor may I any more be called father of Telemachus, if I take thee not and strip from thee thy garments, thy mantle and tunic that cover thy nakedness, and for thyself send thee weeping to the fleet ships, and beat thee out of the assembly with shameful blows."

So spake Odysseus, and with his staff smote Thersites' back and shoulders. And he bowed down and a big tear fell from him, and a bloody weal stood up from his back beneath the golden scepter. Then he sat down and was amazed, and in pain with helpless look wiped away the tear. But the rest, though they were sorry, laughed lightly at him. And thus would one speak looking at another standing by: "Go to, of a truth Odysseus hath wrought good deeds without number ere now, standing foremost in wise counsels, and setting battle in array, but now is this thing the best by far that he hath wrought among the Argives, to wit, that he hath stayed this prating railer from his harangues. Never again, forsooth, will his proud soul henceforth bid him revile the kings with slanderous words." [1]

### 12. Hector and Andromache [2]

So the tumult subsided and the assembly listened to the words of the elders, who bade them make ready for the battle. Then the warriors were marshaled tribe by tribe and clan by clan upon the broad plain of Troy, and over against them were arrayed the Trojans, now no longer fearful of the battle. But when they were come in onset against each other, the godlike Paris played champion to the Trojans and challenged Menelaus to a single combat, with Helen and all her wealth for the victor's prize. Then the Argives and Trojans swore to observe a truce until the combat should be decided. And Menelaus would have triumphed in the duel had not Aphrodite snatched up

[1] It has been well said that the poet who drew this portrait of Thersites must have been perfectly familiar with the mob-orator found in every Greek city.

[2] *Iliad*, vi, 440–502.

Paris very easily, as a goddess may, and hid him in a thick cloud, and so preserved him from black death. And now while the two hosts were still under the truce a Trojan archer treacherously wounded Menelaus. Once more the Achæans raised the loud war-cry and advanced against their foes. And the battle swayed oft this way and that across the plain, as they aimed against each other their bronze-shod javelins. Many Trojans that day and many Achæans were laid side by side upon their faces in the dust. But when the men of Troy began to yield before their enemies, the noble Hector, King Priam's valiant son, quitted the field that he might visit the city and bid the elders and the women pray for succor to the gods. On the city wall he found Andromache, his dear wife, and their infant son Astyanax. With many tears Andromache besought her lord not to go forth again to terrible battle lest he perish and leave her forever desolate.

Then great Hector of the glancing helm answered her: "Surely I take thought for all thy words, my wife; but I have very sore shame of the Trojans and Trojan dames with trailing robes, if like a coward I shrink away from battle. Moreover mine own soul forbiddeth me, seeing I have learnt ever to be valiant and fight in the forefront of the Trojans, winning my father's great glory and mine own. Yea of a surety I know this in heart and soul; the day shall come for holy Ilium to be laid low, and Priam and the folk of Priam of the good ashen spear. Yet doth the anguish of the Trojans hereafter not so much trouble me, neither Hecuba's [1] own, neither King Priam's, neither my brethren's, the many and brave that shall fall in the dust before their foemen, as doth thine anguish in the day when some mail-clad Achæan shall lead thee weeping and rob thee of the light of freedom. So shalt thou abide in Argos and ply the loom at

[1] Wife of Priam and Hector's mother.

another woman's bidding, and bear water from the fountains. . . . And then shall one say that beholdeth thee weep, 'This is the wife of Hector, that was foremost in battle of the horse-taming Trojans when men fought about Ilium.' Thus shall one say hereafter, and fresh grief will be thine for lack of such an husband as thou hadst to ward off the day of thraldom. But me in death the heaped-up earth be covering, ere I hear thy crying and thy carrying into captivity."

So spake glorious Hector, and stretched out his arm to his boy. But the child shrunk crying to the bosom of his fair-girdled nurse, dismayed at his dear father's aspect, and in dread at the bronze and horse-hair crest that he beheld nodding fiercely from the helmet's top. Then his dear father laughed aloud, and his lady mother. Forthwith glorious Hector took the helmet from his head, and laid it, all gleaming, upon the earth; then kissed he his dear son and dandled him in his arms. And Hector spake in prayer to Zeus and all the gods, "O Zeus and all ye gods, vouchsafe ye that this my son may likewise prove even as I, preëminent among the Trojans, and as valiant in might, and be a great king of Ilium. Then may men say of him, 'Far greater is he than his father as he returneth home from battle; and may he bring wth him blood-stained spoils from the foeman he hath slain, and may his mother's heart be glad.'"

So spake he, and laid his son in his dear wife's arms; and she took him to her fragrant bosom, smiling tearfully. And her husband had pity to see her, and caressed her with his hand, and spake and called upon her name: "Dear one, I pray thee be not of over-sorrowful heart; no man against my fate shall hurl me to Hades.[1] Only destiny, I ween, no man hath escaped, be he cowardly or be he valiant, when once he hath been born. But go thou to thine house and see to thine own tasks, the loom and distaff, and bid thine handmaidens ply their work; but for war shall men provide, and I in chief of all men that dwell in Ilium."

So spake glorious Hector, and took up his horse-hair crested

[1] The underworld of the dead.

helmet; and his dear wife departed to her home, oft looking back, and letting fall big tears. Anon she came to the well-stablished house of man-slaying Hector, and found therein her many handmaidens, and stirred lamentation in them all. So bewailed they Hector, while yet he lived, within his house. For they deemed that he would no more come back to them from battle, or escape the fury of the hands of the Achæans.

## 13. The Shield of Achilles[1]

Now Zeus bethought him of his promise to avenge Achilles' wrong on Agamemnon, and when the battle raged again between the hosts he gave the victory to the Trojans. And Hector led his men up to the wall which the Achæans had built for the defense of the ships and broke within and began to burn the vessels where they lined the shore. In sore distress came Patroclus, Achilles' dearest friend, to the sulky chieftain, bidding him lay aside his wrath and once more fight for the Achæans. But Achilles vowed he would never cease from anger until that time when by his own ships the Trojans should raise their loud war-cry. Nevertheless to Patroclus, Achilles lent his splendid armor and his swift-footed immortal horses to draw the war-chariot into battle. Then did Patroclus do a hero's deeds until Hector struck him down and despoiled the corpse of its rich armor. Very terrible was the grief of Achilles when he learned that his friend was slain. And he forgot his wrath against Agamemnon and sought only to have vengeance upon Hector. So Thetis his lady mother secured from Hephæstus a suit of new armor, the work of a god, such as all men afterwards marveled at, whosoever beheld it.

First fashioned Hephæstus a shield great and strong, adorning it all over, and set thereto a shining rim, triple, bright-

[1] *Iliad,* xviii, 478–608.

glancing, and therefrom a silver baldric. Five were the folds of the shield itself; and therein fashioned he much cunning work from his wise heart.[1] There wrought he the earth, and the heavens, and the sea, and the unwearying sun, and the moon waxing to the full, and the signs every one wherewith the heavens are crowned. . . .

Also he fashioned therein two fair cities of mortal men. In the one were espousals and marriage feasts, and beneath the blaze of torches they were leading the brides from their chambers through the city, and loud arose the bridal song. And young men were whirling in the dance, and among them flutes and viols sounded high; and the women standing each at her door were marveling. But the folk were gathered in the assembly place; for there a strife had arisen, two men striving about the blood-price of a man slain. The one claimed to pay full atonement, expounding to the people, but the other denied him and would take naught. . . . And the folk were cheering both, as they took part on either side. And heralds kept order among the folk, while the elders on polished stones were sitting in the sacred circle, and holding in their hands staves from the loud-voiced heralds. Then before the people they rose up and gave judgment each in turn. And in the midst lay two talents of gold, to be given unto him who should plead among them most righteously.

But around the other city were two armies in siege with glittering arms. And two counsels found favor among them, either to sack the town or to share all with the townsfolk even whatsoever substance the fair city held within. But the besieged were not yet yielding, but arming for an ambushment. On the wall there stood to guard it their dear wives and infant children, and with these the old men; but the rest went forth. Their leaders were Ares and Pallas Athena, both wrought in gold, and golden was the vesture they had on. Goodly and

[1] The poet clearly has in mind a round shield, with parallel bands of ornament. The pictures are inlaid with various metals, gold, silver, tin, and with blue glass (cyanus).

great were they in their armor, even as gods, far seen around, and the folk at their feet were smaller. . . .

Furthermore he set in the shield a soft fresh-ploughed field, rich tilth and wide, the third time ploughed; and many ploughers therein drave their yokes to and fro as they wheeled about. Whensoever they came to the boundary of the field and turned, then would a man come to each and give into his hands a goblet of sweet wine, while others would be turning back along the furrows, fain to reach the boundary of the deep tilth. And the field grew black behind and seemed as it were a-ploughing, albeit of gold, for this was the great marvel of the work. Furthermore he set therein the demesne-land of a king, where hinds were reaping with sharp sickles in their hands. Some armfuls along the swathe were falling in rows to the earth, whilst others the sheaf-binders were binding in twisted bands of straw. Three sheaf-binders stood over them, while behind boys gathering corn and bearing it in their arms gave it constantly to the binders; and among them the king in silence was standing at the swathe with his staff, rejoicing in his heart. And henchmen apart beneath an oak were making ready a feast, and preparing a great ox they had sacrificed; while the women were strewing much white barley to be a supper for the hinds.

Also he set therein a vineyard teeming plenteously with clusters, wrought fair in gold; black were the grapes, but the vines hung throughout on silver poles. And around it he ran a ditch of cyanus, and round that a fence of tin; and one single pathway led to it, whereby the vintagers might go when they should gather the vintage. And maidens and striplings in childish glee bare the sweet fruit in plaited baskets. And in the midst of them a boy made pleasant music on a clear-toned viol, and sang thereto a sweet Linus-song [1] with delicate voice; while the rest with feet falling together kept time with the music and song.

Also he wrought therein a herd of kine with upright horns, and the kine were fashioned of gold and tin, and with lowing

---

[1] A lament for the death of vegetation.

they hurried from the byre to pasture beside a murmuring river, beside the waving reed. And herdsmen of gold were following with the kine, four of them, and nine dogs fleet of foot came after them. . . .

Also did the glorious lame god devise a dancing-place. . . . There were youths dancing and maidens of costly wooing, their hands upon one another's wrists. Fine linen the maidens had on, and the youths well-woven doublets faintly glistening with oil. Fair wreaths had the maidens, and the youths daggers of gold hanging from silver baldrics. And now would they run round with deft feet exceeding lightly, as when a potter sitting by his wheel that fitteth between his hands maketh trial of it whether it run. . . . And a great company stood round the lovely dance in joy; and among them a divine minstrel was making music on his lyre, and through the midst of them, leading the measure, two tumblers whirled.[1]

Also he set therein the great might of the River of Ocean[2] around the uttermost rim of the cunningly-fashioned shield.

### 14. Funeral Rites of Patroclus[3]

When Hephæstus had finished the shield and corslet, the massive helmet and greaves of pliant tin, he laid all his work before the mother of Achilles. Then Thetis brought the armor to her son who put it on and went forth terrible to the battle. And Achilles sprang in among the Trojans, his heart clothed with strength, and chased the men of Troy within the city gates. Hector alone remained outside, awaiting Achilles as he drew nigh in giant might. Yet even Hector's heart was now seized with sudden fear

[1] To this day one may see the peasants of Greece dancing in rings and lines, with agile acrobats to lead them, just as represented on the shield of Achilles.

[2] In early Greek fancy the ocean was thought of as a mighty river encircling the earth.

[3] *Iliad*, xxiii, 226–270.

and he fled before Achilles, three times around the wall
of Troy. And when at length Hector stayed his running
and stood up against Achilles, his fight was all in vain.
For he fell beneath his enemy's keen spear and Achilles
stripped him of his armor and brought his body to the
hollow ships. Then Achilles, sated of his vengeance,
ordered Agamemnon to make ready a funeral pyre whereon
to burn the corpse of Patroclus. All through the night
the flames, driven by the winds, consumed the pyre, and
Achilles mourned his friend with many moans.

But at the hour when the morning star goeth forth to herald
light upon the earth, the star that saffron-mantled dawn cometh
after, and spreadeth over the salt sea, then grew the burning
faint, and the flame died down. And the winds went back
again to betake them home over the Thracian main,[1] and it
roared with a violent swell. Then Achilles turned away from
the burning and lay down wearied, and sweet sleep leapt on him.
But they who were with Agamemnon gathered all together,
and the noise and clash of their approach aroused him. And
Achilles sate upright and spake a word to them: "Son of
Atreus and ye other chiefs of the Achæans, first quench with
gleaming wine all the burning so far as the fire hath reached,
and then let us gather up the bones of Patroclus. . . . And
his bones let us put within a golden urn, and double-folded
fat, until that I myself be hidden in Hades. But no huge
barrow I bid you toil to raise — a seemly one, no more:
then afterward do ye Achaeans build it broad and high, whosoever of you after I am gone may be left in the benched ships."
Thus spake he, and they hearkened to the fleet-footed son
of Peleus. First quenched they with gleaming wine the burning as far as the flame went, and the ash had settled deep.
Then with lamentation they gathered the bones of their gentle
comrade into a golden urn and double-folded fat, and placed

[1] The northern Ægean.

the urn in the hut and covered it with a linen veil. And they marked the circle of the barrow, and set the foundations thereof around the pyre, and straightway heaped thereon a mound of earth. Then when they had heaped up the barrow they were for going back.

But Achilles stayed the folk in that place, and made them sit in wide assembly, and from his ships he brought forth prizes, caldrons and tripods, and horses and mules and strong oxen, and fair-girdled women, and gray iron. First for fleet chariot-racers he ordained a noble prize, a woman skilled in fair handiwork for the winner to lead home, and an eared tripod that held two-and-twenty measures. These were for the first man; for the second he ordained a six-year-old mare unbroke. . . and for the third he gave a goodly caldron yet untouched by fire, holding four measures, bright as when first made. And for the fourth he ordained two talents of gold; and for the fifth a two-handled urn untouched by fire.

And now when the funeral games had been celebrated, the aged Priam, under guidance of the god Hermes, came by night to the hut of Achilles. With many gifts he sought to ransom the body of Hector, his dear son. And Achilles hearkened to the old man's entreaties and gave him back the corpse. On a lofty pyre the Trojans burned it, loudly lamenting, and holding funeral for glorious Hector, tamer of horses.

### 15. Nausicaa [1]

The *Iliad* ends with the funeral rites of Hector, who perished in the tenth year of the siege of Troy. After the capture of that city all the Greek chieftains who survived the conflict returned to their homes — all save Odysseus, king of Ithaca. Him the god Poseidon doomed to wander far and wide over the sea to strange lands. His

[1] *Odyssey*, vi, 46–101.

many adventures form the subject of the *Odyssey*. When the poem begins, Odysseus was still far from his rocky island of Ithaca where more than a hundred suitors courted his wife Penelope. Lawless and violent men they were, who feasted all day in the house of Odysseus and wasted his substance. Meantime the hero suffered shipwreck and was carried by the waves to the isle of Scheria where dwelt the Phæacians, a people akin to the gods. There on the shore he lay asleep, the steadfast, goodly Odysseus, foredone with toil and drowsiness. But the goddess Athena, with intent to aid him, appeared in a dream to Nausicaa, the lovely daughter of the Phæacian king, and bade her rise and wash the garments for her wedding day.

Anon came the throned dawn, and awakened Nausicaa of the fair robes, who straightway marveled on the dream, and went through the halls to tell her parents, her father dear and her mother. And she found them within, her mother sitting by the hearth with the women her handmaids, spinning yarn of sea-purple stain, but her father she met as he was going forth to the renowned kings in their council, whither the noble Phæacians called him. Standing close by her dear father she spake, saying: "Father, dear, couldst thou not lend me a high wagon with strong wheels, that I may take the goodly raiment to the river to wash, so much as I have lying soiled? Yea and it is seemly that thou thyself, when thou art with the princes in council, shouldest have fresh raiment to wear. Also, there are five dear sons of thine in the halls, two married, but three are lusty bachelors, and these are always eager for new-washen garments wherein to go to the dances. For all these things have I taken thought." This she said because she was ashamed to speak of glad marriage to her father; but he saw all and answered, saying: "Neither the mules nor aught else do I grudge thee, my child. Go thy ways, and the servants shall get thee ready a high wagon with good wheels, and fitted with an upper frame."

Therewith he called to his men, and they gave ear, and without the palace they made ready the smooth-running mule-wain, and led the mules beneath the yoke, and harnessed them under the car, while the maiden brought forth from her bower the shining raiment. This she stored in the polished car, and her mother filled a basket with all manner of food to the heart's desire, dainties too, she set therein, and she poured wine into a goat-skin bottle, while Nausicaa climbed into the wain. And her mother gave her soft olive oil also in a golden cruse, that she and her maidens might anoint themselves after the bath. . . .

Now when they were come to the beautiful stream of the river, where truly were the unfailing cisterns, and bright water welled up free from beneath, and flowed past, enough to wash the foulest garments clean, there the girls unharnessed the mules from under the chariot. Then they turned them loose and drove them along the banks of the eddying river to graze on the honey-sweet clover. Next they took the garments from the wain, in their hands, and bore them to the black water, and briskly trod them down in the trenches, in busy rivalry. Now when they had washed and cleansed all the stains, they spread all out in order along the shore of the deep, even where the sea, in beating on the coast, washed the pebbles clean. Then having bathed and anointed themselves well with olive oil, they took their mid-day meal on the river's banks, waiting till the clothes should dry in the brightness of the sun. Anon, when they were satisfied with food, the maidens and the princess, they fell to playing at ball, casting away their tires, and among them Nausicaa of the white arms began the song.

### 16   The Palace of Alcinous [1]

Then Odysseus, aroused by the maidens, awoke from his deep sleep and made himself known to Nausicaa and her

[1] *Odyssey*, vii, 81–132.

train. And they gave him meat and drink and covered him with a fair mantle and led him to the city of the Phæacians.

Meanwhile Odysseus went to the famous palace of King Alcinous, and his heart was full of many thoughts as he stood there. . . . For Odysseus saw a gleam as it were of sun or moon through the high-roofed hall of great-hearted Alcinous. Brazen were the walls which ran this way and that from the threshold to the inmost chamber, and round them was a frieze of blue,[1] and golden were the doors that closed in the good house. Silver were the door-posts that were set on the brazen threshold, and silver the lintel thereupon, and the hook of the door was of gold. And on either side stood golden hounds and silver, which Hephæstus wrought by his cunning, to guard the palace of great-hearted Alcinous, being free from death and age all their days. And within were seats arrayed against the wall this way and that, from the threshold even to the inmost chamber, and thereon were spread light coverings finely woven, the handiwork of women. There the Phæacian chieftains were wont to sit eating and drinking, for they had continual store. Yea, and there were youths fashioned in gold, standing on firm-set bases, with flaming torches in their hands, giving light through the night to the feasters in the palace. And Alcinous had fifty handmaids in the house, and some grind the yellow grain on the millstone, and others weave webs and turn the yarn as they sit, restless as the leaves of the tall poplar tree; and the soft olive oil drops off that linen, so closely is it woven. For as the Phæacian men are skilled beyond all others in driving a swift ship upon the deep, even so are the women the most cunning at the loom, for Athena hath given them notable wisdom in all fair handiwork and cunning wit.

And without the courtyard hard by the door is a great garden, and a hedge runs round on either side. And there grow tall

---

[1] A similar "frieze of blue" was found by H. Schliemann in the palace-citadel of Tiryns. The frieze consisted of alabaster inlaid with blue glass.

trees blossoming, pear-trees, and pomegranates, and apple-trees with bright fruit, and sweet figs, and olives in their bloom. The fruit of these trees never perisheth, neither faileth, winter nor summer, enduring through all the year. Evermore the west wind blowing brings some fruits to birth and ripens others. Pear upon pear waxes old, and apple on apple, yea and cluster ripens upon cluster of the grape, and fig upon fig. There too hath he a fruitful vineyard planted, whereof the one part is being dried by the heat, a sunny plot on level ground, while other grapes men are gathering, and yet others they are treading in the wine-press. In the foremost row are unripe grapes that cast the blossom, and others there be that are growing black to vintaging. There too skirting the furthest line, are all manner of garden beds, planted trimly, that are perpetually fresh, and therein are two fountains of water, whereof one scatters his streams all about the garden, and the other runs over against it beneath the threshold of the court-yard, and issues by the lofty house. There did the townsfolk draw water. Such were the splendid gifts of the gods in the palace of Alcinous.[1]

### 17. The Story of Eumæus [2]

And now the Phæacians entreated Odysseus right hos-pitably. And after he had related all his strange adven-tures, the Phæacians bore him back to Ithaca in their hollow ships and set him down in a fair haven of the island. There the goddess, gray-eyed Athena, came to him telling how the wooers beset his house. And the goddess dis-guised Odysseus as an old man, a beggar, and bade him go to the hut of the swineherd Eumæus, who was still faithful to his absent lord. To Eumæus, Odysseus

[1] This description of the palace of Alcinous with its furniture and decora-tions closely accords with actual remains of the Ægean Age as revealed by modern explorations.

[2] *Odyssey*, xv, 403–484.

recited a cunning narrative of his wanderings and his
sufferings; for he would not yet disclose himself to the
swineherd. And Eumæus in turn, when questioned by
Odysseus, related the story of his past life.

"There is a certain isle called Syria; if haply thou hast heard
tell of it, over above Ortygia,[1] and there are the turning-places
of the sun. It is not very great in compass, though a goodly
isle, rich in herds, rich in flocks, with plenty of corn and wine.
Dearth never enters the land, and no hateful sickness falls on
wretched mortals. . . . In that isle are two cities, and the whole
land is divided between them, and my father was king over the
twain . . . a man like to the immortals.

"Thither came the Phœnicians, mariners renowned, greedy
merchant men, with countless gauds in a black ship. Now in
my father's house was a Phœnician woman, tall and fair and
skilled in bright handiwork; this woman the Phœnicians with
their sleights beguiled. First as she was washing clothes, one
of them . . . asked her who she was and whence she came,
and straightway she showed him the lofty home of my father,
saying: 'From out of Sidon[2] I avow that I come, a land rich in
bronze, and I am the daughter of Arybas, the wealthy. But
Taphians,[3] who were sea-robbers, laid hands on me and snatched
me away as I came in from the fields, and brought me hither
and sold me into the house of my master, who paid for me a
goodly price.' Then the man . . . answered, 'Say, wouldst
thou now return home with us, that thou mayest look again
on the lofty house of thy father and mother and on their faces?
For truly they yet live, and have a name for wealth.' Then
the woman answered him, 'Even this may well be, if ye sailors
will pledge me an oath to bring me home in safety?' So spake
she, and they all swore thereto as she bade them. Now when

[1] These islands have a mythical character as the "turning-places" of the
sun.

[2] Sidon was one of the chief cities of Phœnicia.

[3] Inhabitants of Taphos, an island off the coast of Acarnania.

they had sworn and done that oath, again the woman spake among them and answered, saying: 'Hold your peace now, and let none of your fellows speak to me and greet me, if they meet me in the street, or even at the well, lest one go and tell it to the old man at home, and he suspect somewhat and bind me in hard bonds and devise death for all of you. But keep ye the matter in mind, and speed the purchase of your homeward freight. And when your ship is freighted with stores, let a message come quickly to me at the house; for I will likewise bring gold, all that comes under my hand. Yea and there is another thing that I would gladly give for my fare. I am nurse to the child of my lord in the halls, a most cunning little boy, that runs out abroad with me. Him would I bring on board ship, and he should fetch you a great price, wheresoever ye take him for sale among men of strange speech.'

"Therewith she went her way to the fair halls. But they abode among us a whole year, and got together much wealth in their hollow ship. And when their hollow ship was now laden to depart, they sent a messenger to tell the tidings to the woman. There came a man versed in craft to my father's house, with a golden chain strung here and there with amber beads. Now the maidens in the hall and my lady mother were handling the chain and gazing on it, and offering him their price; but he had signed silently to the woman, and therewithal gat him away to the hollow ship. Then she took me by the hand and led me forth from the house. And at the vestibule of the house she found the cups and the tables of the guests that had been feasting, who were in waiting on my father. They had gone forth to the session and the place of parley of the people. And she straightway hid three goblets in her bosom, and bare them away, and I followed in my innocence. Then the sun sank and all the ways were darkened. And we went quickly and came to the good haven, where was the swift ship of the Phœnicians. So they climbed on board and took us up with them, and sailed over the wet ways, and Zeus sent us a favoring wind. For six days we sailed by day and night continually; but when Zeus added the seventh day thereto, then Artemis,[1] the archer, smote the woman that she fell, as a sea-swallow falls, with a plunge into the hold. And they cast her forth to be the prey of seals and fishes, but I was left stricken at heart. And wind and water bare them and brought them to Ithaca where Laertes [2] bought me with his possessions. And thus it came about that mine eyes beheld this land."

While Odysseus still abode with the faithful swineherd, he revealed himself to his son Telemachus, and then planned deadly vengeance on the wicked suitors. Now Penelope had promised that she would wed the man who could draw the bow of Odysseus and send an arrow through the holes in twelve axe-blades set up in a row. But at the trial, not one of the suitors was able even to string the bow. Odysseus, however, bent it easily and sent an arrow through the mark. Then he turned upon the suitors and dealt his shafts among them, and aided by Telemachus and Eumæus, slaughtered all their wicked crew. Thus Odysseus became once more the lord of rocky Ithaca, full twenty years after his departure for the wind-swept plain of Troy.

[1] Artemis, the archer goddess, was sometimes thought of as a deity who slew individuals, especially women, with her deadly arrows. A sudden and mysterious death would be so explained.

[2] Father of Odysseus.

# CHAPTER IV

## STORIES FROM GREEK MYTHOLOGY [1]

THE beautiful and varied mythology of the Greeks came into existence long before the beginnings of Greek history. Until the introduction of writing the myths were preserved in popular traditions, in priestly rituals, and in the songs chanted by minstrel bards as they wandered from city to city. Much of this legendary material was taken over by the authors of the *Iliad* and the *Odyssey* and built into the structure of the Homeric epics. A century or two after Homer, many of the stories about the gods and demigods were gathered together and reduced to order in the poems attributed to Hesiod. Of these the most important was the *Theogony*, which recounts the creation of the world and the generation of the gods and heroes. The Hesiodic poems became to the Greeks a standard repository of the old mythology and the source from which later poets derived much of their legendary lore.

### 18. The Struggle between Zeus and the Titans [2]

The *Theogony* begins with the creation of the world from Chaos and the origin of the forces and phenomena of nature — night and day, earth and the starry heavens, deep-eddying ocean and the lofty hills. From Earth (or

---

[1] *Hesiod, The Poems and Fragments*, translated by A. W. Mair. Oxford, 1908. Clarendon Press.

[2] Hesiod, *Theogony*, 674–721.

Gæa) married to Heaven (or Uranus), sprang the twelve gigantic Titans and the one-eyed Cyclopes. These were personifications of volcanic eruptions, earthquakes, the rolling thunder, and the lightning flash. Other offspring of Earth and Heaven were Briareus, Cottus, and Gyes, hundred-handed giants, supposed to be personifications of the hail, the rain, and the snow. Cronus (Greek, *Kronos*), youngest of the Titans, made war on his father and dethroned him from his seat. Then Cronus married Rhea, who gave birth to the great deities, Hestia, Demeter, Hera, Hades, Poseidon, and Zeus. These, in turn, made war on Cronus. On the one side were the Titans fighting for their brother Cronus; on the opposite side were Zeus and Rhea's other children. For more than ten years they fought, Zeus with his hosts from Mount Olympus, the Titans from Mount Othrys. Then Zeus summoned to his aid the three giants, each with a hundred hands, whom Uranus had sought to bury out of sight beneath the earth.

And now they stood against the Titans in baleful strife, with sheer rocks in their stout hands. And the Titans on the other side eagerly strengthened their ranks. Then these and those together showed forth the work of their hands and their might. The boundless sea roared terribly around them, and the earth crashed aloud, and the wide heaven groaned as it was shaken, and high Olympus was stirred from its foundations at the onset of the immortals, and a grievous convulsion came on misty Tartarus. . . . And the voices of either side came unto the starry heaven as they shouted. And they came together with a mighty din.

Nor did Zeus any longer restrain his soul, but straightway his mind was filled with fury and he showed forth all his might. From heaven and from Olympus he came to join them, lightening as he came. And his bolts flew near at hand with thunder and with lightning, thick bolts from his strong hand rolling a holy flame; and around the life-giving earth crashed as it burned, and the infinite wood cried aloud with fire. And the whole earth boiled, and the streams of Ocean, and the unharvested sea. Hot breath beset the Titans from under the earth, and infinite flame came unto the holy ether, and the flashing glare of thunderbolt and lightning robbed their eyes of sight, albeit they were strong. And a wondrous heat beset Chaos. And it seemed to see with the eyes and to hear the din with the ears, as if earth and the wide heaven above drew nigh to one another. For such a mighty din would have arisen if earth were ruining and heaven above hurling it to ruin. Such was the din when the gods met in strife.

And amid the foremost, Cottus and Briareus and Gyes, insatiate of war, awoke bitter battle. In quick succession they hurled three hundred rocks from their stout hands, and overshadowed the Titans with their shafts, and sent them beneath the wide-wayed earth to Tartarus. . . . As far beneath the earth as the heaven is high above the earth, even so far is it from earth to misty Tartarus.

### 19. Prometheus and Pandora [1]

After the banishment of the Titans to Tartarus, Zeus assumed the sovereignty of the gods. He gave to his brother Poseidon the kingdom of the sea; to Hades, his second brother, the government of the underworld. For himself Zeus retained the dominion of earth and heaven. From his wives sprang many of the gods and goddesses who made up the council of divinities on Mount Olympus.[2] And at the instigation of Zeus, Prometheus, a Titan who

---

[1] Hesiod, *Theogony*, 535–593.

[2] Hesiod enumerates the three Graces, the nine Muses, Persephone, daughter of Zeus by Demeter, Apollo and Artemis, his children by Latona, Hebe and Ares, his children by Hera. From the head of Zeus sprang the goddess Athena. Other offspring of Zeus were Hermes, messenger of the gods, Dionysus, lord of the wine-cup and the revel, and Heracles the mighty hero.

had allied himself with the Olympians in their contest against the Titans, made man in the image of the gods. But Prometheus was wily, and by his deceits drew down upon himself the wrath of Zeus.

For once when the gods and mortal men were contending, Prometheus with willing heart cut up a mighty ox and set it before them, deceiving the mind of Zeus. For he set for them the flesh and the inmeats with rich fat upon a hide, and covered them with an ox paunch; but for Zeus he set the white bones, craftily arraying them, and covering them with glistening fat. Then the father of gods and men spake unto him, "Son of Iapetus,[1] most notable of all princes, how unfairly hast thou divided the portions!"

Then spake to him in turn Prometheus of crooked counsels, smiling quietly, but forgetting not his crafty guile, "Zeus, most glorious, mightiest of the everlasting gods, of these portions choose whichever thy soul within thy breast biddeth thee." So spake he with crafty intent. But Zeus, who knoweth counsels imperishable, knew and failed not to remark the guile; and in his heart he boded evil things for mortal men, which were destined to be fulfilled. With both hands he lifted up the white fat. And he was angered in his heart and wrath came about his soul when he beheld the white bones of the ox given him in crafty guile. And thenceforth do the tribes of men on earth burn white bones to the immortals upon fragrant altars. Then heavily moved, Zeus the cloud gatherer spake unto him, "Son of Iapetus, who knowest counsels beyond all others, thou hast not yet forgotten thy crafty guile."

So in anger spake Zeus, who knoweth counsels imperishable. And henceforward, remembering evermore that guile, he gave not the might of blazing fire to wretched mortals who dwell upon the earth. But the good son of Iapetus deceived him and stole the far-seen gleam of unwearied fire in a hollow fennel

[1] Iapetus the Titan, father of Prometheus.

stalk. And he stung to the depths the heart of Zeus who thundereth on high, and angered his dear heart when he beheld among men the far-shining gleam of fire.

And straightway for fire Zeus devised evil for men. The glorious Lame One [1] fashioned of earth the likeness of a modest maiden as the son of Cronus devised. And the goddess, gray-eyed Athena, girdled her and arrayed her in shining raiment: and over her head she cast with her hands a cunningly-fashioned veil, a marvel to behold; and about her head Pallas Athena set lovely garlands, even wreaths of fresh grass and green. . . . And amazement held immortal gods and mortal men, when they saw the sheer delusion unescapable for men. For from her cometh the race of womankind. Yea, of her is the deadly race and the tribes of women. A great bane are they to dwell among mortal men, no helpmeet for ruinous poverty, but for abundance.[2]

### 20. The Five Races of Man [3]

First of all, a golden race of mortal men did the immortal dwellers in Olympus fashion. These lived in the time of Cronus when he was king in Heaven. Like gods they lived, having a soul unknowing sorrow, apart from toil and travail. Neither were they subject to miserable old age, but ever the same in hand and foot, they took their pleasure in festival apart from all evil. And they died as overcome of sleep. All good things were theirs. The bounteous earth bare fruit for them of her own will, in plenty and without stint. And they in peace and quiet lived on their lands with many good things, rich in flocks and dear to the blessed gods. But since this race was hidden in the earth, spirits they are by the will of mighty Zeus: good spirits, on earth, keepers of mortal men. . . .

---

[1] The god Hephæstus.

[2] These passages from Hesiod contain the earliest Greek version of two famous legends: the origin of fire, and the creation of woman. Pandora might be called the Eve of Greek mythology.

[3] Hesiod, *Works and Days*, 109–179.

Then next the dwellers in Olympus created a far inferior race, a race of silver, no wise like to the golden race in body or in mind. For a hundred years the child grew up by his good mother's side, playing in utter childishness within his home. But when they grew to manhood and came to the full measure of age, for but a little space they lived and in sorrow by reason of their foolishness. For they could not refrain from sinning the one against the other, neither would they worship the deathless gods, nor do sacrifice on the holy altars of the blessed ones, as the manner of men wheresoever they dwell. Wherefore Zeus in anger put them away, because they gave not honor to the blessed gods who dwell in Olympus. Now since this race too was hidden in earth, they beneath the earth are called blessed mortals. Of lower rank, yet they too have their honor.

Then Zeus the father created a third race of mortal men, a race of bronze . . . terrible and strong; whose delight was in the dolorous works of Ares and in insolence. Bread they ate not: but souls they had stubborn, of adamant, unapproachable: great was their might and invincible the arms that grew from their shoulders on stout frames. Of bronze was their armor, of bronze their dwellings, with bronze they wrought. Black iron was not yet. These by their own hands slain went down to the dank house of chill Hades, nameless. And black death slew them, for all that they were mighty, and they left the bright light of the sun.

Now when this race also was hidden in earth, yet a fourth race did Zeus the son of Cronus create upon the bounteous earth, a juster race and better, a god-like race of hero men who are called demigods. . . . And them did evil war and dread battle slay, some at seven-gated Thebes . . . some when war had brought them in ships across the great gulf of the sea to Troy for the sake of fair-tressed Helen. There did the issue of death cover them about. But Zeus the father, the son of Cronus, gave them a life and an abode apart from men, and established them at the ends of the earth afar from the deathless gods. Among them Cronus is king. And they with soul

untouched of sorrow dwell in the Islands of the Blest by deep-
eddying Ocean.  Happy heroes are they, for whom the bounteous earth beareth honey-sweet fruit fresh thrice a year.

I would then that I lived not among the fifth race of men,
but either had died before or had been born afterward.  For
now verily is a race of iron.  Neither by day shall they ever cease
from weariness of woe, neither in the night from wasting, and
sore cares shall the gods give them.  Howbeit even for them shall
good be mingled with evil.[1]

[1] Hesiod's picture of the Gold and Silver ages is purely ideal.  The
Bronze Age and the Iron Age, on the contrary, are historical.  In inserting
an Heroic Age of demigods, the poet is making a concession to the widespread
Greek custom of hero-worship.

# CHAPTER V

## SOME GREEK TYRANTS [1]

In the seventh and sixth centuries B.C. many Hellenic cities passed under the control of illegal rulers whom the Greeks called *tyrants*. By enlisting the common people in his support, or by recruiting a body of mercenary soldiers, an adventurer was often able to overthrow the nobles and to establish himself in the seat of government. The rule of the tyrant formed not seldom a most prosperous period in the history of a Greek city. Yet he sat upon a very unstable throne. The Greeks hated all arbitrary and unconstitutional power. So the tyranny generally came to a sudden end — sometimes during the usurper's lifetime, more frequently after his death, when the rule passed to his sons. The historian, Herodotus, writing at the middle of the fifth century B.C. when many of the tyrannies had disappeared from the Greek cities, reflects the general feeling of hostility to them that was current in his age.

### 21. Cypselus and Periander, Tyrants of Corinth [2]

. . . Cypselus, the first tyrant of Corinth, showed himself a harsh ruler. Many of the Corinthians he drove into banishment, many he deprived of their fortunes, and a still greater number, of their lives. His reign lasted thirty years, and was prosperous to its close; so that he left the government to Periander, his son.

[1] Herodotus. The translation of George Rawlinson, edited by A. J. Grant. 2 vols. London, 1897. John Murray.

[2] Herodotus, v, 92.

This ruler, at the beginning of his reign, was of a milder temper than his father; but after he corresponded by means of messengers with Thrasybulus, tyrant of Miletus, he became even more sanguinary. On one occasion he sent a herald to ask Thrasybulus what mode of government it was safest to set up in order to rule with honor. Thrasybulus led the messenger without the city, and took him into a field of corn, through which he began to walk. While Thrasybulus asked him again and again concerning his coming from Corinth, he broke off and threw away such ears of corn as overtopped the rest. In this way he went through the whole field, and destroyed all the best and richest parts of the crop. Then, without a word, he sent the messenger back. On the return of the man to Corinth, Periander was eager to know what Thrasybulus had counseled, but the messenger reported that he had said nothing. The messenger wondered that Periander had sent him to so strange a man, who seemed to have lost his senses, since he did nothing but destroy his own property. Upon this he told how Thrasybulus had behaved at the interview. Periander, perceiving what the action meant, and knowing that Thrasybulus advised the destruction of all the leading citizens, treated his subjects from this time forward with the greatest cruelty. Where Cypselus had spared any, and had neither put them to death nor banished them, Periander completed what his father had left unfinished. . . .

Corinth, under the brilliant rule of Periander, became the wealthiest and most prosperous city of Greece. After his death his nephew ruled for a few years and then the tyranny of the Cypselids came to an end (581 B.C.). Thenceforth Corinth was governed by an oligarchy of merchant princes.

### 22. Clisthenes of Sicyon [1]

The little state of Sicyon, not far from Corinth, was the seat of a powerful tyranny under its ruler Clisthenes

[1] Herodotus, vi, 125–126, 128–130.

(about 600-570 B.C.). How Clisthenes married his daughter to a member of the noble Athenian family of the Alcmæon-idæ, is related by Herodotus in the following delightful story.

Now the Alcmæonidæ were, even in the days of yore, a family of note at Athens; but from the time of Alcmæon, and again of Megacles, they rose to special eminence. The former of these two personages . . . when Crœsus the Lydian sent men from Sardis to consult the Delphic oracle,[1] gave aid gladly to his messengers, and assisted them to accomplish their task. Crœsus, informed of Alcmæon's kindnesses by the Lydians who from time to time conveyed his messages to the god, sent for him to Sardis, and when he arrived, made him a present of as much gold as he could carry at one time about his person. Finding that this was the gift assigned him, Alcmæon took his measures, and prepared himself to receive it in the following way. He clothed himself in a loose tunic, which he made to bag greatly at the waist, and placed upon his feet the widest buskins that he could anywhere find. Then he followed his guides into the treasure-house. Here he started on a heap of gold-dust, and in the first place packed as much as he could inside his buskins, between them and his legs; after which he filled the breast of his tunic quite full of gold. Then, sprinkling some over his hair, and taking some likewise in his mouth, he came forth from the treasure-house, scarcely able to drag his legs along. . . . On seeing him, Crœsus burst into a laugh, and not only let him have all that he had taken, but gave him presents besides, of fully equal worth. Thus Alcmæon became a man of great wealth; and was able to keep horses for the chariot-race, and won the prize at Olympia.

Afterwards, in the generation which followed, Clisthenes, king of Sicyon, raised the family to still greater eminence among the Greeks. . . . For this Clisthenes . . . had a daughter, called Agarista, whom he wished to marry to the best husband

[1] See page 16.

that he could find in the whole of Greece. At the Olympic games, therefore, having gained the prize in the chariot-race, he caused public proclamation to be made to the following effect: "Whoever among the Greeks deems himself worthy to be the son-in-law of Clisthenes, let him come, sixty days hence, or, if he will, sooner, to Sicyon. Within a year's time, counting from the end of the sixty days, Clisthenes will decide on the man to whom he shall contract his daughter." So all the Greeks who were proud of their own merit, or of their country, flocked to Sicyon as suitors. Clisthenes had a foot-course and a wrestling-ground made ready to try their powers. . . .

Now when they were all come, and the day appointed had arrived, Clisthenes first of all inquired of each concerning his country and his family. After this he kept them with him a year, and made trial of their manly bearing, their temper, their accomplishments, and their disposition. Such as were still youths he took with him from time to time to the gymnasia; but the greatest trial of all was at the banquet-table. During the whole period of their stay he lived with them as I have said; and, further, from first to last, he entertained them sumptuously. Somehow or other the suitors who came from Athens pleased him the best of all. Of these Hippoclides, Tisander's son, was specially in favor, partly on account of his manly bearing, and partly also because his ancestors were of kin to the Corinthian Cypselids.[1]

When at length the day arrived which had been fixed for the espousals, and Clisthenes had to speak out and declare his choice, he first of all made a sacrifice of a hundred oxen, and held a banquet, at which he entertained all the suitors and the people of Sicyon. After the feast was ended, the suitors vied with each other in music, and in speaking on a given subject. Presently, as the drinking advanced, Hippoclides, to the astonishment of the guests, called aloud to the flute-player, and bade him strike up a dance. This the man did, and Hippoclides danced to it. He fancied that he was dancing excellently well;

[1] See page 53.

but Clisthenes, who was observing him, began to misdoubt the whole business. Then Hippoclides, after a pause, told an attendant to bring in a table; and when it was brought, he mounted upon it and danced first of all some Laconian figures, then some Attic ones; after which he stood on his head upon the table, and began to toss his legs about. Clisthenes, notwithstanding that he now loathed Hippoclides for a son-in-law, by reason of his dancing and his shamelessness . . . had restrained himself during the first and likewise during the second dance. When, however, he saw him tossing his legs in the air, he could no longer contain himself, but cried out, "Son of Tisander, thou hast danced thy wife away!" "What does Hippoclides care?" was the other's answer. And hence the proverb arose.

Then Clisthenes commanded silence, and spoke thus before the assembled company: "Suitors of my daughter, well pleased am I with you all; and right willingly, if it were possible, would I content you all, and not by making choice of one appear to put a slight upon the rest. It is, however, out of my power, seeing that I have only one daughter, to grant all your wishes. Now I will present to each of you whom I must needs dismiss a talent [1] of silver, for the honor that you have done me in seeking to ally yourselves with my house, and for your long absence from your homes. But my daughter Agarista, I betroth to Megacles, the son of Alcmæon, to be his wife, according to the usage and wont of Athens." Then Megacles expressed his readiness; and Clisthenes had the marriage solemnized.

Thus ended the affair of the suitors and thus the Alcmæonidæ came to be famous throughout all Greece.

### 23. Pisistratus of Athens [2]

Hippocrates the Athenian, when he was a private citizen, is said to have gone once upon a time to Olympia to see the

---

[1] About $1080.　　[2] Herodotus, i, 59–60.

games. Here a wonderful prodigy happened to him. As he
was employed in sacrificing, the caldrons which stood near,
full of water and the flesh of the victims, began to boil without
the help of fire, so that the water overflowed the pots. Chilon
the Spartan, who happened to be there and to witness the
prodigy, advised Hippocrates, if he was unmarried, never to
take into his house a wife who could bear him a child. . . .
Chilon's advice did not at all please Hippocrates, who disre-
garded it, and some time after became the father of
Pisistratus.

This Pisistratus, at a time when there was civil contention
in Attica between the party of the Sea-coast headed by Megacles [1] the son of Alcmæon, and that of the Plain headed by
Lycurgus, one of the Aristolaïds, formed the project of making himself tyrant. With this end in view he created a third
party.[2] Gathering together a band of partisans, and giving
himself out for the protector of the highlanders, he contrived
the following stratagem. He wounded himself and his mules,
and then drove his chariot into the market place, professing
to have just escaped an attack of his enemies, who had attempted his life as he was on his way into the country. He
besought the people to assign him a guard to protect his person, reminding them of the glory which he had gained when he
led the attack upon the Megarians,[3] and took the town of
Nisæa, at the same time performing many other exploits.
The Athenians, deceived by his story, appointed him a band of
citizens to serve as a guard. They were to carry clubs instead
of spears, and to accompany him wherever he went. Thus
strengthened, Pisistratus broke into revolt and seized the citadel. In this way he acquired the sovereignty of Athens,
which he continued to hold without disturbing the previously
existing offices or altering any of the laws. He administered

---

[1] The same Megacles who married Agarista, daughter of Clisthenes,
tyrant of Sicyon.

[2] Composed of shepherds and peasants living in the mountains of Attica.

[3] When Athens and Megara were at war (570–565 B. C.).

the state according to the established usages, and his arrangements were wise and salutary.

However, after a little time, the partisans of Megacles and those of Lycurgus agreed to forget their differences, and united to drive him out. So Pisistratus, having by the means described first made himself master of Athens, lost his power again before it had time to take root. No sooner, however, had he departed than the factions which had driven him out quarreled anew. At last Megacles, wearied with the struggle, sent a herald to Pisistratus, with an offer to reëstablish him on the throne if he would marry his daughter. Pisistratus consented, and on these terms an agreement was concluded between the two, after which they proceeded to plan the mode of his restoration.

The device on which they hit was the silliest that I find on record, more especially when we consider that the Greeks have been from very ancient times distinguished from the barbarians by superior sagacity, and when we remember also that the persons on whom this trick was played were not only Greeks, but Athenians, who have the credit of surpassing all other Greeks in cleverness. There was in Attica a woman named Phya, whose height only fell short of four cubits by three fingers' breadth, and who was altogether comely to look upon. This woman they first of all clothed in complete armor. Instructing her as to the demeanor which she was to maintain in order to act her part, they placed her in a chariot and drove to the city. Heralds had been sent forward to precede her, and to make proclamation to this effect: "Citizens of Athens, receive again Pisistratus with friendly minds. Athena, who of all men honors him the most, herself conducts him back to her own citadel." This they proclaimed in all directions, and immediately the rumor spread throughout the country districts that Athena was bringing back her favorite. They of the city also, fully persuaded that the woman was the veritable goddess, prostrated themselves before her, and received Pisistratus back.

The tyranny of Pisistratus lasted, with some intermissions noted by Herodotus, for thirty-three years (560–527 B. C.). His two sons, Hippias and Hipparchus, who followed him, enjoyed a briefer rule. Hipparchus was murdered in a private feud. Not long after (510 B. C.), Hippias was expelled from Athens by the Spartans, with the aid of the Alcmæonidæ whom Pisistratus had exiled.

### 24. Polycrates, Tyrant of Samos [1]

One of the most famous of the early tyrants was Polycrates of Samos (about 535–520 B. C.). He owned the largest navy in the eastern part of the Ægean and succeeded in building up a strong maritime empire.

The exceeding good fortune of Polycrates did not escape the notice of Amasis,[2] who was much disturbed thereat. When therefore his successes continued, Amasis wrote him the following letter, and sent it to Samos. "Amasis to Polycrates thus sayeth: It is a pleasure to hear of a friend and ally prospering; but thy exceeding prosperity does not cause me joy, forasmuch as I know that the gods are envious. My wish for myself, and for those whom I love, is, to be now successful, and now to meet with a check. Thus one passes through life amid alternate good and ill, rather than with perpetual good fortune. For never yet did I hear tell of anyone succeeding in all his undertakings, who did not meet with calamity at last, and come to utter ruin. Now, therefore, give ear to my words and meet thy good luck in this way. Consider what treasure thou valuest most and canst least bear to part with; take it, whatsoever it be, and throw it away, so that it may be sure never to come any more into the sight of man. Then, if thy good fortune is not thenceforth mingled with ill, save thyself from harm by again doing as I have counseled."

---

[1] Herodotus, iii, 40–43.   [2] Amasis II, king of Egypt.   See pages 14, 20.

When Polycrates read this letter, and perceived that the advice of Amasis was good, he considered carefully which of the treasures that he had in store it would grieve him most to lose. After much thought he made up his mind that it was a signet-ring which he was wont to wear, an emerald set in gold. So he determined to throw this away. Manning a ship, he went on board, and bade the sailors put out into the open sea. When he was now a long way from the island, he took the ring from his finger, and, in the sight of all those who were on board, flung it into the deep. This done, he returned home, and gave vent to his sorrow.

Now it happened five or six days afterwards that a fisherman caught a fish so large and beautiful, that he thought it well deserved to be presented to the king. So he took it with him to the gate of the palace, and said that he wanted to see Polycrates. Then Polycrates allowed him to come in; and the fisherman gave him the fish with these words of explanation: "O king, when I took this prize, I thought I would not carry it to market, though I am a poor man who live by my trade. I said to myself, It is worthy of Polycrates and his greatness; and so I brought it here to give it to you." This speech pleased the king, who thus spoke in reply: "Thou didst right well, friend; and I am doubly indebted, both for the gift, and for the speech. Come now and sup with me." So the fisherman went home, esteeming it a high honor that he had been asked to sup with the king. Meanwhile the servants, on cutting open the fish, found the signet of their master in its stomach. No sooner did they see it than they seized upon it, and hastening to Polycrates with great joy, restored it to him, and told him in what way it had been found. The king, who saw something providential in the matter, forthwith wrote a letter to Amasis, telling him all that had happened, what he had himself done, and what had been the result — and dispatched the letter to Egypt.

When Amasis had read the letter of Polycrates, he perceived that it does not belong to man to save his fellow-man from the fate which is in store for him. Likewise he felt certain that Polycrates would end ill, as he prospered in everything, even finding what he had thrown away. So he sent a herald to Samos, and dissolved the contract of friendship. This he did, that when the great and heavy misfortune came, he might escape the grief which he would have felt if the sufferer had been his bond-friend.

The apprehensions of the Egyptian monarch were ere long justified. Polycrates' good fortune at length deserted him. He was entrapped by the Persian governor of Sardis and perished miserably "in a way unworthy of his rank and of his lofty schemes. For, if we except the Syracusans, there has never been one of the Greek tyrants who is to be compared with Polycrates for magnificence."

# CHAPTER VI

## SPARTAN EDUCATION AND LIFE [1]

A LITTLE treatise by Xenophon, an Athenian historian and essayist (about 431–355 B. C.), is one of our principal sources of information for the remarkable social institutions of the Spartans. Xenophon lived in Sparta and its vicinity for many years, and so had ample opportunity of studying the Spartan discipline and of comparing it with the methods of training followed in other Greek cities.

### 25. Education of Boys [2]

. . . Throughout the rest of Greece the custom on the part of those who claim to educate their sons in the best way is as follows. As soon as the children are of an age to understand what is said to them, they are immediately placed under the charge of tutors who are also attendants, and sent off to the school of some teacher to be taught "grammar," "music," and the concerns of the palestra.[3] Besides this they are given shoes to wear which tend to make their feet tender, and their bodies are enervated by various changes of clothing. And as for food, the only measure recognized is that which is fixed by appetite. But when we turn to Sparta, we find that Lycurgus . . . set over the young Spartans a public guardian who enjoyed complete authority. This guardian was selected from those

[1] Xenophon, *Polity of the Lacedæmonians. The Works of Xenophon*, translated by H. G. Dakyns. 4 vols. London, 1890–1897. Macmillan and Co.

[2] Xenophon, *Polity of the Lacedæmonians*, 2–3.

[3] The athletic field where outdoor sports were held.

who filled the highest magistracies. He had the right to hold musters of the boys, and as their overseer, in case of any misbehavior, to chastise them severely. The legislator further provided the guardian with a body of youths in the prime of life, and bearing whips, to inflict punishment when necessary. The happy result is that in Sparta modesty and obedience ever go hand in hand, nor is there lack of either.

Instead of softening their feet with shoe or sandal, the rule of Lycurgus was to make them hardy through going barefoot. This habit, if practiced, would, as he believed, enable them to scale heights more easily and clamber down precipices with less danger. In fact, with his feet so trained, the young Spartan could leap and spring and run faster unshod than another shod in the ordinary way. Instead of making them effeminate with a variety of clothes, his rule was to habituate them to a single garment the whole year through, thinking that so they would be better prepared to withstand the variations of heat and cold.

Again, as regards food, the Eiren, or head of the flock, must see that his messmates gathered to the club meal, with such moderate food as to avoid that heaviness which is engendered by repletion, and yet not to remain altogether unacquainted with the pains of penurious living. . . .

Though Lycurgus did not actually allow the boys to help themselves without further trouble to what they needed more, he did give them permission to steal this thing or that in the effort to alleviate their hunger. It was not, of course, from any real difficulty how else to supply them with nutriment that he left it to them to provide themselves by this crafty method. . . .

It is obvious, I say, that the whole of this education tended, and it was intended, to make the boys craftier and more inventive in getting supplies, while at the same time it cultivated their warlike instincts. An objector may retort, "But if Lycurgus thought it so fine a feat to steal, why did he inflict all those blows on the unfortunate who was caught?" My answer is: for the identical reason which induces people, in other matters which are taught, to punish the mal-performance of a service. So they, the Spartans, visit penalties on the boy who is detected thieving, as being but a sorry bungler in the art. . . .

Furthermore, and in order that the boys should not want a ruler, even in case the public guardian himself was absent, he gave to any citizen who chanced to be present authority to lay upon them injunctions for their good, and to chastise them for any trespass committed. By so doing he created in the boys of Sparta a most rare modesty and reverence. And indeed there is no one whom, whether as boys or men, they respect more highly than the ruler. . . .

In his desire firmly to implant in their youthful souls a root of modesty Lycurgus imposed upon the bigger boys a special law. In the very streets they were to keep their two hands within the folds of the cloak; and were to walk in silence and without turning their heads to gaze, now here, now there. They were rather to keep their eyes fixed upon the ground before them. . . . You might sooner expect a stone image to find voice than one of those Spartan youths; to divert the eyes of some bronze statue would be less difficult. And as to quiet bearing, no bride ever stepped in bridal bower with more natural modesty. Note them when they have reached the public table. The plainest answer to the question asked — that is all you need expect to hear from their lips.

## 26. Social Customs [1]

. . . I must now try to describe the style of living which Lycurgus established for the whole body of citizens, irrespective of age. When Lycurgus first came to deal with this question, the Spartans, just as the rest of the Greeks, used to mess privately at home. Tracing more than half the current misdemeanors to this custom, he determined to drag his people out

---

[1] Xenophon, *Polity of the Lacedæmonians*, 5.

of holes and corners into the broad daylight, and so he invented the public messes.[1] . . .

As to food, his ordinance allowed them as much as . . . should guard them from actual want. And, in fact, there are many exceptional dishes in the shape of game supplied from the hunting field. As a substitute for these, rich men will occasionally garnish the feast with wheaten loaves. So that from beginning to end, till the mess breaks up, the common board is never stinted for viands, nor yet is extravagantly furnished.

So also in the matter of drink. Though he put a stop to all unnecessary potations, detrimental alike to a firm brain and a steady gait, he left them free to quench thirst when nature dictated; a method which would at once add to the pleasure, while it diminished the danger, of drinking. And indeed one may fairly ask how, on such a system of common meals, it would be possible for anyone to ruin himself or his family through either gluttony or wine-bibbing. . . . The scene, in fact, but little lends itself to the intrusion of violence or drunken riot; ugly speech and ugly deeds alike are out of place. . . .

In connection with this matter, Lycurgus had not failed to observe the effect of equal amounts of food on different persons. The hard-working man has a good complexion, his muscles are well fed, he is robust and strong. The man who abstains from work, on the other hand, may be detected by his miserable appearance; he is blotched and puffy and devoid of strength. This observation, I say, was not wasted on Lycurgus. On the contrary, turning it over in his mind that anyone who chooses to devote himself to toil may hope to present a very creditable appearance physically, he enjoined upon the eldest for the time being in every gymnasium to see to it that the labors of the class were proportionate to the amount of food. . . . It would be hard to discover a healthier or more

---

[1] As a matter of fact the Spartan custom of communal meals for the men was the survival of a practice widespread among savage and barbarous peoples.

completely developed human being, physically speaking, than the Spartan. His gymnastic training, in fact, makes demands on the legs and arms and neck, etc., simultaneously.

*Ely*

## 27. Characteristics of the Spartan State [1]

There are yet other customs in Sparta which Lycurgus instituted in opposition to those of the rest of Greece, and the following among them. We all know that in most states every one devotes his full energy to the business of making money. One man is a tiller of the soil, another is a mariner, a third is a merchant, while others depend on various arts to earn a living. But Lycurgus forbade his freeborn citizens to have anything whatsoever to do with the concerns of money-making. . . .

And indeed, one may well ask for what reason should wealth be regarded as a matter for serious pursuit in a community where, partly by a system of equal contributions to the necessaries of life, and partly by the maintenance of a common standard of living, the lawgiver placed so effectual a check upon the desire for riches for the sake of luxury? What inducement, for instance, would there be to make money, even for the sake of wearing apparel, in a state where personal adornment is held to lie, not in the costliness of the clothes one wears, but in the healthy condition of the body to be clothed? . . .

Lycurgus went a step further and set up a strong barrier . . . against the pursuit of money-making by wrongful means. In the first place, he established a coinage of so extraordinary a sort,[2] that even a single sum of ten minas [3] could not come into a house without attracting the notice, either of the master himself, or of some member of his household. In fact, it would occupy a considerable space, and need a wagon to carry it. . . .

---

[1] Xenophon, *Polity of the Lacedæmonians*, 7, 9–10.

[2] The celebrated iron money. Although the Spartans attributed their bulky currency to Lycurgus, it seems rather to have been merely a survival from prehistoric times when the baser metals circulated instead of gold and silver. The Spartans had no coined money until the second century B. C.

[3] About $180.

The following also may well excite our admiration for Lycurgus. I speak of the consummate skill with which he induced the whole state of Sparta to regard an honorable death as preferable to an ignoble life. . . . It is clear that the lawgiver set himself deliberately to provide all the blessings of heaven for the good man, and a sorry and ill-starred existence for the coward. In other states the man who shows himself base and cowardly wins an evil reputation and the nickname of a coward — but that is all. For the rest he buys and sells in the same marketplace with the good man; he sits beside him at the play; he exercises with him in the same gymnasium, and all as suits his pleasure. But in Sparta there is not one man who would not feel ashamed to welcome the coward at the common mess-table, or to try conclusions with such an antagonist in a wrestling bout. . . . Such being the weight of infamy which is laid upon all cowards, I, for my part, am not surprised if in Sparta they deem death preferable to a life so steeped in dishonor and reproach. . . .

It may be added that there is no doubt as to the great antiquity of this code of laws. Lycurgus himself is said to have lived in the days of the Heracleidæ.[1] But being of so long standing, these laws, even at this day, are still stamped in the eyes of other men with all the novelty of youth. And the most marvelous thing of all is that, while everybody is agreed to praise these remarkable institutions, there is not a single state which cares to imitate them.

[1] The Heraclidæ (descendants of Heracles), according to Greek legend, were the leaders of the Dorian invasion of the Peloponnesus.

# CHAPTER VII

## XERXES AND THE PERSIAN INVASION OF GREECE [1]

THE Scythian expedition of Darius which added Thrace to the dominions of the Great King,[2] was followed by further European conquests bringing the borders of Persia to the very doors of Greece. It was not long before the Greeks themselves had to face invasion and to engage in that tremendous struggle, the narrative of which forms the leading theme of the history by Herodotus. How the Ionian Greeks revolted against King Darius, how with aid from Athens and Eretria they captured and burned Sardis, how the formidable army sent to punish them met an ignominious repulse on the field of Marathon — all these famous events have been recorded by Herodotus in a story of undying charm. Perhaps the greatest interest attaches to the account of the invasion which Xerxes led in person against the states of Greece. Here the narrative has the power and movement of a dramatic poem. It is even more than the description of a mighty conflict between two nations. It is the picture of a great king, lord of countless peoples, upon whose arrogance and overweening pride there comes suddenly the jealous wrath of Heaven.

### 28. Preparations of Xerxes [3]

Now Xerxes, on first mounting the throne,[4] was coldly disposed toward the Greek war, and made it his business to collect

[1] Herodotus. The translation of George Rawlinson, edited by A. J. Grant. 2 vols. London, 1897. John Murray.

[2] See pages 24–25.    [3] Herodotus, vii, 5–6, 20–21, 24–25.

[4] In 486 B. C. upon the death of his father Darius.

an army against Egypt.[1] But Mardonius, who was at the court, and had more influence with him than any of the other Persians, being his own cousin, plied him with discourses, such as the following: "Master, it is not fitting that they of Athens escape scotfree, after doing the Persians such great injury.[2] Complete the work which thou hast now in hand, and then, when the pride of Egypt is brought low, lead an army against Athens. So shalt thou thyself have good report among men, and others shall fear hereafter to attack thy country." . . . All this he said because he longed for adventures, and hoped to become a satrap [3] of Greece under the king. After a time he had his way, and persuaded Xerxes to do according to his desires. . . .

Xerxes spent four full years in collecting his host and making ready all things that were needful for his soldiers. It was not till the close of the fifth year [4] that he set forth on his march, accompanied by a mighty multitude. Of all the armaments whereof any mention has reached us, this was by far the greatest. . . . For was there a nation in all Asia which Xerxes did not bring with him against Greece? Or was there a river, except those of unusual size, which sufficed for his troops to drink? One nation furnished ships; another was arrayed among the foot-soldiers; a third had to supply horses; a fourth, transports for the horses and men, likewise for the transport service; a fifth, ships of war for the bridges; a sixth, ships and provisions. . . .

In order that his fleet might not be obliged to sail around stormy Mount Athos, where the Persians had lost three hundred ships on a previous occasion, a canal is cut across the isthmus at its narrowest part.

[1] The Egyptians, subdued by Cambyses, had revolted from the Persians in 486 B. C.

[2] Referring to the participation of the Athenians in the Ionian revolt and the burning of Sardis, 499–498 B. C.

[3] Title of a Persian governor.      [4] 481 B. C.

It seems to me that Xerxes, in making the canal, was actuated by a feeling of pride. He wished to display the extent of his power, and to leave behind a memorial to posterity. For notwithstanding that it was open to him, with no trouble at all, to have had his ships drawn across the isthmus, yet he issued orders that a canal should be made through which the sea might flow. It was to be of such a width as would allow of two triremes passing through it abreast with the oars in action. He likewise gave to the same persons who were set over the digging of the trench, the task of making a bridge across the river Strymon.[1]

While these things were in progress, Xerxes had cables prepared for his bridges, some of papyrus and some of white flax, a business which he entrusted to the Phœnicians and the Egyptians. He likewise laid up stores of provisions in various places, to save the army and the beasts of burden from suffering want upon their march into Greece. He inquired carefully about all the sites, and had the stores laid up in such as were most convenient. . . .

### 29. The Persian Host on the March [2]

Meanwhile the land army marches through Asia Minor to Sardis in Lydia.

Here the first care of Xerxes was to send heralds into Greece who were to prefer a demand for earth and water, and to require that preparations should be made everywhere to feast the king. To Athens indeed and to Sparta he sent no such demand; but these cities excepted, his messengers went everywhere. Now this was the reason why he sent for earth and water to states which had already refused. He thought that, although they had refused when Darius made the demand, they would now be too frightened to venture to say him nay. So he sent his heralds, wishing to know for certain how it would be.

---

[1] The boundary between Thrace and Macedonia.
[2] Herodotus, vii, 32–37, 40–41.

After this Xerxes made preparations to advance to Abydos, where the bridge across the Hellespont from Asia to Europe had been lately finished. . . . It is seven furlongs [1] across from Abydos to the opposite coast. But when the channel had been bridged successfully, it happened that a great storm arising broke the whole work to pieces, and destroyed all that had been done.

When Xerxes heard of the disaster, he was full of wrath, and straightway gave orders that the Hellespont should receive three hundred lashes, and that a pair of fetters should be cast into it. Nay, I have even heard it said that he bade the branders take their hot irons and brand the Hellespont. It is certain that he commanded those who scourged the waters to utter, as they lashed them, these wicked words: "Thou bitter water, thy lord lays on thee this punishment because thou hast wronged him without a cause, having suffered no evil at his hands. Verily King Xerxes will cross thee, whether thou wilt or no. Well dost thou deserve that no man should honor thee with sacrifice; for thou art of a truth a treacherous and unsavory river." While the sea was thus punished by his orders, he likewise commanded that the overseers of the work should lose their heads. Then they whose business it was executed the unpleasing task laid upon them; and other men rebuilt the bridge more firmly than before. . . .

When news came to Xerxes that the canal at Athos was completely finished, the host, having first wintered at Sardis, began its march toward Abydos, on the first approach of spring.[2] At the moment of departure, the sun suddenly quitted his seat in the heavens, and disappeared, though there were no clouds in sight, but the sky was clear and serene. Day was thus turned into night. Xerxes, who saw and remarked the prodigy, was seized with alarm, and sending at once for the Magians,[3] inquired of them the meaning of the portent. They replied, "God is foreshowing to the Greeks the destruction of

---

[1] Somewhat less than a mile.    [2] This was the spring of 480 B.C.
[3] The Persian priests.  See page 10.

their cities; for the sun foretells for them, and the moon for us." So Xerxes, thus instructed, proceeded on his way with great gladness of heart. . . .

First of all went the baggage-bearers and the beasts of burden, and then a vast crowd of many nations mingled together without any intervals, amounting to more than one half of the army. After these troops an empty space was left between them and the king. In front of the king went first a thousand horsemen, picked men of the Persian nation — then spearmen a thousand, likewise chosen troops, with their spearheads pointing toward the ground — next ten of the sacred horses called Nisæan,[1] all daintily caparisoned. . . . After the ten sacred horses came the holy chariot of Zeus, drawn by eight milk-white steeds, with the charioteer on foot behind them holding the reins; for no mortal is ever allowed to mount into the car. Next to this came Xerxes himself, riding in a chariot drawn by Nisæan horses, with his charioteer standing by his side.

Thus rode forth Xerxes from Sardis — but he was accustomed every now and then, when the fancy took him, to alight from his chariot and travel in a litter. Immediately behind the king there followed a body of a thousand spearmen, the noblest and bravest of the Persians, holding their lances in the usual manner.[2] Then came a thousand Persian cavalry, picked men — then ten thousand,[3] picked also after the rest, and serving on foot. Of these last one thousand carried spears with golden pomegranates at their lower end, instead of spikes; and these encircled the other nine thousand, who bore on their spears pomegranates of silver. The spearmen, also, who pointed their lances toward the ground, had golden pomegranates; and the thousand Persians who followed close after Xerxes, had golden apples. Behind the ten thousand footmen came a

---

[1] From the Nisæan plain in Media.

[2] That is, with the point upward.

[3] They were called the " Immortals " because their number was always kept at 10,000.

body of Persian cavalry, in number ten thousand. After these there was again a void space for as much as two furlongs; and then the rest of the army followed in a confused crowd.

*Virginia.*

### 30. Passage of the Hellespont [1]

Xerxes now marches northward through Asia Minor. At the site of Troy he makes an offering of a thousand oxen to the Trojan gods and pours out libations to the shades of the heroes who perished in the siege of the city. Then, with his army, he proceeds to Abydos on the Hellespont.

When he had arrived here, Xerxes wished to look upon all his host. Now there was a throne of white marble upon a hill near the city, which the people of Abydos had prepared beforehand, by the king's bidding, for his especial use. Xerxes took his seat on it, and gazing thence upon the shore below, beheld at one view all his land forces and all his ships. While thus employed, he felt a desire to behold a sailing-match between his ships, which accordingly took place. It was won by the Phœnicians of Sidon, much to the joy of Xerxes, who was delighted alike with the race and with his army.

And now, as he looked and saw the whole Hellespont covered with the vessels of his fleet, and all the shore and every plain about Abydos as full as possible of men, Xerxes congratulated himself on his good fortune; but after a little while he wept. Then Artabanus, the king's uncle . . . when he heard that Xerxes was in tears, went to him, and said, "How different, sir, is what thou art now doing from what thou didst a little while ago! Then thou didst congratulate thyself; and now behold! thou weepest." And Xerxes answered, "There came upon me a sudden pity, when I thought of the shortness of man's life, and considered that of all this host . . . no one will be alive when a hundred years are gone by." . . .

[1] Herodotus, vii, 44–46, 54, 56, 60.

All that day the preparations for the passage continued; and on the morrow they burnt all kinds of spices upon the bridges, and strewed the way with myrtle-boughs, while they waited anxiously for the sun, which they hoped to see as he rose. And when the sun appeared, Xerxes took a golden goblet and poured from it a libation into the sea, praying meanwhile, with his face turned to the sun, that no misfortune might befall him such as to hinder his conquest of Europe, until he had penetrated to its uttermost boundaries. After he had prayed, he cast the golden cup into the Hellespont, and with it a golden bowl and a Persian sword. . . . I cannot say for certain whether it was as an offering to the sun god that he threw these things into the deep, or whether he had repented of having scourged the Hellespont, and thought by his gift to make amends to the sea for what he had done. . . . As soon as Xerxes had reached the European side, he stood to contemplate his army as they crossed under the lash. And the crossing continued during seven days and seven nights, without a rest or pause. 'Tis said that here, after Xerxes had made the passage, a Hellespontian exclaimed, "Why, O Zeus, dost thou, in the likeness of a Persian man, and with the name of Xerxes instead of thine own, lead the whole race of mankind to the destruction of Greece? It would have been as easy for thee to destroy it without their aid!" . . .

Upon the wide plain of Doriscus in Thrace, Xerxes counts and reviews his vast host.

What the exact number of the troops of each nation was I cannot say with certainty — for it is not mentioned by any one — but the whole land army together was found to amount to one million seven hundred thousand men.[1] The manner in

---

[1] These figures exclude not only the cavalry and the sailors in the fleet, but also the countless hordes of non-combatants and camp-followers. Adding all these together Herodotus estimates that the expedition of Xerxes brought a host of 5,000,000 individuals into Europe — a veritable human avalanche. But it is clear that such huge numbers are wholly fabulous.

which the numbering took place was the following. A body of
ten thousand men was brought to a certain spot, and the men
were made to stand as close together as possible ; after which
a circle was drawn around them, and the men were let go.
Where the circle had been, a fence was built about the height
of a man's middle ; and the inclosure was filled continually
with fresh troops, till the whole army had in this way been
numbered. When the numbering was over, the troops were
drawn up according to their several nations.

### 31. The Battle at the Pass of Thermopylæ [1]

And now Xerxes, having marched unopposed through
Thrace, Macedonia, and Thessaly, approaches the Pass
of Thermopylæ, the entrance to central Greece. Here
Leonidas of Sparta, with three hundred Spartans and a
few thousand allies, had been posted to hold the pass until
the Greeks should be able to dispatch the main body of
their troops against the invading host.

Xerxes sent a mounted spy to observe the Greeks, and note
how many they were, and see what they were doing. He had
heard, before he came out of Thessaly, that a few men were
assembled at this place, and that at their head were certain
Spartans, under Leonidas, a descendant of Heracles. The
horseman rode up to the camp, and looked about him, but did
not see the whole army; for such as were on the further side of
the wall . . . it was not possible for him to behold. However,
he observed those on the outside, who were encamped in front
of the rampart. It chanced that at this time the Spartans held
the outer guard, and were seen by the spy. Some of them were
engaged in gymnastic exercises, others combing their long hair.
At this the spy greatly marveled, but he counted their number, and when he had taken accurate note of everything, he rode
back quietly. No one pursued after him, or paid any heed to

[1] Herodotus, vii, 208, 210-212, 223-226.

his visit. So he returned and told Xerxes all that he had seen. . . .

Four whole days Xerxes suffered to go by, expecting that the Greeks would run away. When, however, he found on the fifth day that they were not gone, thinking that their firm stand was mere impudence and recklessness, he grew wroth and sent against them the Medes and Cissians, with orders to take them alive and bring them into his presence. Then the Medes rushed forward and charged the Greeks, but fell in vast numbers. Others, however, took the places of the slain, and would not be beaten off, though they suffered terrible losses. In this way it became clear to all, and especially to the king, that though he had plenty of combatants, he had but very few warriors. The struggle, however, continued during the whole day.

Then the Medes, having met so rough a reception, withdrew from the fight; and their place was taken by the band of Persians whom the king called his "Immortals." They, it was thought, would soon finish the business. But when they joined battle with the Greeks, it was with no better success than the Median detachment had met. Things went much as before — the two armies fighting in a narrow space, and the barbarians using shorter spears than the Greeks, and having no advantage from their numbers. The Spartans fought in a way worthy of note, and showed themselves far more skillful in fight than their adversaries. They would often turn their backs, and make as though they were all flying away, on which the barbarians would rush after them with much noise and shouting. Then the Spartans at their approach would wheel round and face their pursuers, in this way destroying vast numbers of the enemy. Some Spartans likewise fell in these encounters, but only a very few. At last the Persians, finding that all their efforts to gain the pass availed nothing, and that, whether they attacked by divisions or in any other way, it was to no purpose, withdrew to their own quarters.

During these assaults, it is said that Xerxes, who was watching the battle, thrice leaped from the throne on which he sat, in terror for his army. Next day the combat was renewed, but with no better success on the part of the barbarians. . . .

At this juncture, a Greek named Ephialtes, stirred by the hope of rich reward, reveals to Xerxes a mountain path by which the Greeks may be taken in the rear. By night he guides a Persian army over the mountain. When the Greeks learn of their betrayal, they withdraw in safety, all save Leonidas and his Spartans, together with the Thespians and Thebans.

At sunrise Xerxes made libations, after which he waited until the time when the market is wont to fill,[1] and then began his advance. . . . So the barbarians under Xerxes began to draw nigh; and the Greeks under Leonidas, as they now went forth determined to die, advanced much further than on previous days, until they reached the more open portion of the pass. Hitherto they had held their station within the wall, and from this had gone forth to fight at the point where the pass was the narrowest. Now they joined battle beyond the defile, and carried slaughter among the barbarians, who fell in heaps. Behind them the captains of the squadrons, armed with whips, urged their men forward with continual blows. Many were thrust into the sea, and there perished; a still greater number were trampled to death by their own soldiers; no one heeded the dying. The Greeks were reckless of their own safety and desperate, since they knew that, as the mountain had been crossed, their destruction was nigh at hand. Accordingly, they exerted themselves with the most furious valor against the barbarians.

By this time the spears of the greater number were all shivered, and with their swords they hewed down the ranks of the Persians. And here, as they strove, Leonidas fell fighting bravely, together with many other famous Spartans, whose names I have taken care to learn on account of their great worthiness, as indeed I have those of all the three hundred. . . .

[1] About ten o'clock.

. . . And now there arose a fierce struggle between the Persians and the Spartans over the body of Leonidas, in which the Greeks four times drove back the enemy, and at last by their great bravery succeeded in bearing off the body. This combat was scarcely ended when the Persians with Ephialtes approached. The Greeks, informed that they drew nigh, made a change in the manner of their fighting. Drawing back into the narrowest part of the pass, and retreating even behind the cross wall, they posted themselves upon a hillock, where they stood all drawn up together in one close body, except only the Thebans. The hillock of which I speak is at the entrance of the straits, where the stone lion stands which was set up in honor of Leonidas. Here they defended themselves to the last. Those who still had swords used them, and the others resisted with their hands and teeth. At length the barbarians, who in part had pulled down the wall and attacked them in front, in part had gone round and now encircled them upon every side, overwhelmed and buried beneath showers of missile weapons the remnant which was left.

Thus nobly did the whole body of Spartans and Thespians behave. Nevertheless, one man is said to have distinguished himself above all the rest, to wit, Dieneces the Spartan. A speech which he made before the Greeks engaged the Medes, remains on record. One of the Trachinians told him, "Such was the number of the barbarians, that when they shot forth their arrows the sun would be darkened by their multitude." Dieneces, not at all frightened at these words, but making light of the Median numbers, answered, "Our Trachinian friend brings us excellent tidings. If the Medes darken the sun, we shall have our fight in the shade." . . .

## 32. Repulse of the Persians from Delphi [1]

The hard-won victory at Thermopylæ allows the Persians to march without interruption through central

[1] Herodotus, viii, 36–38.

Greece.  A detachment from the main army is sent to plunder the Temple of Apollo at Delphi.

When the Delphians heard what danger they were in, great fear fell on them.  In their terror they consulted the oracle concerning the holy treasures, and inquired if they should bury them in the ground, or carry them away to some other country. The god, in reply, bade them leave the treasures untouched. He was able, he said, without help to protect his own.  So the Delphians, when they received this answer, began to think about saving themselves.  First of all they sent their women and children across the Gulf of Corinth into Achæa.  Then the greater number of them climbed up into the tops of Parnassus,[1] and placed their goods for safety in a cave; while some effected their escape to Locris.  In this way all the Delphians quitted the city, except sixty men and the Prophet.

When the barbarian assailants drew near and were in sight of the place, the Prophet beheld, in front of the temple, a part of the sacred armor, which it was not lawful for any mortal hand to touch, lying upon the ground.  It had been removed from the inner shrine where it was wont to hang. Then went he and told the prodigy to the Delphians who had remained behind.  Meanwhile the enemy pressed forward briskly, and had reached the shrine of Athena, when they were overtaken by other prodigies still more wonderful than the first.  Truly it was marvel enough, when instruments of war were seen lying outside the temple, removed there by supernatural power.  What followed, however, exceeded in strangeness all prodigies that had ever before been seen.  The barbarians had just reached in their advance the chapel of Athena, when a storm of thunder burst suddenly over their heads.  At the same time two crags split off from Mount Parnassus, and rolled down upon them with a loud noise, crushing vast numbers beneath their weight.  And from the Temple of Athena there went up the war-cry and the shout of victory.

[1] The mountain, in a defile of which the Delphic oracle was situated.

All these things together struck terror into the barbarians, who forthwith turned and fled. The Delphians, seeing this, came down from their hiding-places, and smote them with great slaughter, from which such as escaped fled straight into Bœotia. These men on their return, declared (as I am told) that besides the marvels mentioned above, they witnessed also other supernatural sights. Two armed warriors, they said, of a stature more than human, pursued after their flying ranks, pressing them close and slaying them.[1]

### 33. Capture of the Athenian Acropolis [2]

Since the passage of the Hellespont and the commencement of the march upon Greece, a space of four months had gone by: one, while the army made the crossing, and delayed about the region of the Hellespont; and three while they proceeded thence to Attica, which they now entered. They found the city forsaken. A few people, only, remained in the temple, either keepers of the treasures, or men of the poorer sort. These persons, having fortified the citadel with planks and boards, held out against the enemy. It was in some measure their poverty which had prevented them from seeking shelter in Salamis. There was likewise another reason which in part induced them to remain. They imagined themselves to have discovered the true meaning of the oracle uttered by the Pythoness, which promised that "the wooden wall" should never be taken. The wooden wall, they thought, did not mean the ships, but the place where they had taken refuge.

The Persians encamped ûpon the hill over against the citadel, which is called the Hill of Ares [3] by the Athenians. They began the siege of the place by attacking the Greeks with arrows

---

[1] It is likely that Xerxes underestimated the difficulty of capturing Delphi and sent an insufficient body of troops against the town. In the narrative by Herodotus, the Persian defeat is attributed to the aid of Apollo — a legend which was invented, doubtless, by Apollo's priests at Delphi.

[2] Herodotus, viii, 51–53.

[3] The seat of the Council of the Areopagus.

to which pieces of lighted tow were attached. These they shot at the barricade. And now those who were within the citadel found themselves in a most woeful case; for their wooden rampart betrayed them; still, however, they continued to resist. It was in vain that the Pisistratidæ [1] came to them and offered terms of surrender. They stoutly refused all parley. Among other modes of defense they rolled down huge masses of stone upon the barbarians as they were mounting up to the gates: so that Xerxes was for a long time very greatly perplexed, and could not contrive any way to take them.

At last, however, in the midst of these many difficulties, the barbarians made discovery of an access to the Acropolis. For verily the oracle had spoken truth, and it was fated that the whole mainland of Attica should fall beneath the sway of the Persians. Right in front of the citadel, but behind the gates and the common ascent — where no watch was kept, and no one would have thought it possible that any foot of man could climb — a few soldiers mounted from the sanctuary of Aglaurus. As soon as the Athenians saw them upon the summit, some threw themselves headlong from the wall, and so perished; while others fled for refuge to the inner part of the temple. The Persians rushed to the gates and opened them, after which they massacred the suppliants. When all were slain, they plundered the temple, and fired every part of the citadel.[2]

### 34. The Battle of Salamis [3]

After the capture of Athens the hopes of the Greeks center in the "wooden walls" of their fleet. In the naval battle of Salamis, the Persians are overwhelmingly defeated.

[1] The adherents of Hippias, son of Pisistratus, after expulsion from Athens, had returned to Greece with the army of Xerxes. See page 60.

[2] The Acropolis of Athens is a position of great natural strength. It is probable that the Athenians thought the place could be held against the Persians and so left a small garrison within the citadel. The story of the oracle about the "wooden wall" may be regarded as a subsequent invention.

[3] Herodotus, viii, 86–88.

The greater number of the Persian ships engaged in this battle were disabled — either by the Athenians or by the Æginetans. Since the Greeks fought in order and kept their line, while the barbarians were in confusion and had no plan in anything that they did, the issue of the battle could scarce be other than it was. Yet the Persians fought far more bravely here than at Eubœa,[1] and indeed surpassed themselves. Each did his utmost through fear of Xerxes, for each thought that the king's eye was upon himself.[2]

What part the several nations, whether Greek or barbarian, took in the combat, I am not able to say for certain. Artemisia,[3] however, distinguished herself in such a way as raised her even higher than she stood before in the esteem of the king. For after confusion had spread throughout the whole of the Persian fleet, and her ship was closely pursued by an Athenian trireme . . . she resolved on a measure which in fact proved her safety. Pressed by the Athenian pursuit, she bore straight against one of the ships of her own party, a Calyndian, which had the Calyndian king himself on board. I cannot say whether or not she had had any quarrel with the man while the fleet was at the Hellespont, neither can I decide whether she of set purpose attacked his vessel, or whether it merely chanced that the Calyndian ship came in her way. Certain it is, however, that she bore down upon his vessel and sank it, and that thereby she had the good fortune to procure herself a double advantage. For the commander of the Athenian trireme, when he saw her bear down on one of the enemy's fleet, thought immediately that her vessel was a Greek, or else had deserted from the Persians, and was now fighting on the Greek side. He therefore gave up the chase, and turned away to attack others.

[1] Referring to the sea fight of Artemisium off the northern coast of Eubœa.

[2] Xerxes watched the battle from a high throne on the hillside overlooking the Bay of Salamis. In the clear atmosphere every detail of the fight must have been visible to the monarch and his courtiers.

[3] Queen of Halicarnassus in Asia Minor.

Thus in the first place she saved her life by the action, and was enabled to get away from the battle. Furthermore, it fell out that in the very act of doing the king an injury she raised herself to a greater height than ever in his esteem. For as Xerxes beheld the fight, he noticed the destruction of the vessel. Whereupon the bystanders said to him, "Seest thou, master, how well Artemisia fights, and how she has just sunk a ship of the enemy?" Then Xerxes asked if it was really Artemisia's doing; and they answered, "Certainly; for we know her ensign": while all were sure that the sunken vessel belonged to the opposite side. Everything, it is said, conspired to prosper the queen — it was especially fortunate for her that not one of those on board the Calyndian ship survived to become her accuser. Xerxes, they say, in reply to the remarks made to him, remarked, "My men have behaved like women, my women like men!"

After Salamis, Xerxes, fearing for his personal safety, hastened back to Persia. He left Mardonius in Greece with a strong army to complete the subjugation of the peninsula. In the closing chapters of Herodotus we learn how the Spartans and Athenians, on the bloody field of Platæa, removed all danger of Persian conquest and gave to Greece that splendid half-century of progress so rudely broken by the Peloponnesian War.

Katherine

# CHAPTER VIII

## EPISODES FROM THE PELOPONNESIAN WAR [1]

THE only work of Thucydides, greatest of Athenian historians, is a history of the Peloponnesian War. In the preface to his book Thucydides indicates the importance of the subject: "Thucydides, an Athenian, wrote the history of the war in which the Peloponnesians and the Athenians fought against one another. He began to write when they first took up arms, believing that it would be great and memorable above any previous war. For he argued that both states were then at the full height of their military power, and he saw the rest of the Greeks either siding or intending to side with one or other of them. No movement ever stirred Greece more deeply than this; it was shared by many of the barbarians, and might be said even to affect the world at large."

### 35. The Athenian and the Spartan Character [2]

The real, though unavowed, cause of the war, Thucydides finds in the growth of the Athenian power, which alarmed the Spartans and forced them into the conflict. The immediate cause was Athenian interference between Corinth and her colonies of Corcyra and Potidæa. In 432 B. C. envoys from Corinth and other states appeared at Sparta and appealed to the Spartans as the leaders of

[1] Thucydides.   The translation by Benjamin Jowett.   1st edition. Oxford, 1881.   Clarendon Press.

[2] Thucydides, i, 70–71.

the Peloponnesus, for aid against Athens. In their speech before the Spartan Assembly the Corinthian envoys drew a striking contrast between the characters and aims of the two great rival cities of Greece.

. . . You have never considered what manner of men are these Athenians with whom you will have to fight, and how utterly unlike yourselves. They are revolutionary, equally quick in the conception and in the execution of every new plan. You are conservative — careful only to keep what you have, originating nothing, and not acting even when action is most necessary. They are bold beyond their strength; they run risks which prudence would condemn; and in the midst of misfortune they are full of hope. It is your nature, though strong, to act feebly; when your plans are most prudent, to distrust them; and when calamities come upon you, to think that you will never be delivered from them. . . . When conquerors, they pursue their victory to the utmost; when defeated, they fall back the least. Their bodies they devote to their country as though they belonged to other men; their true self is their mind, which is most truly their own when employed in her service. . . . To do their duty is their only holiday, and they deem the quiet of inaction to be as disagreeable as the most tiresome business. If a man should say of them, in a word, that they were born neither to have peace themselves nor to allow peace to other men, he would simply speak the truth.

In the face of such an enemy, you persist in doing nothing. . . . But here let your procrastination end; send an army at once into Attica and assist your allies, especially the Potidæans,[1] to whom your word is pledged. Do not allow friends and kindred to fall into the hands of their worst enemies; or drive us in despair to seek the alliance of others. . . . We will remain your friends if you choose to bestir yourselves; for we should be guilty of an impiety if we deserted you without cause; and

[1] Potidæa, a city of Chalcidice, was a tributary ally of Athens. Its revolt in 432 B.C. had led to its investment by an Athenian army.

we shall not easily find allies equally congenial to us.   Take
heed then: you have inherited from your fathers the leadership of the Peloponnesus; see that her greatness suffers no
diminution at your hands.

The Spartan Assembly now voted that Athens had violated the terms of the Thirty Years' Truce.[1]   Soon after
this decision a congress of all the Peloponnesian states
declared war against Athens.

### 36.  Funeral Speech of Pericles [2]

The first year of the war came to an end, and neither
Athens nor Sparta had secured a decided advantage.
During the winter of that year, in accordance with an ancient custom, the Athenians celebrated the public funeral of those who had fallen in the defense of their city.
When the bodies had been laid in earth, Pericles came forward and delivered the funeral oration which was usual
at such an occasion.   His speech was really a splendid
panegyric upon Athens and Athenian civilization.

Our form of government does not enter into rivalry with
the institutions of others.   We do not copy our neighbors, but
are an example to them.   It is true that we are called a democ-
racy, for the administration is in the hands of the many and
not of the few.   But while the law secures equal justice to all
alike in their private disputes, the claim of excellence is also
recognized.   When a citizen is in any way distinguished, he
is preferred to the public service, not as a matter of privilege,
but as the reward of merit.   Even poverty is not a bar, but a
man may benefit his country whatever be the obscurity of his
condition.   There is no exclusiveness in our public life, and in

[1] Arranged between Athens and the Peloponnesian League in 445 B. C.
[2] Thucydides, ii, 37-41.

our private intercourse we are not suspicious of one another, or angry with our neighbor if he does what he likes; we do not put on sour looks at him which, though harmless, are not pleasant. While we are thus unconstrained in our private intercourse, a spirit of reverence pervades our public acts. . . .

And we have not forgotten to provide for our weary spirits many relaxations from toil. We have regular games and sacrifices throughout the year. At home the style of our life is refined; and the delight which we daily feel in all these things helps to banish melancholy. Because of the greatness of our city the fruits of the whole earth flow in upon us; so that we enjoy the goods of other countries as freely as of our own.

Then, again, our military training is in many respects superior to that of our adversaries. Our city is thrown open to the world, and we never expel a foreigner or prevent him from seeing or learning anything of which the secret if revealed to an enemy might profit him. We rely, not upon management or trickery, but upon our own hearts and hands. And in the matter of education, whereas they from early youth are always undergoing laborious exercises which are to make them brave, we live at ease, and yet are equally ready to face the perils which they face. . . .

We are lovers of the beautiful, yet simple in our tastes, and we cultivate the mind without loss of manliness. Wealth we employ, not for talk and ostentation, but when there is a real use for it. To avow poverty with us is no disgrace; the true disgrace is in doing nothing to avoid it. An Athenian citizen does not neglect the state because he takes care of his own household; and even those of us who are engaged in business have a very fair idea of politics. We alone regard a man who takes no interest in public affairs, not as a harmless but as a useless character. If few of us are originators, we are all sound judges, of a policy. The great impediment to action is, in our opinion, not discussion, but the want of that knowledge which is gained by discussion preparatory to action.

For we have a peculiar power of thinking before we act and of
acting too, whereas other men are courageous from ignorance
but hesitate upon reflection. . . .

To sum up: I say that Athens is the school of Hellas, and
that the individual Athenian in his own person seems to have
the power of adapting himself to the most varied forms of action with the utmost versatility and grace. . . . And we shall
assuredly not be without witnesses; there are mighty monuments of our power which will make us the wonder of this and of
succeeding ages.  We shall not need the praises of Homer or
of any other panegyrist whose poetry may please for the moment, although his representation of the facts will not bear
the light of day.  For we have compelled every land and every
sea to open a path for our valor, and have everywhere planted
eternal memorials of our friendship and of our enmity.  Such
is the city for whose sake these men nobly fought and died.
They could not bear the thought that she might be taken
from them; and every one of us who survive should gladly
toil on her behalf.

### 37. The Plague at Athens [1]

In the second year of the war (430 B.C.), a Peloponnesian army entered Attica and ravaged far and wide.  The
Athenians refused a battle with the invaders and gathered
behind their unassailable ramparts.  But within the
crowded city they had to contend with an enemy even more
terrible than the Spartans.  A great pestilence broke out.

. . . Some of the sufferers died from want of care, others
equally who were receiving the greatest attention.  No single
remedy could be deemed a specific; for that which did good
to one did harm to another.  No constitution was of itself
strong enough to resist or weak enough to escape the attacks.
The disease carried off all alike and defied every mode of treat-

[1] Thucydides, ii, 51, 53-54.

ment. Most appalling was the despondency which seized upon anyone who felt himself sickening; for he instantly abandoned his mind to despair and, instead of holding out, absolutely threw away his chance of life. Appalling, too, was the rapidity with which men caught the infection; dying like sheep if they attended on one another. . . . When they were afraid to visit one another, the sufferers died in their solitude, so that many houses were empty because there had been no one left to take care of the sick; or if they ventured they perished, especially those who aspired to heroism. . . . But whatever instances there may have been of such devotion, more often the sick and the dying were tended by the pitying care of those who had recovered, because they knew the course of the disease and were themselves free from apprehension. For no one was ever attacked a second time, at or least not with a fatal result. All men congratulated them, and they themselves, in the excess of their joy at the moment, had an innocent fancy that they could not die of any other sickness. . . .

There were many forms of lawlessness which the plague introduced at Athens. Men who had hitherto concealed their indulgence in pleasure now grew bolder. Seeing the sudden change — how the rich died in a moment, and those who had nothing immediately inherited their property — they reflected that life and riches were alike transitory, and they resolved to enjoy themselves while they could, and to think only of pleasure. . . . No fear of God or law of man deterred a criminal. Those who saw all perishing alike, thought that the worship or neglect of the gods made no difference. For offenses against human law no punishment was to be feared; no one would live long enough to be called to account. Already a far heavier sentence had been passed and was hanging over a man's head; before that fell, why should he not take a little pleasure?

Such was the grievous calamity which now afflicted the Athenians; within the walls their people were dying, and without, their country was being ravaged. In their troubles they naturally called to mind a verse which the elder men among them declared to have been current long ago:

"A Dorian war will come and a plague with it." . . .

### 38. The Sicilian Expedition: Departure of the Fleet [1]

The most remarkable episode in the protracted story of the Peloponnesian War is that of the Sicilian expedition (415–413 B.C.). Largely influenced by the advice of Alcibiades,[2] then a popular hero, the Athenians determined to send out a great armament to capture Syracuse. This was a Sicilian city nearly as populous and powerful as Athens herself. When Nicias, a distinguished statesman, begged the Assembly to ponder well the perils of the expedition before they undertook it, the Athenians cast his warnings to the winds. So a great fleet and army were got ready. Alcibiades, Nicias, and Lamachus were the three commanders.

. . . Early in the morning of the day appointed for their departure, the Athenians and such of their allies as had already joined them went down to Piræus[3] and began to man the ships. The entire population of Athens accompanied them, citizens and strangers alike. The citizens came to take farewell, one of an acquaintance, another of a kinsman, another of a son. The people as they passed along were full of hope and full of tears; hope of conquering Sicily, tears because they doubted whether they would ever see their friends again, when they thought of the long voyage on which they were sending them. At the moment of parting the danger was nearer; and terrors which had never occurred to them when they were voting the expedition now entered into their souls. Nevertheless their spirits revived at the sight of the armament in all its strength. The strangers and the rest of the multitude

---

[1] Thucydides, vi, 30–32.    [2] See chap. IX.    [3] The port of Athens.

came out of curiosity, desiring to witness an enterprise of which the greatness exceeded belief.

No armament so magnificent or costly had ever before been sent out by any single Greek power. . . . This expedition was intended to be long absent, and was thoroughly provided both for sea and land service, wherever its presence might be required. On the fleet the greatest pains and expense had been lavished by the trierarchs [1] and the state. The public treasury gave a drachma [2] a day to each sailor, and furnished empty hulls for sixty swift sailing vessels, and for forty transports carrying hoplites. [3] All these were manned with the best crews which could be obtained. The trierarchs, besides the pay given by the state, added somewhat more out of their own means to the wages of the upper ranks of rowers and of the petty officers. The figure-heads and other fittings provided by them were of the most costly description. Every one strove to the utmost that his own ship might excel both in beauty and swiftness. The infantry had been well selected and the lists carefully made up. There was the keenest rivalry among the soldiers in the matter of arms and personal equipment. . . .

When the ships were manned and everything required for the voyage had been placed on board, silence was proclaimed by the sound of the trumpet, and all with one voice before setting sail offered up the customary prayers. These were recited, not in each ship, but by a single herald, the whole fleet accompanying him. On every deck both officers and men, mingling wine in bowls, made libations from vessels of gold and silver. The multitude of citizens and other well-wishers who were looking on from the land joined in the prayer. The crews raised the Pæan, [4] and when the libations were completed, put to sea. . . .

[1] Wealthy citizens who bore the expense of outfitting the triremes.

[2] About 18 cents.

[3] Heavy-armed foot-soldiers.

[4] A war-song sung before battle in honor of Ares, or after battle as a thanksgiving to Apollo.

### 39. The Sicilian Expedition: Naval Battle at Syracuse [1]

At one time the Athenians very nearly succeeded in capturing Syracuse. But under an able general whom the Spartans had sent them, the Syracusans put up a stubborn defense. Nicias, who had now become the chief Athenian commander, was compelled to demand reinforcements. So the Athenians dispatched another expedition, almost as great as the first. Syracuse likewise received aid from her friends throughout Hellas. Even with fresh troops Nicias and his colleague Demosthenes could not capture the Sicilian city. At length, they resolved to abandon the siege. The Syracusans promptly took the offensive and sought to destroy the host of the enemy before it could get away. They blockaded the mouth of the harbor in order to cut off all escape by sea. The fate of the Athenians depended upon their success in breaking through the barrier.

. . . The last chance of the Athenians lay in their ships, and their anxiety was dreadful. The fortune of the battle varied; and it was not possible that the spectators on the shore should all receive the same impression of it. Some spectators, being quite close and having different points of view, would see their own ships victorious. Their courage would then revive, and they would earnestly call upon the gods not to take from them their hope of deliverance. But others, who saw their ships worsted, cried and shrieked aloud, and were by the sight alone more utterly unnerved than the defeated combatants themselves. Others again, who had fixed their gaze on some part of the struggle which was undecided, were in a state of excitement still more terrible. They kept swaying their bodies to and fro in an agony of hope and fear as the stubborn conflict went on and on; for at every instant they were all but

[1] Thucydides, vii, 71.

saved or all but lost. And while the strife hung in the balance you might hear in the Athenian army at once lamentation, shouting, cries of victory or defeat, and all the various sounds which are wrung from a great host in extremity of danger. Not less agonizing were the feelings of those on board.

At length the Syracusans and their allies, after a protracted struggle, put the Athenians to flight. Triumphantly bearing down upon them, and encouraging one another with loud cries and exhortations, they drove them to land. Then that part of the navy which had not been taken in the deep water fell back in confusion to the shore, and the crews rushed out of the ships into the camp. And the land-forces, no longer now divided in feeling, but uttering one universal groan of intolerable anguish, ran, some of them to save the ships, others to defend what remained of the wall; but the greater number began to look to themselves and to their own safety. Never had there been a greater panic in an Athenian army than at that moment. . . . And so now the Athenians, after the rout of their fleet, knew that they had no hope of saving themselves by land unless events took some extraordinary turn.

### 40. The Sicilian Expedition: Flight and Capture of the Athenians [1]

On the third day after the sea fight, when Nicias and Demosthenes thought that their preparations were complete, the army began to retreat. They were in a dreadful condition. Not only was there the great fact that they had lost their whole fleet, and instead of their expected triumph had brought the utmost peril upon Athens as well as upon themselves, but also the sights which presented themselves as they quitted the camp were painful to every eye and mind. The dead were unburied, and when anyone saw the body of a friend lying on the ground he was smitten with sorrow and fear, while the sick or wounded who still survived but had to be left were even a greater trial to the living, and more to be pitied than those who were gone.

[1] Thucydides, vii, 75, 84–87.

. . . There was also a general feeling of shame and self-reproach. Indeed, they seemed, not like an army, but like the fugitive population of a city captured after a siege; and of a great city too. For the whole multitude who were marching together numbered not less than forty thousand. Each of them took with him anything he could carry which was likely to be of use. Even the heavy-armed soldiers and the cavalry, contrary to their practice when under arms, conveyed about their persons their own food, some because they had no attendants, others because they could not trust them; for they had long been deserting, and most of them had gone off all at once. Nor was the food which they carried sufficient, since the supplies of the camp had failed.

Their disgrace and the universality of the misery, although there might be some consolation in the very community of suffering, was nevertheless at that moment hard to bear, especially when they remembered from what pomp and splendor they had fallen into their present low estate. Never had a Greek army experienced such a reverse. They had come intending to enslave others, and they were going away in fear that they would be themselves enslaved. Instead of the prayers and hymns with which they had put to sea, they were now departing amid appeals to heaven of another sort. They were no longer sailors but landsmen, depending, not upon their fleet, but upon their infantry. Yet in the face of the great danger which still threatened them all these things appeared endurable. . . .

The end soon came. One division of the Athenian forces, under the command of Demosthenes, was surrounded and compelled to surrender. Then on the eighth day of the retreat, the Syracusans caught up with the second body of fugitives at the river Assinarus.

The Syracusans stood upon the further bank of the river, which was steep, and hurled missiles from above on the Athenians, who were huddled together in the deep bed of the stream and for the most part were drinking greedily. The Peloponnesians came down the bank and slaughtered them, falling chiefly upon those who were in the river. Whereupon the water at once became foul, but was drunk all the same, although muddy and dyed with blood, and the crowd fought for it.

At last, when the dead bodies were lying in heaps upon one another in the water and the army was utterly undone, some perishing in the river, and any who escaped being cut off by the cavalry, Nicias surrendered to Gylippus,[1] in whom he had more confidence than in the Syracusans. He entreated him and the Spartans to do what they pleased with himself, but not to go on killing the men. So Gylippus gave the word to make prisoners. Thereupon the survivors, not including, however, a large number whom the soldiers concealed, were brought in alive. . . . The total of the public prisoners when collected was not great; for many were appropriated by the soldiers, and the whole of Sicily was full of them, they not having capitulated as had the troops under Demosthenes. . . .

The Syracusans and their allies gathered their forces and returned with the spoil, and as many prisoners as they could take with them, into the city. The captive Athenians and allies they deposited in the quarries, which they thought would be the safest place of confinement.[2] Nicias and Demosthenes they put to the sword. . . .

Those who were imprisoned in the quarries were at the beginning of their captivity harshly treated by the Syracusans. There were great numbers of them, and they were crowded in a deep and narrow place. At first the sun by day was still scorching and suffocating, for they had no roof over their heads, while the autumn nights were cold, and the extremes of temperature engendered violent disorders. Being cramped for room they had to do everything on the same spot. The corpses of

[1] The Spartan commander.

[2] The vast quarries of Acradina, near Syracuse, are now a hundred feet in depth and many acres in extent.

those who died from their wounds, exposure to the weather and the like, lay heaped one upon another. The smells were intolerable; and they were at the same time afflicted by hunger and thirst. During eight months they were allowed only about half a pint of water and a pint of food a day. Every kind of misery which could befall man in such a place befell them. This was the condition of all the captives for about ten weeks. At length the Syracusans sold them, with the exception of the Athenians and of any Sicilian or Italian Greeks who had sided with them in the war. The whole number of the public prisoners is not accurately known, but they were not less than seven thousand.

Of all the Greek actions which took place in this war, or indeed of all Greek actions which are on record, this was the greatest — the most glorious to the victors, the most ruinous to the vanquished. For the latter were utterly and at all points defeated, and their sufferings were prodigious. Fleet and army perished from the face of the earth. Nothing was saved, and of the many who went forth few returned home. Thus ended the Sicilian expedition.

The disaster at Syracuse occurred in 413 B. C. Athens, though sorely crippled by the loss of so many men and such great treasure upon this fruitless expedition, managed to continue the war with the Peloponnesians for nine years longer. But for the history of these later years we can no longer rely upon the vivid narrative of Thucydides. That breaks off abruptly in the middle of the twenty-first year of the war (411 B.C.). The final scenes of Spartan triumph and Athenian degradation were to be recorded by other and less able historians.

# CHAPTER IX

## ALCIBIADES THE ATHENIAN [1]

THE closing years of the Peloponnesian War, when the Athenians were struggling to recover from the disaster of the Sicilian expedition, are dominated by the personality of the brilliant but misguided Alcibiades. His biography by Plutarch (about 50–120 A. D.) is the fascinating characterization of a man whose virtues and whose faults were those of Athens herself. This account of Alcibiades forms one of the collection of forty-eight *Parallel Lives* of Greek and Roman worthies compiled by Plutarch. Our author was no historian; he cared little for politics; but preferred to study the personal characteristics, the virtues and the failings, of the representative men of antiquity. "It must be borne in mind," he says, "that my design is not to write histories, but lives. And the most glorious exploits do not always furnish us with the clearest examples of virtue or vice in men; sometimes a matter of less moment, an expression or a jest, informs us better of their characters and inclinations, than the most famous sieges, the greatest armaments, or the bloodiest battles whatsoever." [2]

### 41. Boyhood and Early Youth [3]

Alcibiades, it is supposed, was anciently descended from Eurysaces, the son of Ajax,[4] by his father's side; and by his

---

[1] *Plutarch's Lives of Illustrious Men.* The Dryden translation, revised by A. H. Clough. Boston, 1859. Little, Brown, and Co.

[2] Plutarch, *Alexander*, 1.     [3] Plutarch, *Alcibiades*, 1–2, 4–5, 7.

[4] A Greek hero at the siege of Troy.

mother's side from Alcmæon.[1] . . . It is not necessary, perhaps, to say anything of the beauty of Alcibiades, only that it bloomed with him in all the ages of his life, in his infancy, in his youth, and in his manhood; and . . . gave him a peculiar grace and charm. . . .

His conduct displayed many great inconsistencies and variations, not unnaturally, in accordance with the many and wonderful vicissitudes of his fortunes. Among the strong passions of his real character, the one most prevailing was his desire for superiority. This appears in several anecdotes told of his sayings while he was a child. Once being hard pressed in wrestling, and fearing to be thrown, he got the hand of his antagonist in his mouth, and bit it with all his force. The other loosed his hold presently and said, "You bite, Alcibiades, like a woman." "No," replied he, "like a lion." Another time, as he played at dice in the street, being then but a child, a loaded cart came that way, when it was his turn to throw. He called to the driver to stop, because he wished to throw in the way over which the cart was to pass. The man at first gave him no attention and drove on. Alcibiades then flung himself on his face before the cart, and, stretching himself out, bade the carter pass on now if he would. This action so startled the man that he put back his horses. . . .

When Alcibiades began to study, he obeyed all his other masters fairly well, but refused to learn to play on the flute. He said that to play on the lute or the harp does not in any way disfigure a man's body or face, but one is hardly to be known by one's most intimate friends, when playing on the flute. Besides, one who plays on the harp may speak or sing at the same time; but the use of the flute stops the mouth, intercepts the voice, and prevents all articulation. "Therefore," said he, "let the Theban youths pipe, who do not know how to speak. But we Athenians, as our ancestors have told us, have Athena for our patroness and Apollo for our protector, one of

[1] A famous Athenian noble. See page 55.

whom threw away the flute,[1] and the other stripped the Fluteplayer[2] of his skin." Thus, between raillery and good earnest, Alcibiades kept not only himself but others from learning, as it presently became the talk of the young boys, how Alcibiades despised playing on the flute, and ridiculed those who did. In consequence, flute-playing ceased to be reckoned among the liberal accomplishments, and became generally neglected. . . .

It was manifest that the many well-born persons who were continually seeking his company, and making their court to him, were attracted and captivated by his brilliant and extraordinary beauty only. But the affection entertained by Socrates[3] for him is strong evidence of the naturally noble qualities and good disposition of the boy, which Socrates, indeed, detected both in and under his personal beauty. Fearing that his wealth and station, and the great number both of strangers and Athenians who flattered and caressed him, might at last corrupt him, Socrates resolved to interpose and preserve so hopeful a plant from perishing in the flower, before its fruit came to perfection. . . . Such was the happiness of his genius, that he discerned Socrates from the rest, and admitted him, while he drove away the wealthy and the noble who made court to him. . . .

To others who made their addresses to him Alcibiades was reserved and rough, and acted, indeed, with great insolence to some of them. Thus when Anytus, one who was very fond of him, had invited him to an entertainment which he had prepared for some strangers, Alcibiades refused the invitation. Having however, drunk to excess at his own house with some of his companions, Alcibiades went thither with them to play a prank on Anytus. Standing at the door of the room where the guests were enjoying themselves, and seeing the tables covered with

---

[1] Athena is said to have invented the flute which she soon cast aside because its use distorted the features.

[2] The satyr Marsyas.

[3] The great Athenian philosopher. See chap. XI.

gold and silver cups, he commanded his servants to take away half of them, and carry them to his own house. Disdaining so much as to enter the room himself, as soon as he had done this, he went away. The company was indignant, and exclaimed at his rude and insulting conduct. Anytus, however, said that Alcibiades had shown great consideration and tenderness in taking only a part when he might have taken all.

He behaved in the same manner to all others who courted him except to one stranger, who, as the story goes, having but a small estate, sold it all for about a hundred staters,[1] and presented them to Alcibiades. Alcibiades, smiling and well pleased by the act, invited him to supper. After a very kind entertainment, Alcibiades gave him his gold again, requiring him, moreover, not to fail to be present the next day, when the public revenue was offered to farm, and to outbid all others. The man would have excused himself, because the contract was so large, and would cost many talents. But Alcibiades, who had at that time a private pique against the existing farmers of the revenue,[2] threatened to have him beaten if he refused. The next morning, the stranger, coming to the market place, offered a talent more than the existing rate. Thereupon the tax-farmers . . . called upon him to name his sureties, concluding that he could find none. The poor man, being startled at the proposal, began to retire; but Alcibiades, standing at a distance, cried out to the magistrates, "Set my name down, he is a friend of mine; I will be security for him." When the other bidders heard this, they perceived that all their plans were defeated. Their way was, with the profits of the second year to pay the rent for the year preceding. Not seeing any other way to extricate themselves out of the difficulty, they began to entreat the stranger, and offered him a sum of money. Alcibiades would not allow him to accept less than a talent. When that was paid down, he commanded him to relinquish the bargain, having by this device relieved his needs. . . .

[1] The Attic stater, in fine gold, was equivalent to about $5.72.
[2] Contractors who bid for the privilege of collecting the taxes.

When he was past his childhood, he went once to a grammar-school, and asked the master for one of Homer's books. The latter answered that he had nothing of Homer's. Alcibiades then gave him a blow with his fist, and went away. When another schoolmaster told him that he had been correcting Homer, Alcibiades said, "And yet you employ your time in teaching children to read! You, who are able to correct Homer, may well undertake to instruct men." Being once desirous to speak with Pericles, he went to his house, and was told there that he was not at leisure, but busied in considering how to give up his accounts to the Athenians. Alcibiades, as he went away, said, "It would be better for him to consider how he might avoid giving up his accounts at all." . . .

### 42. Public Life [1]

. . . When still a youth, Alcibiades was a soldier in the expedition against Potidæa,[2] where Socrates lodged in the same tent with him, and stood next to him in battle. Once there happened a sharp skirmish, in which they both behaved with signal bravery. Alcibiades receiving a wound, Socrates threw himself before him to defend him, and beyond any question saved him and his arms from the enemy. So in all justice Socrates might have claimed the prize of valor. But the generals appearing eager to adjudge the honor to Alcibiades, because of his rank, Socrates, who desired to increase his thirst after glory of a noble kind, was the first to give evidence for him, and pressed them to crown him, and to decree to him the complete suit of armor. Afterwards, in the battle of Delium, when the Athenians were routed, Socrates with a few others was retreating on foot. Alcibiades, who was on horseback, observing it, would not pass on, but stayed to shelter him from the danger, and brought him safe off. . . .

He gave a box on the ear to Hipponicus, the father of Callias, whose birth and wealth made him a person of great influence

---

[1] Plutarch, *Alcibiades*, 7–11, 16.    [2] See page 86, note 1.

and repute. And this he did unprovoked by any passion or quarrel between them, but only because, in a frolic, he had agreed with his companions to do it. People were justly offended at such insolence when it became known through the city. Early the next morning, Alcibiades went to his house and knocked at the door. Being admitted, Alcibiades took off his outer garment, and, presenting his naked body, desired Hipponicus to scourge and chastise him as he pleased. Upon this Hipponicus forgot all his resentment, and not only pardoned him, but soon after gave him his daughter Hipparete in marriage. . . .

Hipparete was a virtuous and dutiful wife, but, at last, growing impatient at the outrages done to her by her husband . . . she departed from him and retired to her brother's house. Alcibiades seemed not at all concerned at this, and lived on still in the same luxury. Now the law required that a wife should deliver to the archon in person, and not by proxy, the instrument by which she claimed a divorce. When, in obedience to this law, Hipparete presented herself before the archon, Alcibiades came in, caught her up, and carried her home through the market place, no one daring to oppose him or to take her from him. She continued with him till her death, which happened not long after, when Alcibiades had gone to Ephesus.[1] Nor is this violence to be thought so very serious or unmanly. For the law, in making her who desires to be divorced appear in public, seems to design to give her husband an opportunity of treating with her, and of endeavoring to retain her.

Alcibiades had a dog which cost him seventy minas.[2] It was a large animal and very handsome. His tail, which was his principal ornament, Alcibiades caused to be cut off. When some friends of Alcibiades told him that all Athens was sorry for the dog, and cried out upon him for this action, he laughed, and said, "Just what I wanted has happened, then. I wished the Athenians to talk about this, that they might not say something worse of me."

[1] One of the twelve Ionian cities of Asia Minor.      [2] About $1260.

It is said that the first time he came into the Assembly was upon the occasion of a gift of money, which he made to the people. This was not done, however, by design. As he passed along, he heard a shout, and inquiring the cause, and having learned that there was a donative being given to the people, he went in among them and gave money also. The multitude thereupon applauded him, and shouted. Alcibiades was so transported at this applause that he forgot a quail which he had under his robe, and the bird, being frightened with the noise, flew off. Upon this the people made louder acclamations than before, and many of them started up to pursue the bird. One Antiochus, a pilot, caught it and restored it to him, for which action he was ever after a favorite with Alcibiades.

He had great advantages for entering public life. His noble birth, his riches, the personal courage he had shown in various battles, and the multitude of his friends and dependents, threw open, so to say, folding doors for his admittance. But he did not consent to let his power with the people rest on any thing except his own gift of eloquence. That he was a master in the art of speaking, the comic poets bear him witness. And the most eloquent of public speakers,[1] in his oration against Midias, grants that Alcibiades, among other perfections, was a most accomplished orator. If, however, we give credit to Theophrastus,[2] who of all philosophers was the most curious inquirer, and the greatest lover of history, we are to understand that Alcibiades had the highest capacity for discerning what was the right thing to be said for any purpose, and on any occasion. Aiming, however, not only at saying what was required, but also at saying it well . . . he would often pause in the middle of his discourse for want of the apt word, and would be silent and stop till he could recollect himself, and had considered what to say.

His expenses in horses kept for the public games, and in the number of his chariots, was a matter of common observation.

---

[1] Demosthenes, the famous Athenian orator.
[2] A Greek scientist and philosopher (about 372–287 B. C.).

Never did anyone but he, either private person or king, send seven chariots to the Olympic games. And to have carried away at once the first, the second, and the fourth prize, as Thucydides says, or the third, as another relates it, outdoes every distinction that ever was known of that kind. . . .

But with all these words and deeds . . . he intermingled exorbitant luxury and wantonness in his eating, drinking, and dissolute living. He wore long purple robes which dragged after him as he went through the market place. He even caused the planks of his galley to be cut away, so that he might lie the softer, his bed not being placed on the boards, but hanging upon girths. His shield, again, which was richly gilded, had not the usual ensigns of the Athenians, but a painted Cupid, holding a thunderbolt in his hand.

The sight of all this luxury made the people of good repute in the city feel disgust and abhorrence. They had apprehension also, at his free-living, and his contempt of law, as things monstrous in themselves, and indicating designs of usurpation. Aristophanes [1] has well expressed the people's feeling toward him:

> "They love, they hate, but cannot live without him."

And still more strongly, under a figurative expression,

> "Best rear no lion in your state, 'tis true;
> But treat him like a lion if you do."

The truth is that his liberalities, his public shows, and other gifts to the people . . . the glory of his ancestors, the force of his eloquence, the grace of his person, his strength of body, joined with his great courage and knowledge in military affairs, prevailed upon the Athenians to endure patiently his excesses, and to indulge many things to him. . . . For example, he kept Agatharcus, the painter, a prisoner till he had painted his whole house, but then dismissed him with a reward. He publicly struck Taureas, who exhibited certain shows in opposition to

[1] The famous comic dramatist of Athens (about 448–385 B. C.).

him and contended with him for the prize. . . . Once, when Alcibiades succeeded well in an oration which he made, and the whole Assembly attended upon him to do him honor, Timon the misanthrope [1] did not pass slightly by him, or avoid him, as he did others, but purposely met him. Taking him by the hand, Timon said, "Go on boldly, my son, and increase in credit with the people, for thou wilt one day bring them calamities enough." Some that were present laughed at the saying, and some reviled Timon; but there were others upon whom it made a deep impression; so various was the judgment which was made of him, and so irregular his own character.

The subsequent career of Alcibiades fully justified Timon's forebodings. The famous expedition against Syracuse, which ended in such complete disaster to Athens, was undertaken largely by reason of the representations of Alcibiades.[2] Again, when his enemies sought to bring him to trial for his alleged misdoings, Alcibiades took refuge with the Spartans, "assuring them that he would make amends by his future services for all the mischief he had done them while he was still their foe. . . . At his very first coming he succeeded in inducing them to send aid to the Syracusans; and so aroused and excited them that they forthwith dispatched Gylippus to crush the forces which the Athenians had in Sicily." [3]  Upon the collapse of the Sicilian expedition (413 B.C.), Alcibiades, in coöperation with the Spartan generals, was able to arouse almost all the Ionian cities into revolt against Athens. Although the Athenians afterwards recalled their former favorite and gave him the command of their fleet, Alcibiades could never undo the damage he had inflicted upon his native city. The close of the Peloponnesian War found him a

[1] An Athenian who, soured by his disappointments and the ingratitude of his friends, had retired from the world.

[2] See page 91.    [3] See page 93.

fugitive in Asia Minor where by Spartan orders he was treacherously assassinated (404 B. C.). "Those who were sent to kill him had not courage enough to enter the house, but surrounded it first, and set it on fire. Alcibiades, as soon as he perceived it, getting together great quantities of clothes and furniture, threw them upon the fire to choke it, and, having wrapped his cloak about his left arm, and holding his naked sword in his right, he cast himself into the middle of the fire, and escaped securely through it before his clothes were burnt. The barbarians, as soon as they saw him, retreated, and none of them dared to engage with him, but, standing at a distance, they slew him with their darts and arrows."[1]

[1] Plutarch, *Alcibiades*, 39.

# CHAPTER X

## THE EXPEDITION OF THE TEN THOUSAND [1]

ANTIQUITY has bequeathed to us few books more interesting than the *Anabasis* by the Athenian historian, Xenophon.[2] It is the story of that memorable expedition in the course of which an army of ten thousand Greeks penetrated to the very heart of the Persian Empire, overcame their treacherous and watchful foes, and returned by a long and toilsome march to safety in Greek lands. This story is told by one who accompanied the army from beginning to end; at first as the friend and guest of the Greek generals, later as the moving spirit among the soldiers and the real leader of the retreat.

### 43. The March to the Euphrates [3]

Cyrus the Younger, so called to distinguish him from Cyrus the Great, was a brother of Artaxerxes,[4] king of Persia. From his province of Asia Minor [5] he plotted rebellion against King Artaxerxes and raised a great army with which to invade Persia. Besides a multitude of soldiers gathered from his satrapy, Cyrus enlisted a formidable body of Greek mercenaries. Many of them were

---

[1] Xenophon, *Anabasis. The Works of Xenophon*, translated by H. G. Dakyns. 4 vols. London, 1890–1897. Macmillan and Co.

[2] See page 63.

[3] Xenophon, *Anabasis*, i, 5.

[4] Artaxerxes II (404–359 B. C.).

[5] His government extended over the three important districts of Lydia, Phrygia, and Cappadocia.

Spartan hoplites, now freed from service by the close of the Peloponnesian War. When all was ready, the expedition moved out from Sardis in March, 401 B. C. The Greeks believed that they were being led against a certain Tissaphernes [1] with whom Cyrus was then at war. It was not until the soldiers reached Thapsacus on the Euphrates (July, 401 B.C.) that they learned the real object of the expedition. Having crossed to the left bank of the Euphrates, the army marched through a desert country toward Babylon.

. . . Once they found themselves involved in a narrow way, where the deep clay presented an obstacle to the progress of their wagons. Cyrus, with the nobles about him, halted to superintend the operation. He gave orders to take a body of barbarians who should help in extricating the wagons. As they seemed to be slow about the business, he turned round angrily to the Persian nobles and bade them lend a hand to force the wagons out. Then, if ever, what makes up one branch of good discipline was to be witnessed. Each of those addressed, just where he chanced to be standing, threw off his purple cloak, and flung himself into the work with as much eagerness as if it had been a charge for victory. Down a steep hill side they flew, with their costly tunics and embroidered trousers — some with the circlets round their necks and bracelets on their arms. In an instant, they sprang into the miry clay, and in less time than one could have imagined, they brought the wagons safe on solid ground. . . .

Another incident related by Xenophon belongs to this period of the desert march.

Some dispute or other here occurred between the soldiers of Menon and Clearchus,[2] in which Clearchus sentenced one

---

[1] Satrap of Caria and Ionia.

[2] Menon and Clearchus were two of the five Greek generals.

of Menon's men, as the delinquent, and had him flogged. The man went back to his own troops and told them. Hearing what had been done to their comrade, his fellows fretted and fumed, and were highly incensed against Clearchus. The same day Clearchus visited the passage of the river, and after inspecting the market there, was returning with a few followers, on horseback, to his tent, and had to pass through Menon's quarters. Cyrus had not yet come up, but was riding along in the same direction. One of Menon's men, who was splitting wood, caught sight of Clearchus as he rode past, and aimed a blow at him with his axe. The blow took no effect; when another hurled a stone at him, and a third, and then several, with shouts and hisses. Clearchus made a rapid retreat to his own troops, and at once ordered them to get under arms. He bade his hoplites remain in position with their shields resting against their knees, while he, at the head of his Thracians and horsemen, of which he had more than forty in his army . . . advanced against Menon's soldiers. The latter, with Menon himself, were panic-stricken, and ran to seize their arms. Some even stood riveted to the spot, in perplexity at the occurrence.

Just then Proxenus came up from behind, as chance would have it, with his division of hoplites. Without a moment's hesitation he marched into the open space between the rival parties, and grounded arms; then he fell to begging Clearchus to desist. The latter was not too well pleased to hear his trouble mildly spoken of, when he had barely escaped being stoned to death; and he bade Proxenus retire and leave the intervening space open. At this juncture Cyrus arrived and inquired what was happening. There was no time for hesitation. With his javelins firmly grasped in his hands and escorted by some of his faithful bodyguard, he galloped up and exclaimed, "Clearchus, Proxenus, and you other Greeks yonder, you know not what you do. As surely as you come to blows with one another, our fate is sealed — this very day I shall be cut to pieces, and so will you soon after. Let our fortunes once take an evil turn, and these barbarians whom you see around will be worse foes to us than those who are at present serving with the king." At these words Clearchus came to his senses. Both parties paused from battle and retired to their quarters. Order reigned.

### 44. The Death of Cyrus [1]

At Cunaxa, a little village about fifty miles northwest of Babylon, Cyrus and his army encountered the enormous host of the Persian king. The Greek soldiers made short work of the Orientals posted against them. But the battle was not yet won.

. . . Cyrus, seeing the Greeks conquering . . . and in hot pursuit, was well content. But in spite of his joy and the salutations offered him at that moment by those about him, as though he was already king, he was not led away to join in the pursuit. Keeping his squadron of six hundred horsemen in close order, he waited and watched to see what the king himself would do. The king, he knew, held the center of the Persian army. Indeed, it is the fashion for the Asiatic monarch to occupy that position during action. For this there is a twofold reason: he holds the safest place, with his troops on either side of him, while, if he has occasion to dispatch any necessary order along the lines, his troops will receive the message in half the time. The king, accordingly, on this occasion held the center of his army, but for all that, he was outside Cyrus' left wing. Seeing that no one offered him battle in front. . . the king wheeled as if to encircle the enemy. It was then that Cyrus, in apprehension lest the king might get round to the rear and cut to pieces the Greek soldiers, charged to meet him. Attacking with his six hundred, he mastered the line of troops in front of the king, and put to flight the six thousand, cutting down, with his own hand, their commander. But as soon as the rout commenced, Cyrus' own six hundred themselves, in the ardor of pursuit, were scattered, with the

[1] Xenophon, *Anabasis*, i, 8–9.

exception of a handful who remained with Cyrus himself. Left alone with these, he caught sight of the king and the close throng about him. Unable longer to contain himself, with a cry, "I see the man," he rushed at the king and dealt a blow at his chest, wounding him through the corselet. This is according to the statement of Ctesias [1] the surgeon, who further states that he himself healed the wound. As Cyrus delivered the blow, some one struck him under the eye with a javelin. . . . Cyrus fell, and eight of his bravest companions lay on the top of him. The story goes that Artapates, the trustiest squire among his wand-bearers, when he saw that Cyrus had fallen to the ground, leaped from his horse and threw his arms about him. Then, as one account says, the king bade one slay him as a worthy victim to his brother: others say that Artapates drew his scimitar and slew himself with his own hand. . . .

So died Cyrus; a man the kingliest and most worthy to rule of all the Persians who have lived since the elder Cyrus,[2] according to the testimony of all who are reputed to have known him intimately. . . .

## 45. The March to the Black Sea [3]

The death of Cyrus and the dispersal of his Oriental troops placed the Greeks in a position of great peril. They were fifteen hundred miles from home, without provisions, and beset by foes on every side. To add to their troubles, the Greek generals were treacherously entrapped by the Persians and slain. Acting on Xenophon's advice the soldiers chose new generals and began the difficult retreat from Assyria to the Euxine (October, 401 B.C.). Reaching the mountains of Armenia, the Greeks found the warlike inhabitants even more dangerous enemies than the Persians.

[1] A Greek who lived many years at the Persian court as the royal physician. He wrote a history of Persia to the year 399 B.C.

[2] Cyrus the Great.    [3] Xenophon, *Anabasis*, iv, 5, 7–8.

. . . The Greeks now marched through Armenia three desert stages — fifteen parasangs [1] — to the river Euphrates, and crossed it in water up to the waist. The sources of the river were reported to be at no great distance. From this place they marched through deep snow over a flat country. The last of these marches was trying, with the north wind blowing in their teeth, drying up everything and benumbing the men. Here one of the seers suggested to them to do a sacrifice to Boreas,[2] and sacrifice was done. The effect was obvious to all in the diminished fierceness of the blast. But there was six feet of snow, so that many of the baggage animals and slaves were lost, and about thirty of the men themselves.

They spent the whole night in kindling fires, for fortunately there was no dearth of wood at the halting-place. Only those who came late into camp had no wood. Accordingly, those who had arrived first and had kindled fires would not allow these late-comers near their fires, unless they would in return give a share of their corn or of any other food they might have. Here, then, a general exchange of goods was set up. Where the fire was kindled, the snow melted, and great trenches formed themselves down to the bare earth, and it was possible to measure the depth of the snow.

Leaving these quarters, they marched the whole of the next day over snow, and many of the men were afflicted with "boulimia" or hunger-faintness. Xenophon, who was guarding the rear, came upon some men who had dropped down. He did not know what ailed them; but some one who was experienced in such matters suggested to him that they had evidently got "boulimia," and that if they could have something to eat, they would revive. Then Xenophon went the round of the baggage train, and laying an embargo on any eatables he could see, doled out with his own hands, or sent off other able-bodied agents to distribute to the sufferers. The latter, as soon as they

[1] That is, a three days' journey of about 50 miles. The parasang, a Persian measure of distance, was equal to about 3½ miles.

[2] The north wind. At Athens there was a temple dedicated to Boreas.

had taken a mouthful, got on their legs again and continued the march. . . .

On the heels of the army hung perpetually bands of the enemy, snatching away disabled baggage animals and fighting with each other over the carcases. And in its track not seldom were left to their fate disabled soldiers, struck down with snow-blindness or with toes mortified by frostbite. As for the eyes, it was some alleviation against the snow to march with something black before them. For the feet, the only remedy was to keep in motion without stopping an instant, and to take off the sandals at night. If they went to sleep with the sandals on, the thong worked into the feet, and the sandals were frozen fast to them. This was partly due to the fact that, since their old sandals had failed, they wore untanned brogues made of newly-flayed ox-hides.

It was owing to some such dire necessity that a party of men fell out and were left behind. Seeing a black-looking patch of ground where the snow had evidently disappeared, they conjectured it must have been melted. This was actually so, owing to a spring of some sort which was to be seen steaming up in a dell close by. To this spot they turned aside and sat down, and were loth to go a step farther. But Xenophon, with his rearguard, perceived them, and begged and implored them by all manner of means not to lag behind, telling them that the enemy were coming after them in large numbers; and he ended by growing angry. They merely bade him put a knife to their throats; not one step farther would they stir. Then it seemed best to frighten the pursuing enemy, if possible, and prevent their falling upon the invalids. It was already dusk, and the pursuers were advancing with much noise and hubbub, wrangling and disputing over their spoils. Then all of a sudden the rearguard, in the plenitude of health and strength, sprang up out of their lair and ran upon the enemy, while those weary ones bawled out as loud as their sick throats could sound, and dashed their spears against their shields. The enemy in terror hurled themselves through the snow

into the dell, and not one of them ever uttered a sound
again. . . .

After undergoing incredible hardships, the Greeks
succeeded in capturing a native village where they obtained
food and a temporary respite from the exertions of the
march.

Next they marched into the country of the Taochians five
stages — thirty parasangs [1] — and provisions failed. For the
Taochians lived in strong places, into which they had carried
up all their stores. Now when the army arrived before one
of these strong places — a mere fortress, without houses
. . . Chirisophus attacked at once. When the first regiment
fell back tired, a second advanced, and again a third, for it was
impossible to surround the place in full force, as it was encircled
by a river. Presently Xenophon came up with the rearguard,
consisting of both light and heavy infantry, whereupon Chirisophus hailed him with the words, " You have come in the
nick of time. We must take this place, for the troops have
no provisions."

Thereupon they consulted together. To Xenophon's inquiry, "What is it that hinders our simply walking in?"
Chirisophus replied, "There is just this one narrow approach
which you see; but when we attempt to pass by it, they roll
down volleys of stones from yonder overhanging crag. This
is the state in which you find yourself, if you chance to be
caught"; and he pointed to some poor fellows with their legs
or ribs crushed to bits. "But when they have expended their
ammunition," said Xenophon, "there is nothing else, is there,
to hinder our passing? Certainly, except yonder handful of
fellows, there is no one in front of us that we can see; and of
them, only two or three apparently are armed. The distance
to be traversed under fire is, as your eyes will tell you, about
one hundred and fifty feet. Of this space the first hundred

[1] About 100 miles.

feet are thickly covered with great pines at intervals; under cover of these, what harm can come to our men from a pelt of stones, flying or rolling? So then, there are only fifty feet left to cross, during a lull of stones." "Ay," said Chirisophus, "but with our first attempt to approach the bush a galling fire of stones commences." "The very thing we want," said the other, "for they will use up their ammunition all the quicker. But let us select a point from which we shall have only a brief space to run across, if we can, and from which it will be easier to get back, if we wish."

Thereupon Chirisophus and Xenophon set out with Callimachus, the captain in command of the officers of the rearguard that day. The rest of the captains remained out of danger. That done, the next step was for a party of about seventy men to get away under the trees, not in a body, but one by one, each person using his best precaution. Agasias and Aristonymus, who were also officers of the rearguard, were posted as supports outside the trees, for it was not possible for more than a single company to stand safely within the trees. Here Callimachus hit upon a pretty contrivance. He ran forward from the tree under which he was posted two or three paces, and as soon as the stones came whizzing, he retired easily, but at each excursion more than ten wagon-loads of rocks were expended. Agasias, seeing how Callimachus was amusing himself, and the whole army looking on as spectators, was seized with the fear that he might miss his chance of being first to run the gauntlet of the enemy's fire and get into the place. So, without a word of summons to his next neighbor, Aristonymus, or to anyone else, off he set on his own account, and passed the whole detachment. But Callimachus, seeing him tearing past, caught hold of his shield by the rim, and in the meantime Aristonymus ran ahead of both, and after him Eurylochus of Lusia. They were one and all aspirants for valor, and in that high pursuit, each was the eager rival of the rest. So in this strife of honor, the three of them took the fortress, and when they had once rushed it, not a stone more was hurled from overhead.

And here a terrible spectacle displayed itself: the women first cast their infants down the cliff, and then they cast themselves after their fallen little ones, and the men likewise. In such a scene, Æneas, an officer, caught sight of a man with a fine dress about to throw himself over, and seized hold of him to stop him. But the other caught him in his arms, and both were gone in an instant headlong down the crags, and were killed. Out of this place the merest handful of human beings was taken prisoners, but cattle and asses in abundance and flocks of sheep. . . .

And now the Greeks marched rapidly through the territories of barbarian tribes and approached the northern borders of Armenia. They were fortunate in getting a guide who promised to lead them to a summit whence they could behold the sea.

On the fifth day they reached the mountain, the name of which was Theches. No sooner had the men in advance ascended it and caught sight of the sea than a great cry arose. Xenophon, with the rearguard, hearing the sound, conjectured that another set of enemies must surely be attacking in front; for they were followed by the inhabitants of the country. . . .

But as the shout became louder and nearer, and those who from time to time came up, began racing at the top of their speed toward the shouter, and the shouting continually recommenced with yet greater volume as the numbers increased, Xenophon felt certain that something extraordinary must have happened. So he mounted his horse, and taking with him Lycius and the cavalry, he galloped to the rescue. Presently they could hear the soldiers shouting and passing on the joyful word, *The sea! the sea!* ·

Thereupon they began running, rearguard and all, and the baggage animals and horses came galloping up. But when they had reached the summit, then indeed they fell to embracing one another — generals and officers and men — and the tears trickled down their cheeks. And on a sudden . . . the soldiers began bringing stones and erecting a great cairn. On this they dedicated a large number of untanned skins, staves, and captured wicker shields. . . . After this the Greeks dismissed the guide with a present raised from the common store, to wit, a horse, a silver bowl, a Persian dress, and ten darics.[1] What he most begged to have were their rings, and of these he got several from the soldiers. After pointing out to them a village where they would find quarters, and the road by which they would proceed toward the land of the Macrones, as evening fell, he turned his back upon them and was gone.

From the land of the Macrones through the territory of the Colchians it was but a short journey to the sea.

. . . From this place they marched on two stages — seven parasangs — and reached the sea at Trapezus, a populous Greek city on the Euxine. . . . Here they halted about thirty days in the villages of the Colchians, which they used as a base of operations to ravage the whole territory of Colchis. The men of Trapezus supplied the army with a market, entertained them, and gave them oxen and wheat and wine. Further, they negotiated with them in behalf of their neighbors, the Colchians, and from this folk also came gifts of hospitality in the shape of cattle. And now the Greeks made preparation for the sacrifice which they had vowed, and a sufficient number of cattle came in for them to offer thank-offerings for safe guidance to Zeus the Savior, and to Heracles,[2] and to the other gods, according to their vows. They instituted also a gymnastic contest on the mountain side, just where they were quartered, and chose Dracontius, a Spartan. . . to superintend the course and to be president of the games.

As soon as the sacrifices were ended, they handed over the

---

[1] $54.00. A daric was a Persian gold coin worth about $5.40.

[2] The journeys of Heracles were believed to give him special sympathy with wanderers.

hides of the beasts to Dracontius, and bade him lead the way to his racecourse. He merely waved his hand and pointed to where they were standing, and said, "There, this ridge is just the place for running, anywhere, everywhere." "But how," it was asked, "will we manage to wrestle on the hard scrubby ground?" "Oh! worse knocks for those who are thrown," the president replied. There was a mile race for boys, the majority being captive lads; and for the long race more than sixty Cretans competed; there were wrestling, boxing, and the *pancratium*.[1] Altogether it was a beautiful spectacle. . . . There was horse-racing, also. The riders had to gallop down a steep incline to the sea, and then turn and come up again to the altar. On the descent more than half rolled head over heels, and then back they came toiling up the tremendous steep, scarcely out of a walking pace. Loud were the shouts, the laughter, and the cheers.

With the arrival at Trapezus (February, 400 B. C.) the most difficult part of the return of the Ten Thousand was accomplished. The Greeks were now on Greek soil and among Greek people. Here they rested a month and then proceeded, partly by land, partly by sea, to the western extremity of the Euxine. The remnant of the force, after an incursion into Thrace, returned to Asia Minor and took service with the Spartans, then at war with Persia (March, 399 B. C.). After just two years of mingled peril and privation the soldiers of the Ten Thousand had reached their journey's end.

[1] A severe exercise in which wrestling and boxing were combined.

# CHAPTER XI

## THE TRIAL AND DEATH OF SOCRATES [1]

WHILE Xenophon was still absent in Asia with the Ten Thousand Greeks, his master and friend, the philosopher Socrates, suffered death at Athens as a person dangerous to the state. Socrates, who lived during the exciting epoch of the Peloponnesian War, gave himself up to the study of moral problems. His grotesque and even repulsive features contrasted strangely with the noble tone and elevated character of his doctrines. One of his pupils was Plato, a wealthy noble who abandoned a public career for the delights of philosophy. Plato's *Dialogues* furnish us with an attractive picture of Socrates, both as a thinker and as a man. These works are really essays on philosophical themes, but are cast in the form of question and answer which Socrates had employed. In nearly all the dialogues, Socrates is a conspicuous figure; in some of them, indeed, he is throughout the only speaker. As we read these matchless productions of Plato's genius, there rises before our eyes the figure of that poor and homely Athenian who spent all his days in an unwearied search for truth, and who became, at the last, a willing martyr to the cause of truth.

### 46. Socrates Accused [2]

The scene of the following conversation is the porch of the King Archon at Athens. Before this official impeach-

[1] *The Dialogues of Plato*, translated by Benjamin Jowett. 2d edition. 5 vols. Oxford, 1875. Clarendon Press.    [2] Plato, *Euthyphro*, 1–3.

ments for impiety and the answers of the accused were laid. Here Socrates and Euthyphro meet, Socrates having just been indicted, and Euthyphro being engaged in indicting his father for the murder of a laboring man.

*Euth.* Why have you left the Lyceum,[1] Socrates? and what are you doing in the porch of the King Archon? Surely you cannot be engaged in an action before the king, as I am.

*Soc.* Not in an action, Euthyphro; impeachment is the word which the Athenians use.

*Euth.* What! I suppose that some one has been prosecuting you, for I cannot believe that you are the prosecutor of another.

*Soc.* Certainly not.

*Euth.* Then some one else has been prosecuting you.

*Soc.* Yes.

*Euth.* And who is he?

*Soc.* A young man who is little known, Euthyphro; and I hardly know him: his name is Meletus. Perhaps you may remember his appearance; he has a beak, and long straight hair, and a beard which is ill grown.

*Euth.* No, I do not remember him, Socrates. And what is the charge which he brings against you?

*Soc.* What is the charge? Well, a very serious charge, which shows a good deal of character in the young man, and for which he is certainly not to be despised. He says he knows how the youth are corrupted and who are their corrupters. I fancy that he must be a wise man, and seeing that I am anything but a wise man, he has found me out, and is going to accuse me of corrupting his young friends. And of this our mother the state is to be the judge. Of all our political men he is the only one who seems to me to begin in the right way, with the cultivation of virtue in youth. He is a good husbandman, and takes care of the shoots first, and clears away us who are the destroyers of them. That is the first step; he will afterwards

---

[1] A popular resort containing a gymnasium and gardens, on the banks of the Ilissus.

attend to the older branches. If he goes on as he has begun, he will be a very great public benefactor.

*Euth.* I hope that he may; but I rather fear, Socrates, that the reverse will turn out to be the truth. My opinion is that in attacking you he is simply aiming a blow at the state in a sacred place. But in what way does he say that you corrupt the young?

*Soc.* He brings a remarkable accusation against me, which at first hearing excites surprise. He says that I make new gods and deny the existence of old ones; this is the ground of his indictment.

*Euth.* I understand, Socrates. . . . He knows that such a charge is readily received, for the world is always jealous of novelties in religion. And I know that when I myself speak in the Assembly about divine things, and foretell the future to them, they laugh at me as a madman; and yet every word that I say is true. But they are jealous of all of us. I suppose that we must be brave and not mind them.

*Soc.* Their laughter, friend Euthyphro, is not a matter of much consequence. For a man may be thought wise; but the Athenians, I suspect, do not care much about this, until he begins to make other men wise; and then for some reason or other, perhaps, as you say, from jealousy, they are angry.

*Euth.* I have no desire to try conclusions with them about this.

*Soc.* I dare say that you don't make yourself common, and are not apt to impart your wisdom. But I have a benevolent habit of pouring out myself to everybody, and would even pay for a listener, and I am afraid that the Athenians know this; and therefore, as I was saying, if the Athenians would only laugh at me as you say that they laugh at you, the time might pass gayly enough in the court. But perhaps they may be in earnest, and then what the end will be you soothsayers only can predict.

*Euth.* I believe that the affair will end in nothing, Socrates, and that you will win your cause; and I think that I shall win mine.

### 47. Trial of Socrates [1]

The "affair," alas, did not "end in nothing." In the year 399 B. C., Socrates was condemned to death on the charge which Meletus had brought against him. Xenophon tells us that Socrates might easily have obtained a verdict in his favor had he been willing to approach his judges with prayers and flattery. Socrates would not even prepare any defense. However, in one of his dialogues, Plato gives a speech purported to have been delivered by Socrates to the judges after conviction.

. . . You think that I was convicted because I had no words of the sort that would have procured my acquittal — I mean, if I had thought fit to leave nothing undone or unsaid. . . . But I had not the boldness or impudence or inclination to address you as you would have liked me to address you, weeping and wailing and lamenting, and saying and doing many things which you have been accustomed to hear from others, and which, as I maintain, are unworthy of me. I thought at the time that I ought not to do anything common or mean when in danger; or do I now repent of the manner of my defense. I would rather die having spoken after my manner, than speak in your manner and live. For neither in war nor yet at law ought I or any man to use every way of escaping death. . . . The difficulty, my friends, is not in avoiding death, but in avoiding unrighteousness; for that runs faster than death. I am old,[2] and move slowly, and the slower runner has overtaken me, and my accusers are keen and quick, and the faster runner, who is unrighteousness, has overtaken them. . . .

Let us reflect, and we shall see that there is great reason to hope that death is a good. For one of two things is true —

[1] Plato, *Apology*, 29, 32–33.
[2] Socrates at this time was seventy years of age.

either death is a state of nothingness and utter unconsciousness; or, as men say, there is a change and migration of the soul from this world to another. Now if you suppose that there is no consciousness, but a sleep like the sleep of him who is undisturbed even by dreams, death will be an unspeakable gain. For if a person were to select the night in which his sleep was undisturbed even by dreams, and were to compare with it all the other days and nights of his life, and then were to tell us how many days and nights he had passed in the course of his life better and more pleasantly than this one, I think that any man would find them easy to count, when compared with the others. Now if death is like this, I say that to die is gain; for eternity is then but a single night.

But if death is the journey to another place, and there, as men say, all the dead are, what good, O my friends and judges, can be greater than this? If indeed when the pilgrim arrives in the world below, he is delivered from the professors of justice in this world, and finds the true judges who are said to give judgment there, Minos and Rhadamanthus and Æacus and Triptolemus, and other sons of God who were righteous in their own life, that pilgrimage will be worth making. . . . Above all, I shall then be able to continue my search into true and false knowledge; as in this world, so also in that; and I shall find out who is wise, and who pretends to be wise, and is not. . . . In another world they do not put a man to death for asking questions; assuredly not. For besides being happier in that world than in this, they will be immortal, if what is said is true.

Wherefore, O judges, be of good cheer about death, and know of a certainty that no evil can happen to a good man, either in life or after death. He and his are not neglected by the gods; nor has my own approaching end happened by mere chance. But I see clearly that to die and be released was better for me; and therefore the oracle gave no sign. For which reason, also, I am not angry with my accusers, or with those who have condemned me to death. They have done me no harm, although they did not mean to do me any good; and for this I may gently blame them. . . .

## 48. Socrates in Prison [1]

Though condemned to death, Socrates is not to die at once. He must abide in prison until the arrival of a certain sacred ship from the island of Delos. During this interval of waiting, when no legal execution could take place, his friend Crito visits him. Crito begs the philosopher to accept the money which his disciples are ready to give him and with it to bribe his jailers and escape. But Socrates is not to be persuaded. As a reply to Crito, he represents the Laws of his native city as making this speech to him.

. . . "Listen then, Socrates, to us who have brought you up. Think not of life and children first, and of justice afterwards, but of justice first, that you may be justified before the princes of the world below. For neither will you nor any that belong to you be happier or holier or juster in this life, or happier in another, if you do as Crito bids. Now you depart in innocence, a sufferer and not a doer of evil; a victim not of the laws but of men. But if you go forth, returning evil for evil, and injury for injury, breaking the covenants and agreements which you have made with us, and wronging those whom you ought least to wrong, that is to say, yourself, your friends, your country, and us, we shall be angry with you while you live. And our brethren, the Laws in the world below, will receive you as an enemy; for they will know that you have done your best to destroy us. Listen, then, to us, and not to Crito."

*Soc.* This is the voice which I seem to hear murmuring in my ears, like the sound of the flute in the ears of the mystic; that voice, I say, is murmuring in my ears, and prevents me from hearing any other. And I know that anything more which

[1] Plato, *Crito*, 16–17.

you may say will be in vain. Yet speak, if you have anything to say.

*Cr.* I have nothing to say, Socrates.

*Soc.* Leave me then to follow whithersoever God leads.

### 49. Death of Socrates [1]

And now comes the story, so pathetic in its self-restraint, of Socrates' last hours. The philosopher has just concluded a long argument for the immortality of the soul.

When he had done speaking, Crito said, And have you any commands for us, Socrates — anything to say about your children, or any other matter in which we can serve you?

Nothing particular, he said, only, as I have always told you, I would have you look to yourselves; that is a service which you may be always doing to me and mine as well as to yourselves. And you need not make professions; for if you take no thought for yourselves, and walk not according to the precepts which I have given you, not now for the first time, the warmth of your professions will be of no avail.

We will do our best, said Crito. But in what way would you have us bury you?

In any way that you like; only you must get hold of me and take care that I do not walk away from you. Then he turned to us, and added with a smile, I cannot make Crito believe that I am the same Socrates who has been talking and conducting the argument. He fancies that I am the other Socrates whom he will soon see, a dead body, and he asks, How shall he bury me? And though I have spoken many words in the endeavor to show that when I have drunk the poison I shall leave you and go to the joys of the blessed — these words of mine, with which I have comforted you and myself, have had, as I perceive, no effect upon Crito. . . . Be of good cheer, my dear Crito, and say that you are burying my body only, and do with that as is usual, and as you think best. . . .

[1] Plato, *Phædo*, 64, 66.

Crito then made a sign to the servant, who was standing by. He went out, and having been absent for some time, returned with the jailer carrying the cup of poison. Socrates said, You, my good friend, who are experienced in these matters, shall give me directions how I am to proceed. The man answered, You have only to walk about until your legs are heavy, and then to lie down, and the poison will act. At the same time he handed the cup to Socrates, who took it in the easiest and gentlest manner, without the least fear or change of color or feature. Looking at the man with all his eyes, Echecrates,[1] as his manner was, Socrates said, What do you say about making a libation out of this cup to any god? May I, or not? The man answered, We only prepare, Socrates, just so much as we deem enough. I understand, he said, but I may and must ask the gods to prosper my journey from this to that other world — even so — and so be it according to my prayer. Then holding the cup to his lips, quite readily and cheerfully he drank off the poison.

Hitherto most of us had been able to control our sorrow; but now when we saw him drinking, and saw too that he had finished the draught, we could no longer forbear, and in spite of myself my own tears were flowing fast; so that I covered my face, and wept over myself. For certainly I was not weeping over him, but at the thought of my own calamity in having lost such a friend. Nor was I the first, for Crito, when he found himself unable to restrain his tears, had got up and moved away, and I followed; and at that moment Apollodorus, who had been weeping all the time, broke out in a loud and passionate cry which made cowards of us all. Socrates alone retained his calmness. What is this strange outcry? he said. I sent away the women mainly in order that they might not offend in this way, for I have heard that a man should die in peace. Be quiet then, and have patience.

When we heard that we were ashamed, and refrained our

[1] Throughout the dialogue Plato addresses his friend Echecrates, to whom he is relating the circumstances of the philosopher's death.

tears; and he walked about until, as he said, his legs began to fail, and then he lay on his back, according to the directions, and the man who gave him the poison now and then looked at his feet and legs.   After a time the man pressed his foot hard, and asked him if he could feel; and he said, No; and then his leg, and so upward and upward, and showed us that he was cold and stiff.   And he felt them himself, and said, When the poison reaches the heart, that will be the end.   He was beginning to grow cold when he uncovered his face, for he had covered himself up, and said (they were his last words), Crito, I owe a cock to Asclepius[1]; will you remember to pay the debt?   The debt shall be paid, said Crito; is there anything else?   There was no answer to this question; but in a minute or two a movement was heard, and the attendants uncovered him; his eyes were set, and Crito closed his eyes and mouth.

Such was the end, Echecrates, of our friend, whom I may truly call the wisest, justest, and best of all the men whom I have ever known.

[1] The Greek god of healing.

# CHAPTER XII

## DEMOSTHENES AND THE STRUGGLE AGAINST PHILIP [1]

GREEK history, during the half-century following the close of the Peloponnesian War, is a confused and tedious record of the efforts of the leading cities, Sparta, Thebes, Athens, and Corinth, to preserve or to recover a supremacy over their neighbors. In these endless struggles the Greek states wore themselves out. Torn by internal faction and distracted by local jealousies, they were to fall an easy victim to the ambitious designs of Philip of Macedonia. We cannot think of Philip without thinking also of his great antagonist, the Athenian orator Demosthenes. To the task of maintaining the power and independence of Athens against Macedonia, Demosthenes devoted all his splendid talents and, in the end, his life itself. As the crafty Macedonian king gradually extended his power along the coast of Thrace and the peninsula of Chalcidice, Demosthenes saw with ever growing clearness how great a danger threatened the disunited cities of Greece. In several famous speeches (*Philippics*), delivered during the period 351–341 B. C., he exhausted all the resources of the orator's art in the endeavor to awaken his countrymen to their peril.

### 50. The Third Philippic [2]

In 348 B. C. the peninsula of Chalcidice with its many flourishing cities fell into Philip's hands. Two years later

[1] *The Orations of Demosthenes*, translated by C. R. Kennedy. 5 vols. London, 1876–1878. George Bell and Sons.

[2] Demosthenes, *Philippics*, iii, 27–40.

he interfered in the affairs of Phocis, a state of central Greece, and gained the place in the Amphictyonic Council which the Phocians had formerly occupied. The Macedonian monarch thus became one of the recognized powers in Greece proper. Demosthenes saw in this success the death knell of Greek independence unless Philip's further advance was instantly checked. In his *Third Philippic* (341 B. C.) he reviews the steady growth of the Macedonian power and summons all the cities of Greece to unite in alliance against the invader.

That Philip from a mean and humble origin has grown mighty, that the Greeks are jealous and quarreling among themselves, that it was far more wonderful for him to rise from that insignificance, than it would now be, after so many acquisitions, to conquer what is left; these and similar matters, which I might dwell upon, I pass over. But I observe that all people, beginning with you, have conceded to him a right, which in former times has been the subject of contest in every Greek war. And what is this? The right of doing what he pleases, openly fleecing and pillaging the Greeks, one after another, attacking and enslaving their cities. You were at the head of the Greeks for seventy-three [1] years, the Spartans for twenty-nine,[2] and the Thebans had some power in these latter times after the battle of Leuctra. Yet neither you, my countrymen, nor Spartans nor Thebans, were licensed by the Greeks to act as you pleased; far otherwise. When you, or rather the Athenians of that time, appeared to be dealing harshly with certain people, all the rest, even such as had no complaint against Athens, thought proper to side with the injured parties in a war against her. So, when the Spartans became masters and succeeded to your empire, on their

[1] From the conclusion of the Persian invasions to the end of the Peloponnesian War.

[2] Reckoning from the battle of Ægospotami, 405 B. C., to the battle of Naxos, 376 B. C.

attempting to encroach and make oppressive innovations, a general war was declared against them, even by such as had no cause of complaint. . . .

Yet all the faults committed by the Spartans in those thirty years and by our ancestors in the seventy are less, men of Athens, than the wrongs which Philip in thirteen incomplete years has inflicted on the Greeks. Nay, they are scarcely a fraction of these, as may easily be shown in a few words. Olynthus [1] and Methone [1] and Apollonia,[1] and thirty-two cities on the borders of Thrace, I pass over. All these he has so cruelly destroyed, that a visitor could hardly tell if they were ever inhabited. Of the Phocians, so considerable a people exterminated,[2] I say nothing. But what is the condition of Thessaly? Has he not taken away her constitutions and her cities? . . . . Are not the Eubœan states governed now by despots, and that in an island near to Thebes and Athens? Does he not expressly write in his epistles, "I am at peace with those who are willing to obey me?" Nor does he write so and not act accordingly. He is gone to the Hellespont; he marched formerly against Ambracia; Elis, such an important city in the Peloponnesus, he possesses; he plotted lately to get Megara: neither Greek nor barbarian land contains the man's ambition.

And we the Greek community, seeing and hearing this, instead of sending embassies to one another about it and expressing indignation, are in such a miserable state, so intrenched in our separate towns, that to this day we can attempt nothing that interest or necessity requires. We cannot combine or form any association for succor and alliance. We look unconcernedly on the man's growing power, each resolving to enjoy the interval that another is destroyed in, not caring or striving for the salvation of Greece. Yet none can be ignorant that Philip, like some attack of fever or other disease, is coming even on those that yet seem very far removed. And you must be aware that whatever wrong the Greeks sustained from

---

[1] The cities of Chalcidice.     [2] In the Second Sacred War.

Spartans or from us, was at least inflicted by genuine people of Greece. . . . In regard to Philip and his conduct they feel not this, for he is no Greek and in no way akin to Greeks. . . . He is, in fact, a vile fellow of Macedonia from which a respectable slave could not be purchased formerly.[1]

Under the eloquent leadership of Demosthenes the war party at Athens at length secured the upper hand. The final struggle could not be long delayed. In 338 B. C. the men of Athens and Thebes, now united in friendly alliance, met their common foe on the field of Chæronea. Philip triumphed. Greece lay helpless and exhausted at the feet of her Macedonian overlord.

### 51. Oration on the Crown [2]

Two years after the fateful day of Chæronea, on the motion of a certain Ctesiphon, a decree was passed by the Athenian Council that Demosthenes should receive a civic crown of gold and ivory in grateful recognition of his services to the state. This action was opposed as illegal by Æschines, himself a powerful orator, and long a political opponent of Demosthenes. For various reasons the trial was postponed until 330 B. C. Then all Athens gathered to the Assembly to hear the debate between the rival orators. The speech of Æschines, though nominally directed against Ctesiphon, was really a virulent attack upon Demosthenes and his entire public career. In reply, Demosthenes delivered his oration, *On the Crown*, a magnificent defense of his past policy and the greatest oratorical effort of antiquity.

The past is with all the world given up; no one even proposes to deliberate about it: the future it is, or the present, which

[1] Allowance for oratorical exaggeration must be made here. Philip was a Greek, and no barbarian.    [2] Demosthenes, *On the Crown*, 192–208.

demands the action of a counselor. At the time, as it appeared, there were dangers impending, and dangers at hand. Mark the line of my policy at that crisis; don't rail at the event. The end of all things is what the Deity pleases: his line of policy it is that shows the judgment of the statesman. Do not then impute it as a crime to me that Philip chanced to conquer in battle. That issue depended not on me, but on God. Prove that I did not adopt all measures that according to human calculation were feasible; that I did not honestly and diligently and with exertions beyond my strength carry them out; or that my enterprises were not honorable and worthy of the state and necessary. Show me this, and accuse me as soon as you like.

But if the hurricane that visited us has been too powerful, not for us only, but for all Greece besides, what is the fair course? As if a merchant, after taking every precaution, and furnishing his vessel with everything that he thought would insure her safety, because subsequently he met with a storm and his tackle was strained or broken to pieces, should be charged with the shipwreck! "Well, but I was not the pilot" — he might say — just as I was not the general. "Fortune was not under my control: all was under hers."

Consider and reflect upon this. If, with the Thebans on our side, we were destined so to fare in the contest, what was to be expected, if we had never had them for allies, but they had joined Philip, as he used every effort of persuasion to make them do? And if, when the battle [1] was fought three days' march from Attica, such peril and alarm surrounded the city, what must we have expected, if the same disaster had happened in some part of our territory? . . .

All this, at such length, have I addressed to you, men of the jury, and to the outer circle of hearers; for, as to this contemptible fellow, a short and plain argument would suffice. If the future was revealed to you, Æschines, alone, when the state was deliberating on these proceedings, you ought to have forewarned us at the time. If you did not foresee it, you are

[1] Chæronea.

responsible for the same ignorance as the rest. Why then do you accuse me in this behalf, rather than I you? A better citizen have I been than you in respect to the matters of which I am speaking, inasmuch as I gave myself up to what seemed for the general good, not shrinking from any personal danger, or taking thought of any. You, on the contrary, neither suggested better measures (or mine would not have been adopted), nor lent any aid in the prosecuting of mine. Exactly what the basest person and worst enemy of the state would do, are you found to have done after the event. . . . Surely, the man who waited to found his reputation upon the misfortunes of the Greeks deserves rather to perish than to accuse another. . . .

But since he insists so strongly on the event, I will even assert something of a paradox: and I beg and pray of you not to marvel at its boldness, but kindly to consider what I say. If then the results had been foreknown to all, if all had foreseen them . . . not even then should the commonwealth have abandoned her design, if she had any regard for glory, or ancestry, or futurity. . . . For in former times our country has never preferred an ignominious security to the battle for honor. What Greek or what barbarian is ignorant that, by the Thebans, or by the Spartans who were in power before them, or by the Persian king, permission would thankfully and gladly have been given to our commonwealth, to take what she pleased and hold her own, provided she would accept foreign law and let a foreign state command in Greece? But, to the Athenians of that day, such conduct would not have been endurable. None could at any period of time persuade the commonwealth to attach herself in secure subjection to the powerful and unjust. Through every age has she persevered in a perilous struggle for precedency and honor and glory. . . . Never, never can you have done wrong, O Athenians, in undertaking the battle for the freedom and safety of all! I swear it by your forefathers — those that met the peril at Marathon, those that took the field at Platæa, those in the sea fight at Salamis, and those at Artemisium, and many other brave men who repose in the public monuments, all of whom alike, as being worthy of the same honor, the country buried, not only the successful or victorious! Justly! For the duty of brave men has been done by all: their fortune has been such as the Deity assigned to each.

Athens was not false to her glorious past. Demosthenes won his case and received the coveted reward. Æschines, completely discredited, went into voluntary exile. The great orator was to enjoy one more signal triumph before his melancholy end. When tidings of Alexander's death reached Athens, that city, aided by many other states of Greece, broke out in sudden revolt against Macedonia (323 B. C.). At this time Demosthenes was himself in exile, under condemnation on a charge of bribery. Now, however, the Athenians recalled him, as in earlier days they had recalled Alcibiades,[1] and paid out of the public treasury the fine of fifty talents which had been assessed upon him. Demosthenes once more became the center of Athenian resistance to Macedonia. But the revolt was soon suppressed. Antipater, the Macedonian general, demanded, as the price of peace, the surrender of Demosthenes and his fellow orators who had fanned the flame of insurrection. "They dispersed themselves, flying, some to one place, some to another; and Antipater sent about his soldiers into all quarters to apprehend them. Archias was their captain, and was thence called the exile-hunter. . . . Demosthenes, he heard, had taken sanctuary at the Temple of Poseidon in Calauria.[2] Crossing over thither in some light vessels, as soon as he had landed himself, and the Thracian spearmen that came with him, Archias endeavored to persuade Demosthenes to accompany him to Antipater, as if he should meet with

[1] See page 106.    [2] An island off the southeastern coast of Argolis.

no hard usage from him. But Demosthenes, in his sleep
the night before, had a strange dream. It seemed to
him that he was acting a tragedy, and contended with
Archias for the victory; and though he acquitted himself
well, and gave good satisfaction to the spectators, yet for
want of better furniture and settings for the stage, he
lost the day. And so, while Archias was speaking to him
with many expressions of kindness, he sat still in the
same posture, looking steadfastly upon him. 'O Archias,'
said he, 'I am as little affected by your promises
now as I used formerly to be by your acting.' Archias
then began to grow angry and to threaten him. 'Now,'
said Demosthenes, 'you speak like the genuine Macedonian oracle; before you were but acting a part.
Therefore forbear only a little, while I write a word home
to my family.' Having thus spoken, he withdrew into the
temple and taking a scroll, as if he meant to write, he put
the reed into his mouth, and biting it, as he was wont to
do when he was thoughtful or writing, he held it there for
some time. Then he bowed down his head and covered
it. The soldiers that stood at the door, supposing all
this to proceed from want of courage and fear of death,
in derision called him effeminate, and faint-hearted, and
coward. And Archias, drawing near, desired him to rise
up, and repeating the same kind things he had spoken
before, he once more promised him to make his peace with
Antipater. But Demosthenes, perceiving that now the
poison had begun to operate, uncovered his head, and said
to Archias, 'As soon as you please, you may commence
the part of Creon in the tragedy, and cast out this body
of mine unburied. But, O gracious Poseidon, I, for my
part, while I am yet alive, rise up and depart out of this
sacred place; though Antipater and the Macedonians

have not left so much as thy temple unpolluted.' After he had thus spoken he desired to be held up because already he had begun to tremble and stagger. As he was going forward and passing by the altar, he fell down, and with a groan gave up the ghost. . . . Soon after his death, the people of Athens bestowed on him such honors as he had deserved. They erected his statue of bronze; they decreed that the eldest of his family should be maintained in the Prytaneum.[1] On the base of his statue was engraven the famous inscription,

> Had you for Greece been strong, as wise you were,
> The Macedonian had not conquered her." [2]

[1] The public hearth and common table established by the city of Athens.
[2] Plutarch, *Demosthenes*, 28–30.

# CHAPTER XIII

## EXPLOITS OF ALEXANDER THE GREAT [1]

THE subjection of the Greek city-states by Philip of Macedonia was only the first stage of a comprehensive scheme of conquest which that ambitious monarch entertained. At a Panhellenic council held at Corinth shortly after the battle of Chæronea, Philip announced his resolve to free the Greek cities of Asia and to lead an army against Persia in retaliation for the expedition of Xerxes, a century and a half before. Fate, however, had destined that this gigantic task should be achieved by another and even greater man. The murder of Philip in the summer of 336 B. C. placed his young son Alexander on the throne of Macedonia. After two years spent in quelling revolts in Thrace and Greece, Alexander was ready to begin his marvelous career as the conqueror of the East. For the history of his conquests we are fortunate in possessing the work of Arrian, one of the most authentic and accurate of Greek historical compositions. Though Arrian wrote in the second century of our era, he used the best of contemporary records in compiling his narrative. The chief sources upon which he relied were the lives of Alexander by Ptolemy, one of Alexander's generals, and by Aristobulus, who also served under the Macedonian monarch. Arrian's admirable biography is ample compensation for the loss of these two works.

[1] *Arrian's Anabasis of Alexander and Indica*, translated by E. J. Chinnock. London, 1893. George Bell and Sons.

### 52. The Gordian Knot [1]

In the spring of 334 B. C., Alexander crossed the Hellespont and invaded Asia Minor. We are told that when
his army reached the site of Troy, Alexander delayed the
advance to visit the citadel of Ilium and to place a gar-
land upon the tomb of fleet-footed Achilles. The defeat
of the Persian satraps at the river Granicus cleared out of
Alexander's way the only force which was to oppose his
progress in Asia Minor. Within a year from the crossing
of the Hellespont, all Asia Minor lay at the conqueror's
feet. Early in 333 B. C., Alexander advanced to Gordium,
the capital of the ancient kingdom of Phrygia.

When Alexander arrived at Gordium, he was seized with
an ardent desire to go up into the citadel, which contained the
palace of Gordius and his son Midas. He was also desirous of
seeing the wagon of Gordius and the cord of the yoke of this
wagon. . . . The following saying was current, that whosoever
could loosen the cord of the yoke of this wagon was destined
to gain the rule of Asia. The cord was made of cornel bark,
and neither end nor beginning to it could be seen.

It is said by some that when Alexander could find out no way
to loosen the cord and yet was unwilling to allow it to remain
unloosened, lest this should exercise some disturbing influence
upon the multitude, he struck it with his sword. He then cut it
through and said that it had been loosened. But Aristobulus
says that he pulled out the pin of the wagon-pole, which was a
wooden peg driven right through it, holding the cord together.
Having done this, he drew out the yoke from the wagon-pole.
How Alexander performed the feat in connection with this
cord, I cannot affirm with confidence. At any rate both he
and his troops departed from the wagon as if the oracular pre-
diction concerning the loosening of the cord had been fulfilled.

[1] Arrian, *Anabasis of Alexander*, ii, 3.

Moreover, that very night, the thunder and lightning were signs of its fulfillment; and for this reason Alexander offered sacrifice on the following day to the gods who had revealed the signs and the way to loosen the cord.

### 53. Alexander's Treatment of the Family of Darius [1]

The route from Gordium lay through the provinces of Cappadocia and Cilicia into Syria. On the little plain of Issus, where the vast numbers of the enemy were of no avail, Alexander met and overcame the Persian king (October, 333 B. C.). Darius made good his escape, but in his hurried flight he left his choicest treasures in the possession of the victor.

. . . Nor did Alexander treat the mother, wife, and children of Darius with neglect. It is said that on the very night in which he returned from the pursuit of Darius, entering the Persian king's tent, which had been selected for his use, he heard the lamentation of women and other sounds of a similar kind, not far from the tent. Inquiring who the women were, and why they were in a tent so near, he was answered by some one as follows, "O king, the mother, wife, and children of Darius are lamenting for him as slain, since they have been informed that thou hast his bow and his royal mantle, and that his shield has been brought back." When Alexander heard this, he sent Leonnatus, one of his Companions,[2] to them, with injunctions to tell them, "Darius is still alive; in his flight he left his arms and mantle in the chariot; and these are the only things of his that Alexander has." Leonnatus entered the tent and told them the news about Darius. He added that Alexander would allow them to retain the state and retinue befitting their royal rank, as well as the title of queens; for he had not undertaken the war aganst Darius from a feeling of

---

[1] Arrian, *Anabasis of Alexander*, ii, 12.

[2] A cavalry troop, some 1200 strong, composed of Macedonian knights.

hatred, but he had conducted it in a legitimate manner for the empire of Asia. . . .

### 54. A Letter from Alexander to Darius [1]

When Darius had reached safety beyond the Euphrates, he addressed a letter to Alexander in which he complained that Alexander was an unprovoked aggressor upon Persia. "And now he, a king, begged his captured wife, mother and children from a king; and he wished to form a friendship with him and become his ally." Alexander's answer to this request has been preserved.

. . . Come to me, rather, since I am lord of all Asia. But if you are afraid you may suffer any harsh treatment from me, in case you come to me, send some of your friends to receive pledges of safety from me. Come to me, then, and ask for your mother, wife, and children, and anything else you wish. For whatever you ask for, you will receive; and nothing shall be denied you. But for the future, whenever you send to me, send to me as the king of Asia, and do not address to me your wishes as to an equal. If you are in need of anything, speak to me as to the man who is lord of all your territories. If you act otherwise, I shall deliberate concerning you as an evil-doer. And if you dispute my right to the kingdom, stay and fight another battle for it; but do not run away. For wherever you may be, I intend to march against you." . . .

### 55. Visit to the Temple of Amon [2]

The battle of Issus opened the way into Syria. As Alexander marched southward, he came to the ancient city of Tyre, whose inhabitants closed their gates to the Macedonians. The siege of Tyre occupied Alexander nearly eight months (January–August, 332 B. C.). The

---

[1] Arrian, *Anabasis of Alexander*, ii, 14.
[2] *Ibid.*, iii, 3.

place was finally taken by storm. The same fate befell the ancient Philistine fortress of Gaza on the border between Palestine and Egypt. Alexander now marched unopposed into Egypt. While in that country (January, 331 B. C.), he laid the foundations of the great city which to this day perpetuates the conqueror's name.

After these transactions, Alexander was seized with an ardent desire to visit Amon[1] in Libya, partly in order to consult the god, because the oracle of Amon was said to be exact in its information. . . . He also deduced his pedigree from Amon. . . . Accordingly, he made the expedition to Amon with the design of learning his own origin more certainly, or at least that he might be able to say that he had learned it.

According to Aristobulus, Alexander advanced along the seashore through a country which was a desert, but not destitute of water, a distance of about 1600 stades.[2] Then he turned into the interior, where the oracle of Amon was located. The route is desert, and most of it is sand and destitute of water. But there was a copious supply of rain for Alexander, a thing which was attributed to the influence of the Deity; as was also the following occurrence. Whenever a south wind blows in that district, it heaps up sand upon the route far and wide, rendering the tracks of the road invisible, so that it is impossible to discover where one ought to direct one's course in the sand. . . . Consequently, Alexander's army lost the way, as even the guides were in doubt about the course to take. Ptolemy says that two serpents went in front of the army, uttering a voice, and that Alexander ordered the guides to follow them, trusting in the divine portent. He says, too, that they showed the way to the oracle and back again. But Aristobulus, whose account is generally admitted as correct,

[1] The Temple of Amon was in the oasis of Ammon about 220 miles west of Alexandria. An army sent by the Persian king, Cambyses, to destroy the temple was totally lost in the desert. See page 21.

[2] About 187 miles.

says that two ravens flew in front of the army, and that these acted as Alexander's guides. . . .

### 56. The Pursuit and Death of Darius [1]

The advance against the Great King began early in the fateful year 331 B. C. Not far from ancient Nineveh, on a broad plain some sixty miles north of Arbela, Alexander encountered the Persian host (September, 331 B. C.). Again the Macedonian triumphed and again Darius turned his chariot and fled, this time into the highlands of Media. For the moment Alexander did not pursue him, but continued the march on Babylon. That great city yielded to the conqueror without a struggle. Susa, the summer residence of the Persian monarch, and Persepolis, with all its treasures, were soon captured. In the meantime Darius remained in Media, surrounded by those satraps of the eastern provinces who were still faithful to his fallen fortunes. It was late in the spring of 330 B. C. when Alexander took up the chase of Darius and advanced on Ecbatana, the Median capital. As Alexander proceeded, he learned that Darius had been made prisoner by his own satraps who were hurrying him toward Bactria. Alexander now resolved on a swift and hot pursuit.

. . . He came upon the barbarians just before daybreak, going along without any order and unarmed; so that only a few of them rushed to defend themselves. Most of them, as soon as they saw Alexander himself, took to flight without even coming to blows. A few of those who had turned to resist were killed, and then the rest also fled away. Up to this time Bessus and his party were still conveying Darius with them in a covered carriage; but when Alexander was already close upon them, they wounded him and left him there,

[1] Arrian, *Anabasis of Alexander*, iii, 21–22.

and with six hundred horsemen took to flight. Darius died from his wounds soon after, before Alexander had seen him. The body of Darius was sent to Persepolis, to be buried in the royal sepulcher, in the same way as the other Persian kings before him had been buried. . . . Such was the end of Darius.

This king was a man very effeminate and lacking in self-reliance in military enterprises. As to civil matters he never exhibited any disposition to indulge in arbitrary conduct; nor indeed was it in his power to exhibit it. For it happened that he was involved in a war with the Macedonians and Greeks at the very time he succeeded to the regal power; and consequently it was no longer possible for him to act the tyrant toward his subjects, even if he had been so inclined, standing as he did in greater danger than they.

As long as Darius lived, one misfortune after another befell him. He did not experience any cessation of calamity from the time when he first succeeded to the throne. In the first place the cavalry defeat was sustained by his viceroys at the Granicus, and forthwith all Asia Minor was occupied by his foe. . . . Then came his own discomfiture at Issus, where he saw his mother, wife, and children taken prisoners. Upon this Phœnicia and the whole of Egypt were lost. Next at Arbela he himself fled disgracefully among the first, and lost a very vast army composed of all the nations of his empire. After this, wandering as an exile from his own kingdom, he died after being betrayed by his personal attendants to the worst treatment possible, being at the same time the Great King and a prisoner. . . . When he died he was about fifty years of age.

### 57. Capture of the Sogdian Rock [1]

Though the royal dynasty of Persia had come to an end, the eastern provinces of the Persian Empire were yet unsubdued. Their conquest proved no easy task. During the next two years Alexander led his undaunted army through

[1] Arrian, *Anabasis of Alexander*, iv, 18–19.

the little known regions of Iran. The spring of 328 B. C.
found him crossing the almost insurmountable heights of
the Hindu-Kush and occupying the fertile provinces of
Bactria and Sogdiana. Here the captured Bessus met
his doom and here also occurred the tragic episode of the
death of Alexander's foster-brother, Clitus, murdered by
the Macedonian king during a drunken carousal. While
Alexander was still in Sogdiana, its wild tribes broke out
in renewed hostilities.

. . . At the first appearance of spring,[1] Alexander advanced
toward the rock in Sogdiana, to which, he was informed, many
of the people had fled for refuge. Among these were said to
be the wife and daughters of Oxyartes the Bactrian, who had
deposited them for safety in that place, as if, indeed, it was
impregnable. . . . When Alexander approached it, he found
that it was precipitous on all sides and that the barbarians had
collected provisions for a long siege. The great quantity of
snow which had fallen helped to make the approach more
difficult to the Macedonians, while at the same time it kept
the barbarians supplied with plenty of water. But notwithstanding all this, Alexander resolved to assault the place. . . .
He then issued a proclamation that the first man who mounted
should have a reward of twelve talents,[2] the man who came
next to him the second prize, and so on in proportion, so that
the last reward should be three hundred darics [3] to the last
prize-taker who reached the top. This proclamation excited
the valor of the Macedonians still more, though they were
even before very eager to begin the assault.

All the men who had gained practice in scaling rocks in sieges
banded themselves together to the number of three hundred,
and provided themselves with the small iron pegs by which
their tents had been fastened to the ground. These they
intended to fix into the snow, wherever it might be seen to be

---

[1] Of the year 327 B. C.          [2] About $14,000.          [3] About $1600.

frozen hard, or into the ground, if it should anywhere exhibit itself free from snow.  Tying strong ropes made of flax to these pegs, they advanced in the night toward the most precipitous part of the rock, which was on this account most unguarded. Then they fixed some of these pegs into the earth, where it made itself visible, and others into the snow, where it seemed least likely to crumble, and so hoisted themselves up the rock, some in one place and some in another.  Thirty of them perished in the ascent; and as they fell into various parts of the snow, not even could their bodies be found for burial.  The rest, however, reached the top of the mountain at the approach of dawn.  They took possession of it and then waved linen flags toward the camp of the Macedonians, as Alexander had directed them to do.  He now sent a herald with instructions to shout to the sentries of the barbarians to make no further delay, but surrender at once. . . . At the same time the herald pointed at the soldiers upon the crest of the mountain.  The barbarians were alarmed by the unexpectedness of the sight and suspected that the men who were occupying the peaks were more numerous than they really were, and that they were completely armed.  They surrendered at once, so frightened did they become at the sight of those few Macedonians.

The wives and children of many important men were there captured, including those of Oxyartes.  This chief had a daughter, a maiden of marriageable age, named Roxana, who was asserted by the men who served in Alexander's army to have been the most beautiful of all the Asiatic women whom they had seen, with the single exception of the wife[1] of Darius. They also say that no sooner did Alexander see her than he fell in love with her, and did not think it beneath his dignity to marry her. . . .

### 58. Alexander and Porus[2]

From Bactria and Sogdiana, Alexander turned to the conquest of India.  He again crossed the Hindu-Kush

[1] See page 140.     [2] Arrian, *Anabasis of Alexander*, v, 19.

and descended upon the broad plains of the Punjab, the region of the five rivers. One hard-fought battle with the Indian monarch Porus, by the banks of the Hydaspes (326 B. C.), sufficed to remove the only power in the land which could hope to stay Alexander's progress. Porus was himself taken prisoner.

When Alexander heard that Porus was being brought before him, he rode in front of the line with a few of the Companions to meet the Indian king. Stopping his horse, he admired the king's handsome figure, and his stature, which reached somewhat above five cubits. He was also surprised that Porus did not seem to be cowed in spirit; but advanced to meet him as one brave man would meet another brave man, after having gallantly struggled in defense of his own kingdom against another king.

Then indeed Alexander was the first to speak, bidding him say what treatment he would like to receive. The story goes that Porus replied, "Treat me, O Alexander, in a kingly way!" Alexander being pleased at the expression, said, "For my own sake, O Porus, thou shalt be thus treated; but for thy own sake do thou demand what is pleasing to thee!" But Porus said that everything was included in his former statement. Alexander being still more pleased at this remark, not only granted him the rule over his own Indians, but also added another country to that which he had before, of larger extent than the former. Thus he treated the brave man in a kingly way, and from that time found him faithful in all things. . . .

### 59. The March through the Desert of Gedrosia [1]

Alexander now advanced to the Hyphasis. That river was destined to mark the eastward limit of his invasion. Though he would have led his men in an exploration of the

[1] Arrian, *Anabasis of Alexander*, vi, 24, 26.

rich Ganges region, the exhausted soldiers refused to go another step farther. Retracing their road to the Hydaspes, part of the army embarked on transports and the remainder marched southward along the two branches of the river to its junction with the Indus. Army and fleet now proceeded down the Indus to its mouth. The fleet under Nearchus was then sent west to explore the Indian Ocean and to discover, if possible, a sea route from India to the Euphrates. Alexander, with the army, was to return to Persia by a land route. The way led through the inhospitable regions of Gedrosia.

. . . The scorching heat and lack of water destroyed a great part of the army, and especially the beasts of burden. Most of these perished from thirst and some of them even from the depth and heat of the sand, because it had been thoroughly scorched by the sun. For they met with lofty ridges of deep sand, not closely pressed and hardened, but such as received those who stepped upon it just as if they were stepping into mud, or rather into untrodden snow. At the same time, too, the horses and mules suffered still more, both in going up and coming down the hills, from the unevenness of the road as well as from its instability. The length of the marches between the stages also exceedingly distressed the army, since the lack of water often compelled them to make the marches unusually long. When they traveled by night on a journey which it was necessary to complete, and at daybreak came to water, they suffered no hardship at all. If, while still on the march, on account of the length of the way, they were caught by the heat, then they did indeed suffer terribly from the blazing sun, being at the same time oppressed by thirst. . . .

Here I have resolved not to pass over in silence perhaps the most noble deed ever performed by Alexander. . . . The army was continuing its march through the sand, though the heat of the sun was already scorching, because it was necessary to reach water before halting.  They were far on the journey, and Alexander himself, though oppressed by thirst, was nevertheless with great pain and difficulty leading the army on foot. . . . At this time some of the light-armed soldiers, starting away from the army in quest of water, found some collected in a shallow cleft, a small and mean spring.  Collecting this water with difficulty, they came with all speed to Alexander, as if they were bringing him some great gift.  As soon as they approached the king, they poured the water into a helmet and carried it to him.  He took it, and commending the men who brought it, immediately poured it upon the ground in sight of all.  As a result of this action, the entire army was reinvigorated to so great a degree that anyone would have imagined that the water poured away by Alexander had furnished a draught to every man. . . .

### 60. Plans of Alexander [1]

After a terrible three months' march through desert sands, Alexander reached Persia and its ancient capital cities (325 B. C.).  He still had dreams of further conquests.

For my own part I cannot conjecture with any certainty what were now his plans; and I do not care to guess.  But this I think I can confidently affirm, that he meditated nothing small or mean; and that he would never have remained satisfied with any of the acquisitions he had made.  Even if he had added Europe to Asia, or the islands of the Britons to Europe, he would still have gone on seeking for some unknown land beyond those mentioned.  I verily believe that, if he had found no one else to strive with, he would have striven with himself.

On this account I commend some of the Indian philosophers, who are said to have been caught by Alexander as they were walking in the open meadow where they were accustomed to spend their time.  At the sight of him and his army they did

[1] Arrian, *Anabasis of Alexander*, vii, 1.

nothing else but stamp with their feet on the earth. . . .
When he asked them by means of interpreters what was the
meaning of their action, they replied as follows: "O King Alexander, every man possesses as much of the earth as this upon
which we have stepped; but thou being only a man like the
rest of us, except in being meddlesome and arrogant, art come
over so great a part of the earth from thy own land, both
having trouble thyself and giving it to others. And yet thou
also wilt soon die, and possess only as much of the earth as is
sufficient for thy body to be buried in."

### 61. A Speech by Alexander [1]

In the spring of 324 B. C., Alexander left Susa for Ecbatana in Media. Sailing up the Tigris, he halted at Opis,
and there formally discharged the Macedonian soldiers,
some ten thousand in number, who by reason of old age
or wounds were no longer fit for service. Although he
promised to return them safely to Macedonia and to give
them "as much extra reward as would make them special
objects of envy at home," the soldiers did not take kindly
to the proposal. They broke out in open mutiny and
urged Alexander to dismiss, not only the worn-out veterans,
but all the Macedonians in the army. The king promptly
quelled the sedition by ordering the ringleaders to be
executed. When the rest, stricken with terror, became
silent, Alexander mounted a platform and addressed his
former companions-in-arms.

"But some one may say that, while you endured toil and
fatigue, I have acquired wealth and glory as your leader without myself sharing the toil and fatigue. But who is there of
you who knows that he has endured greater toil for me than
I have for him? Come now! whoever has wounds, let him
strip and show them, and I will show mine in turn. There is no

[1] Arrian, *Anabasis of Alexander*, vii, 10.

part of my body, in front, at any rate, remaining free from wounds; nor is there any kind of weapon used either for close combat or for hurling at the enemy, the traces of which I do not bear on my person. For I have been wounded with the sword in close fight, I have been shot with arrows, and I have been struck with missiles projected from engines of war. Though oftentimes I have been hit with stones and bolts of wood for the sake of your lives, your glory, and your wealth, I am still leading you as conquerors over all the land and sea, all rivers, mountains, and plains. I have celebrated your weddings with my own, and the children of many of you will be akin to my children. Moreover, I have paid the debts of all those who had incurred them, without inquiring too closely for what purpose they were contracted, though you receive such high pay, and carry off so much booty whenever there is booty to be got after a siege. Most of you have golden crowns, the eternal memorials of your valor and of the honor you receive from me. Whoever has been killed, has met with a glorious end and has been honored with a splendid burial. Brazen statues of most of the slain have been erected at home and their parents are held in honor, being released from all public service and from taxation. But no one of you has ever been killed in flight under my leadership. And now I was intending to send back those of you who are unfit for service, objects of envy to those at home; but since you all wish to depart, depart all of you! . . ."

It is pleasant to relate that this fiery speech by the angry monarch brought his soldiers to their senses. Before long a reconciliation took place and henceforth Alexander and his troops resumed their cordial relations.

### 62. Alexander's Character [1]

Toward the end of the year 324 B. C., Alexander set out from Ecbatana and reached Babylon. It was to be

[1] Arrian, *Anabasis of Alexander*, vii, 28–30.

his last journey. He had passed only a few months in the capital city of his vast empire when the deadly Babylonian fever struck him down (June, 323 B. C.).

Alexander died in the hundred and fourteenth Olympiad. According to the statement of Aristobulus, he lived thirty-two years, and had reached the eighth month of his thirty-third year. He had reigned twelve years and these eight months. He was very handsome in person, and much devoted to exertion. He was very active in mind, very heroic in courage, very tenacious of honor, exceedingly fond of incurring danger, and strictly observant of his duty to the Deity. In regard to the pleasures of the body, he had perfect self-control; and of those of the mind, praise was the only one of which he was insatiable. . . . In marshaling, equipping, and ruling an army, he was exceedingly skillful. He was very renowned for rousing the courage of his soldiers, filling them with hopes of success, and dispelling their fear in the midst of danger by his own freedom from fear. Therefore, even what he had to do in uncertainty of the result, he did with the greatest boldness. . . .

That Alexander should have committed errors in conduct from impetuosity or from wrath, and that he should have been induced to act like the Persian monarchs to an immoderate degree, I do not think remarkable, if we fairly consider both his youth and his uninterrupted career of good fortune. . . . However, I am certain that Alexander was the only one of the ancient kings who, from nobility of character, repented of the errors which he had committed. . . . I do not think that even Alexander's tracing his origin to a god [1] was a great error on his part, if it was not perhaps merely a device to induce his subjects to show him reverence. . . . His adoption of the Persian mode of dressing also seems to me to have been a political device in regard to the foreigners, that the king might not appear altogether alien to them; and in regard to the Macedonians, to show them that he had a refuge from their rashness

[1] See page 142.

of temper and insolence. For this reason, I think, he mixed the Persian royal guards, who carried golden apples at the end of their spears,[1] among the ranks of the Macedonians, and the Persian peers with the Macedonian body-guards. Aristobulus also asserts that Alexander used to have long drinking parties, not for the purpose of enjoying the wine, as he was not a great wine-drinker, but in order to exhibit his sociability and friendly feeling to his Companions.

Whoever, therefore, reproaches Alexander as a bad man, let him do so; but let him first not only bring before his mind all his actions deserving reproach, but also gather into one view all his deeds of every kind. Then, indeed, let him reflect . . . who that man was whom he reproaches as bad, and to what a height of human success he attained, becoming without any dispute a king of both continents,[2] and reaching every place by his fame. . . . For my own part, I think there was at that time no race of men, no city, or even a single individual to whom Alexander's name and fame had not penetrated. For this reason it seems to me that a hero, totally unlike any other human being, could not have been born without the agency of the Deity. . . .

[1] See page 73.     [2] Europe and Asia.

# CHAPTER XIV

## LEGENDS OF EARLY ROME [1]

MOST eloquent of all Roman historians is Livy (59 B. C.–
17 A. D.).   His history of Rome begins with Romulus and
extends to the reign of Augustus.   The first ten books of
the work relate the fortunes of the Roman city from its
foundation to the consolidation of Roman power in Italy
by the subjugation of the Samnites.   Modern scholars
are not inclined to attach much value as sober history
to this earlier part of Livy's narrative.   And indeed the
author himself declares that for the first four centuries of
Roman history "the facts were obscure by reason of their
remote antiquity, like objects which from their great distance are seen with difficulty, and also because in those
times written records, which are the only faithful guard-
ians of the memory of events, were few and rare." [2]
Whatever their historical importance, the earlier chapters of Livy's great production are a treasure house of
those heroic legends, of those splendid stories of patriotic
devotion, which never failed to fire the hearts of noble
Romans.

### 63. The Founding of Rome [3]

Æneas, son of Priam, after the destruction of Troy by
the Greeks, led a colony of Trojans into Latium, the fated
end of his long wanderings by land and sea.   And here

---

[1] Livy.  *History of Rome*, books i–vi, ix.   The translation of D. Spillan,
revised by J. H. Freese, E. S. Weymouth, and Francis Storr.   London,
1893–1894.   George Bell and Sons.

[2] Livy, vi, 1.              [3] Livy, i, 6–7.

he married Lavinia, daughter of King Latinus, and founded a city called, after her name, Lavinium. When Æneas died, his son Ascanius succeeded his father as king of the Latins and built a new city under the Alban Hills, named Alba Longa (the "Long White Town"). Now many generations afterwards, King Amulius sat upon the throne of Alba Longa, having wickedly expelled his elder brother, Numitor, from the royal power. And he forced Rhea Silvia, Numitor's daughter, to become a Vestal Virgin, lest she marry and raise a son to avenge the wrongs of her house. It was decreed by the Fates, however, that she should bear to Mars, the god of war, twin sons, Romulus and Remus. When Numitor learned of their birth, he ordered the babes to be set adrift on the Tiber. But Heaven guarded them: the river, subsiding, left the trough and its occupants safe on dry land; and a she-wolf, hearing their cries, came and nursed them. In this situation they were discovered by a shepherd, who rescued the children and brought them to his home. After the boys had grown to manhood, they killed the wicked Amulius and restored their grandfather Numitor to his kingdom.

. . . The government of Alba Longa being thus intrusted to Numitor, Romulus and Remus were seized with the desire of building a city on the spot where they had been exposed and brought up. . . . But ambition to be sole ruler interrupted their plans, and provoked them to a shameful quarrel. Since they were twins, and neither could claim the rights of an elder brother, they agreed to leave it to the gods, under whose protection the place was, to choose by augury which of them should give a name to the new city, and govern it when built. Romulus chose the Palatine [1] and Remus the Aventine,[1] as points of observation for taking the auguries.

[1] Two of the "seven hills" of Rome.

It is said that an omen came to Remus first, in the shape of six vultures. When, after the omen had been declared, twice that number presented themselves to Romulus, each was hailed king by his own party. Remus claimed sovereign power because he had been the first to see any birds; Romulus likewise claimed to have triumphed because he saw more birds than his brother. . . . A common account is that Remus, in derision of his brother, leaped over the newly-erected walls of Rome, and was thereupon slain by Romulus in a fit of passion. "So," said Romulus, "may every one perish hereafter, who shall leap over my walls." Thus Romulus obtained supreme power for himself alone. The city, when built, was called after the name of its founder. . . .

### 64. Rape of the Sabine Women [1]

The Roman state was now so powerful, that it was a match for any of the neighboring states in war. But owing to the scarcity of women, its greatness was not likely to outlast the existing generation. . . . By the advice of the senators, Romulus sent ambassadors around to the neighboring states, to solicit an alliance and the right of intermarriage for his new subjects. . . . The embassy nowhere obtained a favorable hearing. Although the neighboring peoples treated it with great contempt, yet at the same time they dreaded the growth of such a mighty power in their midst. In most cases, when the ambassadors were dismissed, they were asked whether they had opened an asylum for women also; [2] for in that way only could they obtain suitable matches.

The Roman youths were bitterly indignant at this treatment, and the matter began unmistakably to point to open violence. Romulus, in order to provide a fitting opportunity and place for this, instituted games to be solemnized every year in honor of equestrian Neptune. He then ordered the show to be pro-

[1] Livy, i, 9.

[2] To increase the population of his city Romulus had made it an asylum for all the reckless and discontented individuals in the neighboring tribes.

claimed among the neighboring peoples. The Romans prepared to celebrate it with all the pomp which they were able to exhibit. Great numbers of strangers then flocked to Rome to witness the games and see the new city. . . . They were hospitably invited to the different houses. When they noticed the position of the city, its fortified walls, and how crowded with houses it was, they were astounded that the power of Rome had increased so rapidly.

When the time of the show arrived, and their eyes and minds alike were intent upon it, then, according to preconcerted arrangement, a disturbance was made. At a given signal, the Roman youths rushed in different directions to seize the unmarried women. A great number were carried off at haphazard, by those into whose hands they fell. . . . As the festival was interrupted by the alarm thus caused, the sorrowing parents of the maidens retired, complaining of the violated compact of hospitality, and crying for vengeance to the god, to whose solemn festival and games they had come. . . .

### 65. War with the Sabines [1]

And now the Sabines arose in fierce anger, seeking vengeance for their wrongs. Rome was besieged by a Sabine army under King Titus Tatius.

. . . Spurius Tarpeius was in command of the Roman citadel. Now it happened that his maiden daughter . . . was bribed by Tatius to admit some armed soldiers into the citadel. After they were admitted, they crushed her to death by heaping their arms upon her. They did this, either that the citadel might rather appear to have been taken by storm, or for the sake of setting forth a warning that faith should never on any occasion be kept with a betrayer. . . .

Although the Sabines had captured the citadel on the Capitoline Hill, the Romans were not ready to concede

[1] Livy, i, 11, 13.

defeat. In the valley, afterwards occupied by the Forum, the two armies drew up for a decisive struggle.

At this crisis the Sabine women, with disheveled hair and torn garments . . . flung themselves into the midst of the flying weapons, and parted the incensed combatants. They implored their fathers on the one hand and their husbands on the other, not to besprinkle themselves with impious blood or to fix the stain of murder on their offspring. "If," said they, "you are dissatisfied . . . with our marriage, turn your resentment against *us;* it is we who are the cause of war, of wounds and bloodshed to our husbands and parents. It will be better for us to perish than to live widows or orphans without one or other of you." This incident so affected the people that silence and sudden quiet followed. The leaders thereupon came forward to conclude a treaty; and not only made a peace, but formed one state out of two. They united the kingly power, but transferred the entire sovereignty to Rome. . . .

### 66. Death of Romulus [1]

The Sabines were now settled on the Capitoline Hill and the Romans under Romulus on the Palatine. For a time the two kings ruled in common, but after the death of Tatius, Romulus became the sole king of the united community. During his long reign he vanquished many of the surrounding peoples and firmly established the power of the Roman city.

One day when Romulus was reviewing his army in the plain [2] a storm suddenly came on. It was accompanied by loud thunder and lightning, and enveloped the king in so dense a mist that it entirely hid him from the sight of the assembly. After this Romulus was never seen again on earth. . . . All

---

[1] Livy, i, 16.   [2] On the field of Mars, the Campus Martius.

the people now saluted Romulus as a god, the son of a god, the king and parent of the Roman city. They also prayed that with gracious kindness he would always preserve his offspring. . . .

Proculus Julius, while the state was still troubled at the loss of the king . . . came forward into the assembly. "Quirites," said he, "Romulus, the father of this city, suddenly descending from heaven, appeared to me this day at dawn. . . . 'Go,' said he, 'tell the Romans, that the gods have decreed that my Rome should become the capital of the world. Therefore let them cultivate the art of war, and let them know and so hand it down to posterity, that no human power can withstand the Roman arms.' Having said this, he vanished up to heaven." It is surprising how much credit was given to that person when he made the announcement. It is no less remarkable how much the regret of the common people and army for the loss of Romulus was relieved when the certainty of his immortality was made known.

### 67. The Affair at Gabii [1]

Romulus, according to legend, was followed by six other kings. The last of these was an Etruscan, Tarquinius the Proud. He ruled Rome harshly and made many enemies. One of his exploits was the capture of the city of Gabii by fraud and stratagem; "arts," says Livy, "by no means Roman." Representing himself as a fugitive from his father's cruelty, young Sextus Tarquinius fled to Gabii whose unsuspecting citizens received him kindly. He was immediately admitted into their public councils and before very long was chosen as commander in the war against Rome.

. . . When he saw that he had sufficient strength collected to support him in any undertaking, he sent one of his confidants

[1] Livy, i, 54.

to his father at Rome to inquire what he wished him to do. To this courier no answer by word of mouth was given, because, I suppose, he appeared of questionable fidelity. The king went into a garden of the palace, as if in deep thought, followed by his son's messenger. Walking there for some time without uttering a word, he is said to have struck off the heads of the tallest poppies with his staff.[1] The messenger, wearied with asking and waiting for an answer, returned to Gabii apparently without having accomplished his object, and told what he had himself said and seen. He added that Tarquin, either through passion, aversion to him, or his innate pride, had not uttered a single word. As soon as it was clear to Sextus what his father wished, he put to death the most eminent men of the city. . . . Some who wished to go into voluntary exile were allowed to do so, others were banished, and their estates, as well as the estates of those who were put to death, publicly divided in their absence. Out of these the gifts and plunder were distributed. By the sweets of private gain the sense of public calamities became extinguished. At last the state of Gabii, destitute of counsel and assistance, surrendered itself without a struggle into the power of the Roman king.

### 68. Execution of the Sons of Brutus [2]

Some time after this exploit, Sextus Tarquinius, coming by night to the house of a cousin, Tarquinius Collatinus, did violence to Lucretia, his chaste and beautiful wife. The next day Lucretia summoned her husband and her father, told them the story of her injury, and made them swear vengeance on the guilty man. Then in their presence she stabbed herself to death. Another witness to the tragedy was Lucius Junius Brutus, the friend of

---

[1] The original of this story is found in Herodotus where it is told of the tyrant Thrasybulus. See page 54.

[2] Livy, ii, 5.

Collatinus and a nephew of the king.   He it was who now delivered the Romans from the tyrant and his evil race. Brutus and Collatinus were then chosen as the first consuls of the new republic (509 B. C.).    Not long afterward the two sons of Brutus joined a conspiracy to restore Tarquinius Superbus to his throne.   The plot was detected and the children of Brutus were seized and condemned to death.

. . . This punishment was the more noticeable, because the consulship imposed on the father the office of punishing his own children. . . . Young men of the highest rank stood bound to the stake; but the consul's sons diverted the eyes of all the spectators from the rest of the criminals, as from persons unknown.   The people felt pity, not so much on account of their punishment, as of the crime by which they had deserved it. . . . The consuls advanced to take their seats, and the lictors were dispatched to inflict punishment.   The young men were stripped naked, beaten with rods, and their heads struck off with the axe.   The looks and countenance of the father presented a touching spectacle, as his natural feelings displayed themselves during the discharge of his duty in inflicting public punishment. . . .

### 69. The Exploit of Horatius [1]

Tarquinius now sought aid from his countrymen, the Etruscans.   The battle which ensued brought no decided success to either side.   Then the cause of the exiles was taken up by Lars Porsena, the powerful king of Clusium. He appeared before Rome with a great army.   Never before was the Roman state in such deadly peril.   On the approach of the hostile forces all withdrew for protection from the country into the city.   The Sublician Bridge, connecting with the Janiculum across the Tiber,

[1] Livy, ii, 10.

wellnigh afforded the enemy an entrance into Rome. But in one man, Horatius Cocles, the protecting spirit of Rome on that day found a defense. He strode to the front of the bridge and single-handed defied the enemy.

A sense of shame kept back with him two other Romans, Spurius Larcius and Titus Herminius, both men of high birth, and renowned for their gallant exploits. With them Horatius for a short time stood the first storm of danger and the severest brunt of the battle. Afterwards, as those who were cutting down the bridge called upon them to retire, and only a small portion of it was left, he obliged them also to withdraw to a place of safety. Then, casting his stern eyes threateningly upon all the nobles of the Etruscans, he now challenged them singly, now reproached them all as the slaves of haughty tyrants, who, unmindful of their own freedom, came to attack that of others. For a considerable time they hesitated, looking round one upon another, and waiting to commence the fight. A feeling of shame then stirred the army, and raising a shout, they hurled their weapons from all sides on their single adversary. When these had all stuck in the shield he held before him, and he with no less obstinacy kept possession of the bridge, they sought to thrust him down from it by their united attack. But the crash of the falling bridge, and at the same time the shout raised by the Romans for joy at having completed their task, checked their assault. Then Horatius said, "Father Tiberinus,[1] holy one, I pray thee, receive these arms and this thy soldier, in thy favoring stream." Then, in full armor, he leaped into the Tiber, and, amid showers of darts that fell upon him, swam across unharmed to his comrades. The state showed itself grateful towards such distinguished valor. A statue of Horatius was erected in the Forum, and as much land was given to him as he could draw a furrow round in one day with a plough.

[1] Tiberinus was the tutelary divinity of the river.

### 70. The Deed of Mucius Scævola [1]

Porsena, unable to capture Rome by storm, turned the siege into a blockade. And now a high-born Roman youth, Mucius by name, obtained leave from the Senate to enter the enemy's lines in disguise, "not for plunder," he said, "but for a deed of higher mark, with the help of the gods." He penetrated to the tribunal of the Etruscan monarch and sought to kill him, but by accident dispatched the royal secretary instead. Mucius was promptly seized by the guards and brought before the king.

. . . "I am," said the undaunted youth, "a Roman citizen; men call me Gaius Mucius. An enemy, I wished to slay an enemy. Nor have I less courage to suffer death than I had to inflict it. Both to do and to suffer bravely is a Roman's part. Nor have I alone harbored such feelings toward you. There follows after me a long succession of aspirants to the same honor. Therefore, if you choose, prepare yourself for this peril: to be in danger of your life from hour to hour; to find the sword and the enemy at the very entrance of your tent. Such is the war we, the young men of Rome, declare against you. Dread not an army in the field, or a battle; you will have to contend alone and with each of us one by one."

When the king, furious with rage, and at the same time terrified at the danger, commanded fires to be kindled about him, if he did not speedily disclose the plots at which he had darkly hinted, Mucius said, "See here, that you may understand of how little account the body is to those who have great glory in view." Immediately he thrust his right hand into the fire that was lighted for sacrifice. There he allowed it to burn as if his spirit were quite insensible to any feeling of pain. The king, who was astounded at this surprising sight, leaped from his seat and commanded the young man to be removed from the altar. "Depart," said he, " thou who hast acted more like

[1] Livy, ii, 12.

an enemy toward thyself than toward me. I would bid thee
go on and prosper in thy valor, if that valor was on the side of
my country. I now dismiss thee unharmed and unhurt, exempt
from the right of war." Then Mucius, as if in return for the
kindness, said, "Since bravery is held in honor with you, that
you may obtain from me by your kindness what you could
not obtain by threats, know this: we are three hundred, the
chief of the Roman youth, who have conspired to attack you
in this manner. The lot fell upon me first. The rest will be
with you, each in his turn . . . until fortune or some favorable opportunity shall have delivered you into our hands."

This deed of Mucius, thenceforward known in legend
by the surname Scævola (left-handed), determined Porsena to withdraw from the investment of the city. So
Tarquinius, foiled once more, stirred up the Latin Confederacy to make war upon the Romans. But at the great
battle of Lake Regillus the Latins and their royal allies
were totally defeated. Rome was at length delivered
from the rule of kings (497 B. C.).

### 71. Coriolanus and the Roman Matrons [1]

Among the enemies surrounding the young republic
were the Volscians, who lived in the southern part of Latium. With these rude mountaineers Rome had many
border wars. One of her most successful generals was
Coriolanus. He, however, was a patrician and when the
plebeian tribunes unjustly prosecuted him on the charge of
treason against the liberties of the people, Coriolanus took
refuge among his former foes. Under his able leadership
the Volscians recovered many of their lost possessions and
at last pitched their camp within a few miles of Rome.
In the presence of this emergency, the plebeians refused

[1] Livy, ii, 40.

to fight.  The Senate in vain sent envoy after envoy to Coriolanus to detach him from his unnatural alliance. To all their requests he gave a harsh reply.  It is recorded, too, that the priests in their sacred garb went as suppliants to the enemy's camp; and that they did not influence the mind of Coriolanus any more than had the deputies of the Senate.  Then Veturia, the mother of Coriolanus, and his wife Volumnia, accompanied by her two sons and a crowd of Roman matrons, sought out the haughty conqueror.

. . . Coriolanus rushed from his seat and offered to embrace his mother as she met him.  She, however, turning from entreaties to wrath, said, "Before I permit your embrace, let me know whether I have come to an enemy or to a son, whether I am in your camp a captive or a mother?  Has length of life and a hapless old age reserved me for this — to behold you first an exile, then an enemy?  Have you had the heart to lay waste this land, which gave you birth and nurtured you? Though you came in an incensed and vengeful spirit, did not your resentment abate when you entered its borders? When Rome appeared in view, did not the thought enter your mind — within those walls are my house and household gods, my mother, wife, and children?  So then, had I not been a mother, Rome would not now be besieged.  Had I not a son, I might have died free in a free country." . . . The lamentation proceeding from the entire crowd of women, and their bemoaning their own lot, and that of their country, at length overcame the man.  After embracing his family, he sent them away and withdrew his camp from the city.

### 72. The Fabian Gens and the War Against Veii [1]

Across the Tiber, not far from Rome, lay the powerful Etruscan city of Veii.  The enmity between the two

[1] Livy, ii, 48–49.

cities was of long standing. One of the legends of this period relates how the single Roman family of the Fabii undertook to carry on the war out of their own resources and by means of their own numbers alone.

. . Then the Fabian family approached the Senate and the consul spoke in the name of the family, "Conscript fathers, the Veientine war requires, as you know, an unremitting rather than a strong defense. Do you attend to other wars: assign the Fabii as enemies to the Veientines. We pledge ourselves that the majesty of the Roman name shall be safe in that quarter. This war, as if it was a family matter, it is our determination to conduct at our own private expense. In regard to it, let the republic be spared the expense of soldiers and money." For this offer the warmest thanks were returned to them. . . .

On the following day, the Fabii took up arms and assembled where they had been directed. The consul, coming forth in his military robe, beheld the whole family drawn up in the order of march. . . . Never did an army proceed through the city, either smaller in number, or more distinguished in renown and more admired by all. Three hundred and six soldiers, all patricians, all of one family, not one of whom an honest Senate would reject as a leader under any circumstances whatever, went on their way, threatening the Veientine state with destruction by the might of a single family. . . . As they passed the Capitol and the citadel, and the other sacred edifices, the people offered up prayers to the gods that they would send forward that band with prosperity and success, and soon return them safe to their country. In vain were these prayers uttered. . . .

For two years (479–477 B.C.) the Fabii kept garrison against Veii. Then they were surprised and cut to pieces, only one young man escaping from the massacre to become the new founder of the house of Fabius.

### 73. Cincinnatus the Dictator [1]

Not many years after this ill-fated enterprise of the Fabii, the Romans were involved in a desperate struggle with the Æquians (458 B. C.). These hardy mountaineers from their strongholds in the Apennines made constant descents upon the fertile and unprotected plains of Latium. Once they shut up a Roman consul and his army in a valley. When the Senate met in hurried council upon this crisis, one man's name was upon the lips of all. It was Lucius Quintius, whom the people called Cincinnatus from his "crisped" hair. He was appointed dictator with absolute power over Rome and her armies.

. . . It is worth while for those persons who despise all things human in comparison with riches, and who suppose that there is no room either for exalted honor or for virtue, except where riches abound in great profusion, to listen to the following story. Lucius Quintius, the sole hope of the Roman people, cultivated a farm of four acres on the other side of the Tiber. . . . While engaged on some work in the fields, he was requested by the ambassadors to put on his toga, and listen to the commands of the Senate. Asking whether all was well, he bade his wife immediately bring his toga from the hut. As soon as he had put it on, having first wiped off the dust and sweat, the ambassadors congratulated him and united in saluting him as dictator. They then summoned him to the city and told him what terror prevailed in the army. . . .

Cincinnatus immediately took the field. He attacked the blockading Æquians, compelled them to surrender, and returned to Rome victorious. The Senate granted him a splendid triumph. After a rule of sixteen days he laid down his absolute power and retired, once more a humble peasant, to his little farm.

[1] Livy, iii, 26.

## 74. Capture of Veii [1]

By the end of the fifth century B. C., the Romans had recovered Latium from their enemies, the Volscians and Æquians. They now renewed the war with Veii. The city endured a siege of ten years. Its capture by the dictator Camillus (396 B. C.) removed Rome's longest and most bitter rival for supremacy.

. . . When all the property of the people of Veii had been carried away, the Romans began to remove the offerings to their gods and the images of the gods themselves. But they proceeded more after the manner of worshipers than of plunderers. Certain youths, selected from the entire army, were assigned the duty of conveying Queen Juno to Rome. Having thoroughly washed their bodies and arrayed themselves in white garments, they entered her temple with profound adoration. They applied their hands to the image of Juno with religious awe, because, according to the Etruscan usage, no one but a priest of a certain family had been accustomed to touch the statue. When some one, either moved by divine inspiration or in youthful jocularity, said, "Juno, art thou willing to go to Rome," the rest all declared that the goddess nodded assent. It was also said that Juno was heard to declare that she was willing to go. At any rate her image was raised from its place by machines of trifling power, and was easily removed. . . .

## 75. Sack of Rome by the Gauls [2]

Only a few years after the fall of Veii the Roman state met with a great disaster. Barbarian Gauls from beyond the Alps, having overrun northern Italy, invaded Etruria and totally defeated a Roman army by the little stream of the Allia, eleven miles from Rome (390 B. C.). Most of the fugitives took refuge in the deserted city of Veii. At Rome all who could bear arms shut themselves up in the

[1] Livy, v, 22.    [2] Livy, v, 41.

citadel on the Capitoline Hill. The aged senators and patricians, who would not burden the defenders of the Capitol, refused to leave their homes and proudly awaited death at the hands of the enemy. The Gauls reached the walls of Rome on the evening of the battle, and found the gates open and the city deserted. Fearing a stratagem, they postponed their entrance till the morning.

. . . On the next day the Gauls entered the city, advanced through the Colline Gate, which lay open, into the Forum . . . and dispersed in quest of plunder through the empty streets. Some of them in a body rushed into the houses which were nearest; some repaired to those which were most distant, considering that those certainly would be untouched and abounding in spoil. Afterward, being terrified by the very solitude, they returned in a mass to the Forum and the parts adjoining the Forum, in order that no stratagem of the enemy should surprise them while dispersed. There, as the houses of the common people had barred doors, and the halls of the leading men stood open, almost greater hesitation was felt about attacking the open, than the closed, houses. With what veneration did they behold men sitting in the porches of their houses, men who . . . were like to gods in the majesty which their looks and the gravity of their countenance displayed! While they stood gazing at the senators, as if the latter were statues, it is said that Marcus Papirius roused the anger of a Gaul by striking him on the head with his ivory staff, because he stroked Marcus' long beard. Irritated by this action, the Gauls slew Marcus and then the rest of the nobles as they sat in their seats. No person whatever was spared; the houses were plundered, and when emptied, were set on fire.

### 76. Repulse of the Gauls from the Capitol [1]

Meanwhile, the citadel and Capitol of Rome were in great danger. For the Gauls had either perceived the track of a

[1] Livy, v, 47.

human foot where a messenger from Veii had passed, or had themselves noticed the rock with its easy ascent at the Temple of Carmentis. On a starlight night, after they had first sent forward an unarmed man to make trial of the way, they attempted the ascent of the rock. Handing over their arms whenever any difficult passage occurred, and alternately supported by and supporting each other, they reached the summit in such silence that they not only escaped the notice of the sentinels, but of the dogs also. But the Gauls did not escape the notice of the geese. These, as being sacred to Juno, had been spared by the Romans, though there was the greatest scarcity of food. As it turned out, this was a very fortunate circumstance. For Marcus Manlius, who three years before had been consul, was aroused from sleep by their cackling and the clapping of their wings. He snatched up his arms, at the same time calling the others to do the same, and proceeded at once to the spot. He then struck with the boss of his shield a Gaul who had already got footing on the summit, and tumbled him down. Since the fall of this man threw down those who were next, Manlius slew others, who in their consternation had cast aside their arms and were grasping tight the rocks to which they clung. And now the other Romans, having assembled, beat down the enemy with javelins and stones, and the whole line of Gauls was hurled headlong with a crash. The alarm then subsiding, the remainder of the night was given up by the Romans to repose, as far as could be done considering the disturbed state of their minds. . . .

Though the citadel still held out, the famine was sore among its defenders. At length the Gauls, who had little liking for a siege, were bribed to withdraw from the city. A thousand pounds' weight of gold was agreed upon "as a ransom of a people who were soon after to be the rulers of the world. To a transaction so very humiliating in itself, insult was added. False weights were brought by the Gauls, and, on the tribune objecting to them, the insolent

Gallic chieftain threw in his sword in addition to the weights, and was heard to utter an expression intolerable to Roman ears, 'Woe to the vanquished.'" But before this disgraceful bargain was completed, the great dictator, Camillus, marched in from Veii at the head of his troops. He bade the treasure be taken back and told his countrymen that Rome was ransomed with steel, not with gold. Then in two pitched battles he so thoroughly defeated the Gauls that, according to Livy, "not a man was left to carry home the news of their disaster."

### 77. Condemnation of Marcus Manlius [1]

When all danger from the Gauls had passed away, the Romans hurriedly rebuilt their city. Under the leadership of Camillus they triumphed over the Volscians and Etruscans, who had seized the hour of Rome's adversity to renew the long war for the supremacy of Latium. Camillus gained great glory, and in after years the grateful Romans styled him the second founder of their city. But the brave Marcus Manlius, the defender of the Capitol, met a different fate. He was accused by the patricians of ingratiating himself with the plebeians with intent to make himself a king.

. . . He is said to have brought forward nearly four hundred persons to whom he had lent money without interest, whose goods he had prevented from being sold, or whom he had saved from being led off as bondsmen. Besides this, he not only enumerated his military records, but even set them forth to view. These included spoils of slain enemies up to thirty and presents from generals to the number of forty. Among the latter the most remarkable were two mural crowns and eight civic crowns. He also brought forward citizens whom

[1] Livy, vi, 20.

he had preserved from the enemy. . . . Then, after he had recounted his exploits in war . . . he bared his breast, marked with scars received in battle. . . . He entreated the people to form their judgment of him with their eyes fixed on the Capitol and citadel and with their faces turned to the immortal gods.

As the people were summoned by centuries on the field of Mars,[1] and as the accused, extending his hands toward the Capitol, directed his prayers from men to the gods, it became evident to the tribunes that Manlius could never be condemned within sight of the Capitol. So the day of trial was postponed, and a meeting of the people was summoned in the Peteline grove outside the Flumentan Gate, from which there was no view of the Capitol. There the charge was made good.

In the stubbornness of their determination an awful sentence — one which excited horror even in his judges — was passed on him. . . . The tribunes cast him down from the Tarpeian rock.[2] . . . Marks of infamy were offered to him when dead: a public one, in that, since his home had been where the Temple of Moneta and the Mint now stand, it was proposed to the people that no patrician should dwell in the citadel and Capitol. The other was inflicted by his clan, it being provided by a decree of the Manlian clan that none of their descendants should ever bear the name of Marcus Manlius. Such was the fate of a man who, had he not been born in a free state, would have been celebrated. . . .

The discomfiture of the Gauls gave the Romans only a temporary respite from their foes. In the great Latin War (340–338 B.C.), Rome had to contend against a union of all the Latin cities. Victorious in this struggle, she soon became involved in another with the Samnites, the most powerful people of central Italy. Livy's narrative, as it has reached us, breaks off before the close of this final

[1] The Campus Martius.          [2] See page 157.

conflict, but not until the historian has exhibited to us Rome triumphant over her foes and the mistress of central Italy.[1]

[1] Books xi–xx of Livy's history covering the seventy-three years (292–219 B. C.) are lost.   We must rely upon other writers for the events of this period, including the war with Tarentum which ended in the subjugation of southern Italy (282–272 B. C.), and the First Punic War (264–241 B. C.) which added Sicily to the Roman dominions.

# CHAPTER XV

## HANNIBAL AND THE GREAT PUNIC WAR[1]

OF the many chapters in Livy's history of Rome, none are more memorable than those which relate the long and checkered story of the Second Punic War.[2] The theme is the life and death struggle of two proud and powerful nations for the dominion of the world. The hero is Hannibal, the supreme military genius of his age. Rome, at first helpless against his attack, is brought to the very verge of destruction. Nor does her final triumph detract from the grandeur of her foe. In all the episodes of this wonderful period, there stands out the royal figure of the mighty Carthaginian, waging on an alien soil and against overwhelming odds, the most famous contest in antiquity.

### 78. Passage of the Alps[3]

The contest arose as the result of Hannibal's capture of the Spanish city of Saguntum. Since this place was protected by a treaty with Rome, Hannibal's action was regarded by the Romans as a direct provocation to war. The Carthaginian Senate refused to disavow the brilliant exploit of their young commander. Rome at once declared war (218 B. C.). In the summer of the same year, Hannibal began the invasion of Italy. The route led from

[1] Livy, *History of Rome*, books xxi-xxv. *The Second Punic War*, translated by A. J. Church and W. J. Brodribb. London, 1883. Macmillan and Co.

[2] Books xxi-xxx cover the entire period of the war (218–201 B. C.).

[3] Livy, xxi, 32, 35, 37.

Spain through the passes of the Pyrenees and across the Rhone to the foot of the Alps.

. . . From the Druentia [1] Hannibal marched through a country generally flat to the Alps, wholly unmolested by the Gauls in those parts. And then, though rumor which usually magnifies the unknown far beyond truth, had given some anticipation of the facts, still the near sight of the mountain heights with their snows almost mingling with the sky, the rude huts perched on the rocks, cattle and beasts of burden shriveled with cold, human beings unkempt and wild, and all things animate and inanimate stiffened with frost, with other scenes more horrible to behold than to describe, revived their terror. . . .

On the ninth day they reached the top of the Alps, passing for the most part over trackless steeps, and by devious ways, into which they were led by the treachery of their guides. Two days they encamped on the height, and the men, worn out with hardships and fighting, were allowed to rest. Some beasts of burden, also, which had fallen down among the crags, found their way to the camp by following the army's track. The men were already worn out and wearied with their many miseries, when a heavy fall of snow added to their sufferings. At daybreak the march commenced, and as the army moved wearily over ground all buried in snow, languor and despair were visibly written on every face. Then Hannibal stepped to the front, and having ordered a halt on a peak which commanded a wide and distant prospect, he pointed to Italy and to the plains round the Po, as they lay beneath the heights of the Alps. "These are the walls," he told his men, "not of Italy only but of Rome itself that you are now scaling. What remains," he added, "will be a smooth descent; in one, or at the most, in two battles we shall have the citadel and capital of Italy in our grasp and power."

The army then began to advance, and now even the enemy attempted nothing but some stealthy ambuscades, as opportunity offered. The remainder, however, of the march proved

[1] One of the eastern tributaries of the Rhone.

far more difficult than the ascent, as the Alps on the Italian side have a shorter, and therefore a steeper, slope. In fact the whole way was precipitous, narrow, and slippery, so much so that they could not keep themselves from falling, or could those who had once stumbled retain their foothold. Thus they fell over one another and the beasts of burden over the men. . . .

At last, when both men and animals were worn out with fruitless exertion, they encamped on a height, in a spot which with the utmost difficulty they had cleared of the snow. The soldiers were then marched off to the work of making a road through the rock, as there only was a passage possible. Having to cut into the stone, they heaped up a huge pile of wood from great trees in the neighborhood, which they had felled and lopped. As soon as there was strength enough in the wind to create a blaze, they lighted the pile, and melted the rock, as it heated, by pouring vinegar on it. The burning stone was then cleft open with iron implements. . . . Four days were spent in this rocky pass, and the beasts almost perished of hunger, as the heights generally are quite bare and such herbage as grows is buried in snow.

Amid the lower slopes were valleys, sunny hills, too, and streams and woods. These were spots now at last more worthy to be the habitations of man. Here they sent the beasts to feed, and the men, worn out with the toil of road-making, were allowed to rest. In the next three days they reached level ground, and now the country was less wild, as was also the character of the inhabitants.[1]

### 79. Dictatorship of Fabius Maximus[2]

The long march was at an end. Hannibal at last stood on Italian soil. Of his original army scarcely thirty thou-

---

[1] The particular pass by which Hannibal entered Italy cannot be identified from Livy's narrative. The author's description is powerfully written, but it is not the account of an eyewitness and participant in the experiences described.

[2] Livy, xxii, 7–9, 16–17.

sand men remained, with whom to meet and master the
gigantic power of his adversary.   But if the Romans were
inclined to regard the invaders with haughty scorn, they
were soon undeceived.   Two battles in northern Italy,
one on the banks of the Ticinus, the other at the river
Trebia, were complete victories for the Carthaginians
(218 B. C.).   The next year Hannibal crossed the Apennines, entered Etruria, and totally defeated the consul
Flaminius at Lake Trasimenus.

. . . At Rome the first tidings of this defeat brought a terror-
stricken and tumultuous crowd into the Forum.   The matrons
wandered through the streets and asked all whom they met
what was this disaster of which news had just arrived, and how
the army had fared.   A crowd, thick as a thronged assembly,
with eyes intent upon the Senate-house, called aloud for the
magistrates.   At last, not long before sunset, the prætor,
Marcus Pomponius, said, "We have been beaten in a great
battle."   Nothing more definite than this was stated by him;
but each man had reports without end to tell his neighbor.
The news which they carried back to their homes was that the
consul had perished with a great part of his troops, that the few
who had survived were either dispersed throughout Etruria or
taken prisoners by the enemy. . . .

. . . The country hastily betook itself to a remedy which had
not been either wanted or employed for many years — the
creation of a dictator.   But the consul was absent, and it was
the consul only, it would seem, who could create him.   It was
no easy matter to send him a messenger or a letter, with
the Carthaginian armies in possession of Italy; nor could the
Senate make a dictator without consulting the people.   In the
end a step wholly unprecedented was taken.   The people
created Quintus Fabius Maximus dictator.   The Senate
charged him to strengthen the walls and towers of the city, to
put garrisons in whatever places he thought best, and to

break down the bridges over the rivers. Italy they could not defend, but they could still fight for their city and their homes. . . .

. . . On the day that Fabius Maximus, who was now dictator for the second time, entered upon his office, he convoked the Senate. He began with mention of the gods. It was, he proved to the senators, in neglect of religious rites and auspices rather than in rashness and want of skill, that the error of Flaminius had lain. Heaven itself, he urged, must be asked how the anger of heaven could be propitiated. He thus prevailed upon them to do what is scarcely ever done except when the most sinister marvels have been observed, that is, to order the Ten to consult the books of the Sibyl.[1] They inspected the volumes of destiny, and reported to the Senate that, since a vow to Mars was the cause of the war, this vow, not having been duly performed, must be performed anew and on a larger scale. Moreover, they announced that games of the first class must be vowed to Jupiter, and a temple to Venus and another to Reason erected. There must also be a public litany, a banquet of the gods, and a year of consecration vowed, if the arms of Rome were to prosper and the state to·remain in the same position which it had occupied before the war. The Senate, knowing that Fabius would be occupied with the business of the campaign, directed the prætor, Marcus Æmilius, who had been nominated by the college of pontiffs, to see all things speedily done. . . .

Instead of attacking Rome, Hannibal crossed the peninsula to the Adriatic and marched into Apulia. Fabius, with a new army, now appeared in his rear. The Roman dictator followed Hannibal's movements but refused to

[1] According to the legend, the Sibyl, a priestess of Apollo at Cumæ, had sold to King Tarquinius Superbus three books of prophecies concerning the future of Rome. These books, a Greek collection of sacred verse, were in charge of a body of priests who consulted them whenever the Roman state was in especial danger.

fight a pitched battle.   It was at this time that the Carthaginian army, having been placed in a dangerous position,
was extricated in a remarkable manner.

To deceive his foe, Hannibal contrived an optical illusion of
most alarming appearance, and resolved to move stealthily up
the hills at nightfall.   The deception was thus arranged.   Fire-
wood was collected from all the country around, and bundles
of twigs and dry faggots were fastened to the horns of oxen
from the plundered rural districts. . . . Nearly two thousand
oxen were thus treated, and Hasdrubal was intrusted with the
business of driving this herd, with their horns alight, upon the
hills, especially to those above the passes occupied by the
enemy.

In the dusk of evening, Hasdrubal silently struck his camp.
. . . When the Carthaginians reached the foot of the mountain,
where the roads narrowed, the signal was immediately given
to hurry the herd with their horns alight up the slope of the hills.
The animals rushed on, goaded into madness by the terror of
the flames which flashed from their heads, and by the heat
which soon reached the flesh at the root of their horns.   At this
sudden rush all the thickets seemed to be in a blaze, and the very
woods and mountains to have been fired.   When the beasts
vainly shook their heads, it seemed as if men were running about
in every direction.   The troops posted in the pass, seeing fires
on the hilltops and above them, fancied that they had been
surrounded, and left their position.   They made for the loftiest
heights as being their safest route, for it was there that the fewest
flashes of light were visible.   But even there they fell in with
some of the oxen which had strayed from the herd.   When
they saw them at a distance, they stood thunder-struck at what
seemed to be the miracle of oxen breathing fire.   As soon as it
was seen to be nothing but a human contrivance, they suspected
some deep stratagem and fled in wilder confusion than ever. . . .
Hannibal, meanwhile, had led his whole army through the pass,
cutting off, as he went, some of his opponents.

### 80. Battle of Cannæ [1]

The policy of delay followed by Fabius was so far successful that it compelled Hannibal to go into winter quarters without inflicting upon the Romans another signal defeat. The next year (216 B. C.), Rome made preparations for a decisive conflict with the invader. The cautious tactics of the dictator were abandoned. Varro and Æmilius Paulus, the two consuls for the year, with eighty thousand troops, met the Carthaginians at Cannæ on the Aufidus. The two consuls commanded on alternate days. Paulus steadily refused to risk an engagement. Varro, when his turn came, with that rashness that had already cost the Romans so dear, staked all upon a single throw. He led out his troops and offered battle. Hannibal at once accepted the challenge.

At dawn Hannibal sent in advance his slingers and light-armed troops and crossed the river. To each division, as it crossed, he assigned its position. His Gallic and Spanish cavalry he posted near the river bank on the left wing, facing the Roman horse. The right wing was given to the Numidian cavalry. The center showed a strong force of infantry, having on either side the African troops, with the Gauls and Spaniards between them. These Africans might have been taken for a Roman force; so largely were they equipped with weapons taken at Trebia, and yet more at Trasimenus. The Gauls and Spaniards had shields of very nearly the same shape, but their swords were widely different in size and form. The Gauls had them very long and pointless, while the Spaniards, who were accustomed to assail the enemy with thrusts rather than with blows, had them short, handy, and pointed. These nations had a specially terrible appearance, so gigantic was their stature and so strange their look. The Gauls were naked above the middle; the

Spaniards wore tunics of linen bordered with purple, of a whiteness marvelously dazzling. The total number of the infantry who were that day ranged in line was forty thousand, that of the cavalry, ten thousand. Hasdrubal commanded the left wing; Maharbal the right; Hannibal himself, with his brother Mago, was in the center. The sun — whether the troops were purposely so placed or whether it was by chance — fell very conveniently sideways on both armies, the Romans facing the south, the Carthaginians the north. The wind, however, blew straight against the Romans and whirled clouds of dust into their faces till they could see nothing. . . .

The battle was stubbornly contested but at length turned in favor of the Carthaginians.

Paulus was on the other side of the field. He had been seriously wounded at the very beginning of the battle by a bullet from a sling. Yet he repeatedly encountered Hannibal with a compact body of troops, and at several points restored the fortune of the day. He was protected by the Roman cavalry, which at last sent away their horses when the consul became too weak to manage his charger. Some one told Hannibal that the consul had ordered the cavalry to dismount. "He might better hand them over to me bound hand and foot," said he. The horsemen fought on foot as men were likely to fight, when, the victory of the enemy being beyond all doubt, the vanquished preferred dying where they stood, to flight. . . . All were soon scattered, and such as were able, sought to recover their horses and fly.

Lentulus, as he galloped by, saw the consul sitting on a stone and covered with blood. "Lucius Æmilius," he cried, "the one man whom heaven must regard as guiltless of this day's calamity, take this horse while you have some strength left, and I am here to be with you, to lift you to the saddle, and to defend you. Do not make our defeat yet sadder by a consul's death. There is weeping and sorrow enough without that." The consul replied,

"It is a brave thought of thine, Cornelius; but waste not in fruitless pity the few moments you have for escaping from the enemy. My public message to the senators is that they must fortify Rome and make its garrison as strong as possible before the victorious enemy arrives. My private message to Quintus Fabius is that Lucius Æmilius remembered his teaching in life and death. As for me, let me breathe my last among my slaughtered soldiers. I would not again leave my consulship to answer for my life, nor would I stand up to accuse my colleague, and by accusing another, protect my own innocence." While they thus talked together, they were overtaken, first by a crowd of Roman fugitives and then by the enemy. The latter buried the consul under a shower of javelins, not knowing who he was. Lentulus galloped off in the confusion.

The Romans now fled wildly in every direction. Seven thousand men escaped into the smaller, ten thousand into the larger, camp, ten thousand more into the village of Cannæ itself. These last were immediately surrounded by the Carthaginian cavalry, for no fortification protected the place. The other consul, who, whether by chance or of set purpose, had not joined any large body of fugitives, fled with about five hundred horsemen to Venusia.[1] Forty-five thousand five hundred infantry, two thousand seven hundred cavalry, and almost as many more citizens and allies are said to have fallen. Among these were the quæstors of both consuls, twenty-nine tribunes of the soldiers, not a few ex-consuls, ex-prætors, and ex-ædiles . . . and eighty who were either actual senators or had filled such offices as made them eligible for the Senate. . . .

Such was the battle of Cannæ, as famous as the disaster at the Allia,[2] and though less serious in its consequences, thanks to the inaction of the enemy, yet in loss of men still more ruinous and disgraceful. The flight at the Allia lost the city but saved the army. At Cannæ the consul who fled was followed by

[1] A town of Apulia not far from Cannæ.

[2] Referring to the defeat of Romans by the Gauls in 390 B.C. See page 168.

barely fifty men; with the consul who perished, perished nearly
the whole army. . . .

### 81. After Cannæ [1]

Round the victorious Hannibal crowded his officers with
congratulations and entreaties that, since this mighty war was
finished, he should take what remained of that day and the
following night for rest, and give the same to his wearied soldiers.
Maharbal, the general of his cavalry, thought that there should
be no pause. "Nay," he cried, "you are aware what has
been achieved by this victory. You can hold a conqueror's
feast in the Capitol within five days. Pursue them; I will go
before you with my cavalry, and they shall know that you have
come before they know you are coming." Hannibal felt that
his success was too great for him to be able to realize it at the
moment. "I commend," he said, "Maharbal's zeal, but I
must take time to deliberate." Maharbal replied, "Well, the
gods do not give all gifts to one man. Hannibal, you know how
to conquer; not how to use a conquest." That day's delay is
believed to have saved Rome and its empire. . . .

At Rome report said. . . that the army with the two consuls
had been utterly destroyed, and that the whole force had ceased
to exist. Never before, with Rome itself still safe, had there
been such panic and confusion within our walls. I shall decline
the task of attempting a lengthened description which could
not but be far inferior to the truth. The year before, a consul
with his army had fallen at Trasimenus; it was not wound after
wound, but multiplied disasters that were announced. Two consuls and the armies of two consuls had perished. Rome had
now no camp, no general, no soldiers. Hannibal was master of
Apulia, of Samnium, of nearly the whole of Italy. Certainly
there was not a nation in the world which would not have been
overwhelmed by such a weight of calamity. . . .

How greatly this disaster surpassed all previous disasters is
clearly shown by the fact that the loyalty of our allies, steadfast

[1] Livy, xxii, 51, 54, 61.

until that day, now began to waver. It was simply, indeed, because they despaired of the maintenance of our empire. Yet all these disasters and defections never made the Romans so much as mention peace, either before the consul [1] went back to Rome, or after his return had renewed the remembrance of the terrible loss sustained. On this latter occasion, indeed, such was the high spirit of the country, that, when the consul returned after this great disaster of which he had himself been the chief cause, all classes went in crowds to meet him. He was publicly thanked because "he had not despaired of the commonwealth." Had he been a Carthaginian general, they knew that there was no torture which he would not have had to suffer.

The battle of Cannæ was Hannibal's last and greatest triumph. The war did not end here. Hannibal was to lead his Carthaginians for thirteen years longer, up and down the length of Italy, capturing her towns, devastating her lands, but unable to take the Roman city itself. Step by step Rome recovered her strength. At length Scipio's invasion of Africa compelled the Carthaginian Senate to recall Hannibal for the defense of Carthage. His defeat by Scipio at the battle of Zama (202 B. C.) ended the Second Punic War. Peace was declared with Carthage, but not with Hannibal. He fled from his native country, and after many wanderings took refuge at the court of Prusias, the king of Bithynia in Asia Minor. Thither came Flamininus, sent from Rome to demand the surrender of her ancient enemy. "The Carthaginian had always foreseen some such end of his life; for he knew the implacable hatred which the Romans bore him, and placed little confidence in the faith of kings. Besides, he had experienced the fickle temper of Prusias, and had, for some time, dreaded the arrival of Flamininus, as an

[1] Varro.

event fatal to him. Encircled by enemies on every side, in order to have always some path open for flight, he had made seven passages from his house, of which some were concealed, lest they might be invested by a guard. But the imperious government of kings suffers nothing to remain secret which should be discovered. The circuit of the entire house was surrounded with guards, in such a manner that no one could escape from it. Hannibal, on being told that some of the king's soldiers were in the porch, endeavored to escape through a back door, which was the most private, and from which the passage was most secret. Perceiving that door, also, to be guarded by a body of soldiers, and every avenue round to be blocked up by the guards, he called for poison, which he had long kept in readiness to meet such an event, and said, 'Let us release the Romans from their anxiety, since they think it too long to wait for the death of an old man.[1] Flamininus will gain no very great or memorable victory over one unarmed and betrayed. What an alteration has taken place in the behavior of the Roman people, this day affords abundant proof. Their fathers gave warning to Pyrrhus, their armed foe, then heading an army against them in Italy, to beware of poison. The present generation have sent an ambassador, of consular rank, to persuade Prusias villainously to murder his guest.' Then, imprecating curses on the head of Prusias and on his kingdom, and calling on the gods who presided over hospitality and were witnesses of his breach of faith, he drank off the contents of the cup. This was the end of the life of Hannibal."[2]

[1] Hannibal was then (184 B. C.) sixty-three years of age.
[2] Livy, xxxix, 51.

# CHAPTER XVI

## CATO THE CENSOR: A ROMAN OF THE OLD SCHOOL[1]

PLUTARCH'S [2] life of Marcus Porcius Cato (234–149 B. C.) describes a statesman and moralist who lived during the period when Roman society was undergoing a series of profound and far-reaching changes. The influx of Greek ideas and Greek customs that followed the Second Punic War and Rome's conquests in the eastern Mediterranean, threatened to overthrow those earlier ideals of simplicity and honesty, of industry and economy, of patriotism and fidelity to the state, the possession of which had distinguished the Romans above all other ancient peoples. Cato spent his entire life in an endeavor to stem this revolutionary tide, and to turn his countrymen back into the old paths wherein their forefathers had walked so long. It was because Rome had once been the home of many men like Cato that the city had risen to her position of imperial power. In himself Cato summed up the qualities — often very unlovely qualities — that made Rome great among the nations.

### 82. Anecdotes of his Public Career [3]

Cato grew very powerful by his eloquence, so that he was commonly called the Roman Demosthenes. But his manner of life was yet more famous. For oratorical skill was, as an accom-

---

[1] *Plutarch's Lives of Illustrious Men.* The Dryden translation, revised by A. H. Clough. Boston, 1859. Little, Brown, and Co.

[2] For a notice of Plutarch see page 98.

[3] Plutarch, *Marcus Cato*, 4, 6–9.

plishment, commonly studied and sought after by all young men. It was, however, very rare for a man to cultivate the old habits of bodily labor, or to prefer a light supper and a breakfast which never saw the fire; or to be in love with poor clothes and a homely lodging, or to set his ambition rather on doing without luxuries than on possessing them. . . . With reason, therefore, everybody admired Cato. When they saw others sink under labors, and grow effeminate by pleasures, they beheld him unconquered by either, and this, not only when he was young and desirous of honor, but also when old and gray-headed, after a consulship and triumph. He was like some famous victor in the Olympic games, persevering in his exercise and maintaining his character to the very last. . . .

For his general temperance and self-control, he really deserves the greatest credit. When he commanded the army, he never took for himself and for those that belonged to him, above three bushels of wheat for a month, and somewhat less than a bushel and a half a day of barley for his baggage-cattle. When he entered upon the government of Sardinia, where his predecessors had been used to require tents, bedding, and clothes upon the public account, and to charge the state heavily with the cost of provisions and entertainments for a great train of servants and friends, the difference Cato showed in his economy was something incredible. There was nothing of any sort for which he would put the public to expense. He would walk without a carriage to visit the cities, with only one of the common town officers, who carried his dress and a cup with which to offer libations. Yet, though he seemed thus easy and sparing to all who were under his power, he, on the other hand, showed most inflexible severity and strictness in what related to public justice. . . . The Roman government never appeared more terrible or yet more mild, than under his administration.

His manner of speaking was courteous, yet forcible; pleasant, yet overwhelming; facetious, yet austere; sententious, yet vehement. He was like Socrates, in the description of Plato, who seemed outwardly to those about him to be but a simple, talkative, blunt fellow; though at the bottom he was full of such gravity and matter, as would even move tears and touch the very hearts of his auditors. . . . We must now write down some of Cato's memorable sayings; being of the opinion that a man's character appears much more by his words, than by his looks.

Being once anxious to dissuade the common people of Rome, from their unseasonable and impetuous clamor for gifts and distributions of corn, he began thus to harangue them, "It is a difficult task, O citizens, to make speeches to the stomach, which has no ears." Reproving, also, their sumptuous habits, he said that it was hard to preserve a city, where a fish sold for more than an ox. He had a saying, also, that the Roman people were like sheep; for they, when single, do not obey, but when together in a flock, they follow their leaders. "So you," said he, "when you have got together in a body, let yourselves be guided by those whom singly you would never think of being advised by." Discoursing on the power of women, he remarked, "Men usually command women; but we command all men, and the women command us". . . .

The Romans once dispatched three ambassadors to Bithynia,[1] of whom one was gouty, another had his skull trepanned, and the other seemed little better than a fool. Hereupon, Cato said that the Romans had sent an embassy which had neither feet, head, nor heart. His interest was once entreated by Scipio,[2] on account of Polybius, for the Achæan exiles. There happened to be a great discussion in the Senate about it, some being for, and some against, their return. Cato, standing up, thus delivered himself, "Here we sit all day long, as if we had nothing to do but beat our brains whether these old Greeks should be carried to their graves by the bearers here, or by those

---

[1] Bithynia, a division of Asia Minor, was at this time an independent kingdom.

[2] Publius Cornelius Scipio Æmilianus. His friend Polybius, famous as the historian of Rome, was one of the 1000 Greek hostages brought from Achæa in 167 B. C. and detained in Italy for sixteen years.

in Achæa." . . . He used to assert, also, that wise men profited more by fools, than fools by wise men; since wise men avoided the faults of fools, but fools would not imitate the good examples of wise men. He would profess, too, that he was more taken with young men who blushed, than with those who looked pale; and that he never desired to have a soldier who moved his hands too much in marching, and his feet too much in fighting; or snored louder than he shouted. . . . When one who was much given to the pleasures of the table desired his acquaintance, Cato answered that he could not live with a man whose palate was of a quicker sense than his heart. He would likewise say. . . that in his whole life he most repented of three things: one, that he had trusted a secret to a woman; another, that he went by water when he might have gone by land; the third, that he had remained one whole day without doing any business of importance. . . .

### 83. Cato's Censorship[1]

. . . He gave most general annoyance while censor by re-trenching people's luxury; for . . . he caused all dress, carriages, women's ornaments and household furniture, of which the price exceeded a certain value, to be rated at ten times as much as they were worth. By thus making the assessments greater, he intended to increase the taxes paid upon them. . . .

. . . Cato also caused the pipes, through which some persons brought the public water into their own houses and gardens, to be cut, and threw down all buildings which jutted out into the common streets. He beat down, also, the price in contracts for public works to the lowest, and raised it in contracts for farming the taxes[2] to the highest sum. By such proceedings he drew a great deal of hatred on himself. . . .

However the people liked his censorship wondrously well. Setting up a statue for him in the temple of the goddess of Health, they put an inscription under it. The latter did not record his commands in war or his triumph. It was to the

---

[1] Plutarch, *Marcus Cato*, 18–19.      [2] See page 101, note 2.

effect, that this was Cato the Censor, who, by his good discipline
and wise and temperate ordinances, reclaimed the Roman
commonwealth when it was sinking down into vice.  Before
this honor was done to himself, he used to laugh at those who
loved such things.  He said that they did not see that they
were taking pride in the workmanship of brass-founders and
painters; whereas the citizens bore about his best likeness in
their breasts.  And when anyone seemed to wonder that he
should have never a statue, though many ordinary persons had
one, he said, "I would much rather be asked, why I have no
statue, than why I have one."  In short, he could not endure to
have any honest citizen praised, unless it might prove advan-
tageous to the commonwealth. . . .

## 84. Cato in His Family[1]

Cato was a good father, an excellent husband to his wife, and
an extraordinary economist. . . . He married a wife more noble
than rich.  He was of the opinion that the rich and the high-
born are equally haughty and proud; but that those of noble
blood would be more ashamed of base things, and consequently
more obedient to their husbands in all that was fit and right.
A man who beat his wife or child, laid violent hands, he said,
on what was most sacred.  A good husband he reckoned worthy
of more praise than a great senator.  He admired the ancient
Socrates for nothing so much, as for having lived a temperate
and contented life with a wife who was a scold, and with children who were half-witted.

As soon as he had a son born . . . he would be present when his
wife washed it, and dressed it in its swaddling clothes. . . . When
the child began to reach years of discretion, Cato would teach
him to read, although he had a servant, a very good grammarian,
who taught many others.  Cato, however, thought it not fit
to have his son reprimanded by a slave, or pulled, it may be,
by the ears, when found backward in his lesson.  Nor would he

[1] Plutarch, *Marcus Cato*, 20.

have him owe to a servant the obligation of so great a thing as
his learning. Cato, therefore, taught his son grammar, law, and
gymnastic exercises. He showed him, too, how to throw a dart,
to fight in armor, and to ride, how to box, how to endure both
heat and cold, and how to swim over the most rapid and rough
rivers. He says, likewise, that he wrote histories, in large characters, with his own hand, so that his son might learn to know
about his countrymen and forefathers. Nor did he less abstain
from speaking anything obscene before his son, than if it had
been in the presence of the sacred virgins, called vestals. . . .
Thus, like an excellent work, Cato formed and fashioned his son
to virtue; nor had he any occasion to find fault with his readiness
and docility. . . .

### 85. Later Life [1]

Some consider the overthrow of Carthage [2] to have been one
of Cato's last acts of statesmanship. . . . The war, chiefly by the
counsel and advice of Cato, was undertaken on the following
occasion. Cato was sent to the Carthaginians and to Masinissa, king of Numidia, to learn why they were enemies and at
war with each other. Masinissa, it seems, had been a friend
of the Romans from the beginning. The Carthaginians, also,
since their conquest by Scipio, were of the Roman confederacy,
having been shorn of their power by loss of territory and a
heavy tax. When he found Carthage, not (as the Romans
thought) low and in an ill condition, but well manned, full of
riches and all sorts of arms and ammunition, Cato believed that
it was not a time for the Romans to adjust affairs between them
and Masinissa. He thought rather that they themselves would
fall into danger, unless they should find means to check this
rapid growth of Rome's ancient and irreconcilable enemy.
Returning quickly to Rome, he informed the Senate that the
former defeats and blows given to the Carthaginians had not
so much diminished their strength, as it had abated their
imprudence and folly. . . .

[1] Plutarch, *Marcus Cato*, 26–27.     [2] By the Third Punic War, 149–146 B. C.

Moreover, they say that, shaking his gown, he took occasion to let drop some African figs before the senators. On their admiring the size and beauty of them, he added, that the place that bore them was but three days' sail from Rome. Nay, he never after this made a speech but at the end he would be sure to come out with this sentence, "ALSO CARTHAGE, METHINKS, OUGHT UTTERLY TO BE DESTROYED." But Publius Scipio Nasica would always declare his opinion to the contrary, in these words, "It seems requisite to me that Carthage should still stand." . . . He looked upon the Carthaginians as too weak to overcome the Romans, and too great to be despised by them. On the other side, it seemed a perilous thing to Cato, that a city which had been always great, and was now grown sober and wise by reason of its former calamities, should still lie, as it were, in wait for the follies and dangerous excesses of the over-powerful Roman people. Hence he thought it the wisest course to have all outward dangers removed, when they had so many inward ones among themselves.

Thus Cato, they say, stirred up the third and last war against the Carthaginians. No sooner was the said war begun, than he died. . . .

# CHAPTER XVII

## CICERO THE ORATOR[1]

AFTER the death of Cato the Censor, some three quarters of a century elapsed before there came to the front the commanding personality of Cicero. Marcus Tullius Cicero (106–43 B. C.) was the greatest orator and likewise the most eminent man of letters of his time. His place in Latin literature is as secure and unapproachable as his position among the few great statesmen whom republican Rome produced. He wrote copiously upon philosophical subjects; he conducted an extensive correspondence which throws a flood of light upon the condition of the age; and for more than thirty years he spoke constantly in the law courts, before the popular assemblies, and in the Senate. Nearly sixty of his speeches have come down to us.

### 86. First Verrine Oration[2]

Cicero's reputation as an orator was securely established by his seven speeches against Verres, a former governor of Sicily. At the earnest request of the Sicilians, Cicero undertook the prosecution and was so successful that Hortensius, the famous advocate retained by Verres, threw up the case when Cicero had concluded his second oration. Verres went into exile (70 B. C.). The five remaining

---

[1] *The Orations of Marcus Tullius Cicero*, translated by C. D. Yonge. 4 vols. London, 1851–1856. George Bell and Sons.

[2] Cicero, *Against Verres*, i, 1, 3–5.

speeches of this series, though never delivered, were afterwards published by Cicero, in order that the evidence as
to the misgovernment of Verres might be known to all
the world. They afford a disheartening picture of the
tyranny and oppression which the provincials could suffer
under an unscrupulous governor.

. . . An opinion has now become established, pernicious to us
and pernicious to the republic . . . that in the courts of law as
they exist at present no wealthy man, however guilty he may
be, can possibly be convicted.  Now, at this time of peril to your
order[1] and to your tribunals, when men are ready to attempt by
harangues and by the proposal of new laws, to increase the existing unpopularity of the Senate, Gaius Verres is brought to trial
as a criminal.  He is a man condemned in the opinion of every
one by his life and actions, but acquitted by the greatness of
his wealth, according to his own hope and boast.

I, O judges, have undertaken this cause as prosecutor with the
sincerest good wishes and expectation on the part of the Roman
people, not in order to increase the unpopularity of the Senate
but to relieve it from the discredit which I share with it.  For I
have brought before you a man, by acting justly in whose case
you have an opportunity of retrieving the lost credit of your
judicial proceedings, of regaining your credit with the Roman
people, and of giving satisfaction to foreign nations. . . . And if
you come to a decision about this man with severity and a due
regard to your oaths, that authority which ought to remain in
you will cling to you still.  If, however, that man's vast riches
shall break down the sanctity and honesty of the courts of justice,
at least I shall achieve this, that it shall be plain that it was
rather honest judgment that was wanting to the republic, than
a criminal to the judges, or an accuser to the criminal. . . .

What are the circumstances on which Verres founds his hopes
. . . I see clearly.  But how he can have the confidence to think

---

[1] The judges at this period were taken from the senatorial order.

that he can effect anything with the present prætor and the present bench of judges, I cannot conceive. This one thing I know. . . that his hopes were of that nature that he placed all his expectations of safety in his money; and that if this protection was taken from him, he thought nothing would be any help to him. . . .

Verres has established great and numerous monuments and proofs of all his vices in the province of Sicily, which he for three years so harassed and ruined that it can by no possibility be restored to its former condition. It appears, indeed, scarcely able to recover at all after a long series of years. . . . While this man was prætor, the Sicilians enjoyed neither their own laws nor the decrees of our Senate nor the common rights of every nation. . . . No legal decision for three years was given on any other ground but his will. No property was so secure to any man, even if it had descended to him from his father and grandfather, but he was deprived of it at the command of Verres. Enormous sums of money were exacted from the property of the cultivators of the soil by a new and nefarious system. The most faithful of the allies were classed in the number of enemies. Roman citizens were tortured and put to death like slaves. The worst criminals were acquitted in the courts of justice through bribery. . . . The most fortified harbors, the greatest and strongest cities, were laid open to pirates and robbers. The sailors and soldiers of the Sicilians, our own allies and friends, died of hunger. The best built fleets on the most important stations were lost and destroyed, to the great disgrace of the Roman people. This same man, while prætor, plundered and stripped those most ancient monuments, some erected by wealthy monarchs and intended by them as ornaments for their cities; some, too, the work of their own generals, which they either gave or restored as conquerors to the different states in Sicily. And he did this not only in the case of public statues and ornaments, but he also plundered all the consecrated temples. In short, he did not leave to the Sicilians one god which appeared to him to be made in a tolerably workmanlike manner. . . .

## 87. First Oration against Catiline [1]

Perhaps the best known of all of Cicero's speeches are the four orations against Catiline, delivered in the year of his consulship, 63 B. C. Catiline, a ruined and dissolute patrician, had formed a conspiracy which included the most vicious and desperate men of Italy, to overthrow the government, murder the magistrates, and establish a tyranny upon the ruins of the republic. But the vigilant consul detected the plot and when the arch-conspirator boldly appeared in his seat in the Senate, he was met by the storm of fiery denunication which forms the *First Oration against Catiline*.

When, O Catiline, do you mean to cease abusing our patience? How long is that madness of yours still to mock us? When is there to be an end of your unbridled audacity? Do not the nightly guards placed on the Palatine Hill [2] — do not the watches posted throughout the city — do not the alarm of the people and the union of all good men — do not the precautions taken of assembling the Senate in this most defensible place — do not the looks and countenances of this venerable body here present, have any effect upon you? Do you not feel that your plans are detected? Do you not see that your conspiracy is already arrested and rendered powerless by the knowledge which every one here possesses of it? What is there that you did last night, what the night before — where is it that you were — whom did you summon to meet you — what design was there which was adopted by you, with which you think that anyone of us is unacquainted?

Shame on the age and on its principles! The Senate is aware of these things; the consul sees them; and yet this man lives.

[1] Cicero, *Against Catiline*, i, 1–2, 13.

[2] The Palatine Hill was the original seat of the city of Rome. In Cicero's day, after the city had spread gradually over the other hills in the neighborhood, the Palatine became the fashionable quarter of Rome.

Lives! ay, he comes even into the Senate. He takes a part in the public deliberations; he is watching and marking down and checking off for slaughter every individual among us. And we, gallant men that we are, think that we are doing our duty to the republic if we keep out of the way of his frenzied attacks. . . .

I wish, O conscript fathers, to be merciful; I wish not to appear negligent amid such danger to the state; but I do now accuse myself of remissness and culpable inactivity. A camp is pitched in Italy, at the entrance of Etruria, in hostility to the republic. The number of the enemy increases daily. And yet the general of that camp, the leader of those enemies, we see within the walls — ay, and even in the Senate — planning every day some internal injury to the republic. If, O Catiline, I should now order you to be arrested, and to be put to death, I should, I suppose, have to fear lest all good men should say that I had acted tardily, rather than that anyone should affirm that I had acted cruelly. But what ought to have been done long ago, I have good reason for not doing as yet. I will put you to death only when there cannot be found a single person so wicked, so abandoned, so like yourself, as not to admit that it has been rightly done. As long as one person exists who dares to defend you, you shall live. But you shall live as you do now, surrounded by my trusty guards, so that you shall not be able to stir one finger against the republic. Many eyes and ears shall still observe and watch you, as they have hitherto done, though you shall not perceive them. . . .

Take yourself off, O Catiline, to your impious and nefarious war, to the great safety of the republic, to your own misfortune and injury, and to the destruction of those who have joined themselves to you in every wickedness and atrocity. Then do you, O Jupiter, who were consecrated by Romulus with the same auspices as this city, whom we rightly call the stay of this city and empire, repel this man and his companions from your altars and from the other temples — from the houses and walls of the city — from the lives and fortunes of all the citizens.

And overwhelm all the enemies of good men, the foes of the republic, the robbers of Italy . . . with eternal punishments.

### 88. Second Oration against Catiline [1]

When Catiline ventured to reply to Cicero's accusations, he was interrupted by cries of "traitor" and "parricide" from the angry senators. Rushing from the chamber, he took refuge with his friends outside the city and proceeded to the army awaiting him in Etruria. The next day Cicero assembled the people and announced Catiline's departure in a triumphant speech.

At length, O Romans, we have dismissed from the city, or driven out, or, when he was departing of his own accord, we have pursued with words, Lucius Catiline, mad with audacity, breathing wickedness, impiously planning mischief to his country, threatening fire and sword to you and to this city. He has gone, he has departed, he has disappeared, he has rushed out. No injury will now be prepared against these walls, within the walls themselves, by that monster and prodigy of wickedness. And we have, without controversy, defeated him, the sole general of this domestic war. For now that dagger will no longer hover about our sides. We shall not be afraid in the Campus Martius, in the Forum, in the Senate-house — ay, and within our own private walls. He was moved from his place when he was driven from the city. Now we shall openly wage without hindrance a regular war with an enemy. Beyond all question we shall ruin the man. We have defeated him splendidly when we have driven him from secret treachery into open warfare. But that he has not taken with him his sword red with blood as he intended — that he has left us alive — that we wrested the weapon from his hands — that he has left the citizens safe and the city standing, what great and overwhelming grief must you think that this is to him! Now he lies prostrate, O Romans, and feels

[1] Cicero, *Against Catiline*, ii, i.

himself stricken down and abject, and often casts back his eyes toward this city, which he mourns over as snatched from his jaws, but which seems to me to rejoice at having thrown forth such a pest and cast it out of doors.

After the departure of Catiline, Cicero arrested those of his associates who remained in Rome. Then, in a third speech, also addressed to the people, the consul described the steps he had taken to implicate them in the conspiracy. His fourth and final oration, delivered before the Senate, dealt with the fate of the prisoners. Cæsar argued for their imprisonment, but Cicero believed that they should be put to death. The consul's advice was taken and the conspirators were strangled in their underground prison. Not long after, Catiline and his entire army were put to the sword. Cicero's success in saving the state made him for a time the most eminent man in Rome. The grateful citizens saluted him as *Pater Patriæ*, "Father of his Fatherland."

### 89. The Second Philippic[1]

After the assassination of Cæsar in 44 B. C., a new tyrant in the person of Antony succeeded to Cæsar's power at Rome. Though Cicero had taken no part in the plot against Cæsar, he approved of it and he now determined that Antony should not long enjoy his position of virtual dictator. As leader of the Senate, Cicero delivered during the next few months a series of fourteen orations against Antony. These orations, from their likeness to the speeches of Demosthenes against Philip of Macedonia,[2] have always been known as *Philippics*. The *Second Philippic* is generally esteemed the masterpiece of Cicero's eloquence. Circumstances prevented its delivery in the Senate. Cicero,

---

[1] Cicero, *Philippics*, ii, 44–46.　　[2] See page 129.

however, wrote it out and circulated it among his friends. In the following passage, concluding the oration, he implores Antony not to tread in Cæsar's footsteps.

. . . The name of peace is sweet, the thing itself is most salutary. But between peace and slavery there is a wide difference. Peace is liberty in tranquillity; slavery is the worst of all evils — to be repelled, if need be, not only by war, but even by death. But if those deliverers of ours have taken themselves away out of our sight, still they have left behind the example of their conduct. They have done what no one else has done. Brutus pursued Tarquinius,[1] who was a king when it was lawful for a king to exist in Rome. Spurius Cassius,[2] Spurius Mælius,[3] and Marcus Manlius [4] were all slain because they were suspected of aiming at regal power. These are the first men who have ever ventured to attack, sword in hand, a man who was not aiming at regal power, but actually reigning. And their action is not only of itself a glorious and godlike exploit, but it is also one put forth for our imitation; especially since by it they have acquired such glory as appears hardly to be bounded by heaven itself. . . .

Recollect then, O Marcus Antonius, that day on which you abolished the dictatorship. Set before you the joy of the Senate and people of Rome. Compare it with this infamous market held by you and by your friends; and then you will understand how great is the difference between praise and profit. But, in truth, just as some people, through some disease which has blunted the senses, have no conception of the niceness of food, so men who are lustful, avaricious, and criminal, have no taste for true glory. But if praise can not allure you to act rightly, still can not even fear turn you away from the most shameful actions? . . .

[1] See pages 160–161.

[2] Spurius Cassius, the leading statesman of the early republic, was put to death in 485 B. C. on the charge of treason to the state.

[3] Mælius was a rich plebeian accused of conspiring to overthrow the republic (439 B. C.).

[4] See pages 171–172.

But if you are not afraid of brave men and illustrious citizens, because they are prevented from attacking you by your armed retinue, still, believe me, your own fellows will not long endure you. And what a life it is, day and night to be fearing danger from one's own people! Unless, indeed, you have men who are bound to you by greater kindnesses than some of those men by whom he was slain were bound to Cæsar; or unless there are points in which you can be compared with him.

In that man were combined genius, method, memory, literature, prudence, deliberation, and industry. He had performed exploits in war which, though calamitous for the republic, were nevertheless mighty deeds. Having for many years aimed at being king, he had, with great labor and much personal danger, accomplished what he intended. He had conciliated the ignorant multitude by presents, by monuments, by gifts of food, and by banquets. He had bound his own party to him by rewards, and his adversaries by the appearance of clemency. Why need I say much on such a subject? He had already brought a free city, partly by fear, partly by patience, into a habit of slavery. With him I can, indeed, compare you as to your desire to reign; but in all other respects you are in no degree to be compared with him. . . .

Consider, I beg you, Marcus Antonius, do some time or other consider the republic. Think of the family of which you are born, not of the men with whom you are living. Be reconciled to the republic. However, do you decide on your conduct. As for mine, I myself will declare what that shall be. I defended the republic as a young man; I will not abandon it now that I am old. I scorned the sword of Catiline; I will not quail before yours. No, I will rather cheerfully expose my own person, if the liberty of the city can be restored by my death.

May the indignation of the Roman people at last bring forth what it has been so long laboring with. In truth, if twenty years ago·in this very temple I asserted that death could not come prematurely upon a man of consular rank, with how much more truth must I now say the same of an old man? To me, indeed,

O conscript fathers, death is now even desirable, after all the honors which I have gained and the deeds which I have done. I only pray for these two things: one, that dying, I may leave the Roman people free. No greater boon than this can be granted me by the immortal gods. The other, that every one may meet with a fate suitable to his deserts and conduct toward the republic.

These *Philippics* were the last orations ever delivered by Cicero, and the last voice, as well, of republican Rome. When Antony united with Lepidus and the young Octavius in the Second Triumvirate, Cicero was one of his first victims. Hired assassins, headed by Papillius, a tribune, and Herennius, a centurion, tracked the old man to his country seat at Caieta. "A youth who had been educated by Cicero in the liberal arts and sciences . . . informed the tribune that Cicero in a litter was on his way to the sea. The tribune, taking a few with him, ran to the place where he was to come out. Cicero, perceiving Herennius running in the path, commanded his servants to set down the litter. Stroking his chin, as he used to do, with his left hand, he looked steadfastly at his murderers, his person covered with dust, his beard and hair untrimmed, and his face worn with his troubles. The greater number of those that stood by covered their faces while Herennius slew him. And thus was he murdered, stretching forth his neck out of the litter. He was in his sixty-fourth year. Herennius cut off his head, and, by Antony's command, his hands also, by which his *Philippics* were written; for so Cicero styled those orations he wrote against Antony, and so they are called to this day. . . . Antony commanded that the head and hands be fastened up over the Rostra, where the orators spoke; a sight which the Roman people shuddered to behold. They believed they saw there not the face of Cicero, but the image of Antony's own soul. Some long time after, Cæsar,[1] I have been told, visiting one of his daughter's sons, found him with a book of Cicero's in his hand. The boy for fear endeavored to hide it under his gown; which Cæsar perceiving, took it from him, and, turning over a great part of the book gave it to him again, and said, 'My child, this was a great orator, and a man who loved his country well.'" [2]

[1] Octavius, afterwards Cæsar Augustus.
[2] Plutarch, *Cicero*, 48–49.

# CHAPTER XVIII

## THE CONQUEST OF GAUL, RELATED BY CÆSAR [1]

THE *Commentaries on the Gallic War* by Julius Cæsar is a book of unique interest. The greatest Roman of his time describes in it the wonderfully successful campaigns by which he extended the dominion of Rome over western Europe to the North Sea and the Rhine. Cæsar was brought in contact with the inhabitants of this region during the years 58–51 B. C. When Cæsar had finished his work, all Gaul had been added to the Roman Empire and a beginning had been made toward its subsequent extension over part of Germany and Britain.

### 90. The First Invasion of Germany [2]

In 58 B. C. Cæsar proceeded to his province of Transalpine Gaul and there immediately found himself confronted with a serious situation. The Helvetii, inhabitants of northern Switzerland, were then attempting an armed immigration through the heart of the Roman territories. Cæsar met them with his legions and hurled back the tide of invasion at the cost of more than two hundred thousand barbarian lives. Later in the same year, he expelled from Gaul and drove across the Rhine a German people under their king Ariovistus. During his second year as governor (57 B. C.), Cæsar was engaged in

---

[1] *Cæsar's Commentaries on the Gallic War*, translated by T. R. Holmes. London, 1908. Macmillan and Co.

[2] Cæsar, *Commentaries on the Gallic War*, iv, 17–19.

subduing the inhabitants of northern Gaul (modern Belgium). The third year (56 B. C.) saw a campaign against
the Veneti, a warlike people living in the peninsula of Brit-
tany. Though the Veneti were expert sailors, Cæsar
built a navy, met them on the sea, administered a
sharp defeat, and reduced the entire nation to slavery. The *Commentaries* for the year 55 B. C. relate two
events of commanding interest — the invasion of Germany
and the expedition to Britain. The hurried inroad into
Germany fixed the Rhine as the military frontier between
the Roman Empire and the barbarian world.

Cæsar was determined to cross the Rhine, but he thought it
hardly safe to pass over in boats, and considered that to do so
would not be consistent with his own dignity or that of the
Roman people. Although the construction of a bridge presented great difficulties, on account of the breadth, swiftness,
and depth of the stream, he nevertheless thought best to make
the attempt, or else not to cross at all. . . .

Within ten days after the collection of the timber began, the
whole work was finished, and the army crossed over.[1]  Cæsar
left a strong force at both ends of the bridge, and marched
rapidly for the country of the Sugambri. Meanwhile, envoys
came in from several tribes; and Cæsar replied graciously to
their prayer for peace and friendship and directed them to bring
him hostages. But the Sugambri, who from the moment when
the construction of the bridge began . . . had prepared for
flight, left their country with all their belongings, and hid
themselves in the recesses of the forests.

Cæsar remained a few days in their country, burned all their
villages and homesteads, cut down their corn, and returned to the
territory of the Ubii. Promising to help them in case they were
molested by the Suebi, he ascertained from them that the Suebi,

[1] Cæsar's passage of the Rhine was probably between Andernach and
Coblenz.

on learning from their scouts that the bridge was being made, had
called a council according to their custom, and had sent messengers in all directions, bidding the people to abandon the
strongholds, convey their wives and children and all their belongings into the forests, and assemble — all of them who could
bear arms— at a fixed place. . . . Here they were waiting the
arrival of the Romans, and here they had determined to fight a
decisive battle.    Cæsar had now achieved every object for which
he had determined to lead his army across — he had overawed
the  Germans, punished the Sugambri, and relieved the Ubii
from hostile pressure.    He felt, therefore, that honor was
satisfied and that he had served every useful purpose.    Accordingly, when he heard the news about the Suebi, he returned to
Gaul, having spent just eighteen days on the further side of the
Rhine, and destroyed the bridge.

### 91. The First Invasion of Britain [1]

Upon his return from the foray into Germany, Cæsar
made his famous expedition to Britain.    Until this time
the country had remained almost entirely unknown to the
Greeks and Romans.    Cæsar's landing in Britain is thus of
much historical interest, although it did not lead immediately to the conquest of the island.

Cæsar took advantage of favorable weather and set sail
about the third watch, having first directed the cavalry to march
to the further harbor, embark there, and follow him.    They
were rather slow in getting through their work; but Cæsar,
with the leading ships, reached Britain about the fourth hour;
and there, standing in full view on all the heights, he saw an
armed force of the enemy.    The formation of the ground was
peculiar, the sea being so closely walled in by abrupt heights
that it was possible to throw a missile from the ground above
onto the shore.    Cæsar thought the place most unsuitable for

[1] Cæsar, *Commentaries on the Gallic War*, iv, 23–26.

landing, and accordingly remained till the ninth hour, waiting at anchor for the other ships to join him.

Cæsar, meanwhile, assembled the generals and tribunes . . . and explained his own plans, charging them to bear in mind the requirements of war and particularly of seamanship, involving as it did rapid and irregular movements, and to see that all orders were carried out smartly and at the right moment.  The officers then dispersed.  When wind and tide were together in his favor, Cæsar gave the signal, weighed anchor, and, sailing on about seven miles further, ran the ships aground on an open and evenly-shelving shore.[1]

The natives knew what the Romans intended.  Sending on ahead their cavalry and charioteers — a kind of warriors whom they habitually employ in action — they followed with the rest of their force and attempted to prevent our men from disembarking.  It was very difficult to land, for these reasons.  The size of the ships made it impossible for them to approach except in deep water; the soldiers did not know the ground, and with their hands loaded, and weighted by their heavy, cumbrous armor, they had to jump down from the ships, keep their foothold in the surf, and fight the enemy all at once.  The enemy, on the contrary, had all their limbs free, they knew the ground perfectly, and standing on dry land or moving forward a little into the water, they threw their missiles boldly and drove their horses into the sea, which they were trained to enter. Our men were unnerved by the situation.  Having no experience of this kind of warfare, they did not show the same dash and energy that they generally did in battles on land.

Cæsar, noticing this, ordered the galleys, with the look of which the natives were not familiar, and which were easier to handle, to sheer off a little from the transports, row hard, and range alongside of the enemy's flank.  Slingers, archers, and artillery were to shoot from their decks and drive the enemy out of the way.  This manœuvre was of great service to our men.

[1] The landing was between Deal and Walmer near the white cliffs of Dover; the date, August 26, 55 B. C.

The natives, alarmed by the build of the ships, the motion of the oars, and the strangeness of the artillery, stood still, and then drew back a little. And now, as our soldiers were hesitating, chiefly because of the depth of the water, the standard-bearer of the 10th legion, praying that his attempt might redound to the success of the legion, cried, "Leap down, men, unless you want to abandon the eagle to the enemy. I, at all events, shall have done my duty to my country and my general." Uttering these words in a loud voice, he threw himself overboard and advanced, bearing the eagle, against the foe. Then, calling upon each other not to suffer such a disgrace, the men leaped all together from the ship. Seeing this, their comrades in the nearest ships followed them, and moved close up to the enemy.

There was fierce fighting on both sides. Our men, however, were in great confusion, because they could not keep their ranks unbroken or get firm foothold or follow their respective standards. . . . The enemy, on the other hand, knew all the shallows. When, from their standpoint on shore they saw a few men disembarking one by one, they urged on their horses and . . . attacked them before the Romans were ready. Others again got on the exposed flank of an entire company and plied them with missiles. Cæsar, noticing this, ordered the men-of-war's boats and also the scouts to be manned, and, whenever he saw any of his soldiers in difficulties, sent them to the rescue. Our men, as soon as they got upon dry land, followed by all their comrades, charged the enemy and put them to flight, but could not pursue them far, because the cavalry had not been able to keep their course and make the island. This was the only drawback to Cæsar's usual good fortune.

## 92. Britain and Its Inhabitants [1]

After holding a difficult position in Britain for about three weeks, Cæsar was glad to make peace with its war-

[1] Cæsar, *Commentaries on the Gallic War*, v, 12-14.

like natives and to return with his fleet to Gaul. The following year (54 B. C.) he again visited Britain. If his two months' stay in the island led to no lasting conquests, it added considerably to the Roman knowledge of the country and its people.

The interior of Britain is inhabited by a people who, according to oral tradition . . . are aboriginal; the maritime districts by immigrants who crossed over from Belgium to plunder and attack the aborigines. . . . When the war was over, they remained in the country and settled down as tillers of the soil. The population is immense. Homesteads, closely resembling those of the Gauls, are met with at every turn; and cattle are very numerous. Gold coins are in use, or, instead of coins, iron bars of fixed weight.[1] Tin is found in the country in the inland, and iron in the maritime, districts, but the latter only in small quantities; bronze is imported. Trees exist, of all the varieties which occur in Gaul, except the beech and the fir. Hares, fowls, and geese they think it impious to taste; but they keep them for pastime or amusement. The climate is more equable than in Gaul, the cold being less severe.

The island is triangular in shape, one side being opposite Gaul. One corner of this side, by Kent — the landing-place for almost all ships from Gaul — has an easterly, and the lower one a southerly aspect. The extent of this side is about five hundred miles. The second trends westward toward Spain.[2] Off the coast here is Ireland, which is considered only half as large as Britain, though the passage is equal in length to that between Britain and Gaul. Halfway across is an island called Man; and several smaller islands also are believed to be situated opposite this coast. . . .

By far the most civilized of all the natives are the inhabitants of Kent . . . whose culture does not differ much from that of the Gauls. The people of the interior do not, for the most

[1] Many of these iron bars have been found in hoards.
[2] A curious geographical error.

part, cultivate grain, but live on milk and flesh-meat, and clothe themselves with skins. All the Britons, without exception, stain themselves with woad, which produces a bluish tint; and this gives them a wild look in battle. They wear their hair long, and shave the whole of their body except the head and the upper lip. . . .

### 93. The Gauls[1]

Throughout Gaul there are two classes of that part of the population which is of any account or rank. The common people are regarded almost as slaves. They never venture to act on their own initiative, and are not admitted to any council. Generally, when crushed by debt, heavy taxation, or ill treatment by powerful individuals, they bind themselves to serve men of rank, who exercise over them all the rights that masters have over their slaves.

One of these two classes consists of the Druids, the other of the Knights. The former officiate at the worship of the gods, regulate sacrifices, private as well as public, and expound questions of religion. Young men resort to them in large numbers for study, and the people hold them in great respect. They are judges in nearly all disputes, whether between tribes or individuals. When a crime is committed, when a murder takes place, when a dispute arises about inherited property or boundaries, the Druids settle the matter and fix the awards and fines. If any ligitant, whether an individual or a tribe, does not abide by their decision, they excommunicate the offender — the heaviest punishment which they can inflict. Persons who are under such a sentence are looked upon as impious monsters; everybody avoids them, everybody shuns their approach and conversation, for fear of incurring pollution. . . .

The Druids, as a rule, take no part in war, and do not pay taxes like the rest of their countrymen. They also enjoy exemption from military service and immunity from all burdens. Attracted by these great privileges, many persons voluntarily

[1] Cæsar, *Commentaries on the Gallic War*, vi, 13–16.

come to learn from them, while many are sent by their parents and relatives. During their novitiate it is said that they learn by heart a great number of verses; and accordingly some remain twenty years under instruction. It is against the principles of the Druids to commit their doctrines to writing, though, for most other purposes, such as public and private documents, they use Greek characters. They seem to me to have established this custom for two reasons. They neither wish their doctrines to become common property, nor their disciples to trust to documents and neglect to cultivate their memories. For with most people it usually happens that, if they rely upon documents, they become less diligent in study and their memory is weakened. A doctrine which the Druids are very earnest in inculcating is that the soul does not perish, but that after death it passes from one body to another.[1] They regard this belief as a powerful incentive to valor, since it inspires a contempt for death. They also hold long discussions about the heavenly bodies and their motions, the size of the universe and of the earth, the origin of all things, and the might and power of the immortal gods. . . .

The second of the two classes consists of the Knights. On occasion, when war breaks out, as happened almost every year before Cæsar's arrival . . . they all take the field, and surround themselves with as many armed servants and retainers as their birth and resources permit. This is the only sign of influence and power which they recognize.

The Gallic people, in general, are remarkably addicted to religious observances. . . . They have colossal images the limbs of which, made of wickerwork, they fill with living men and set on fire; and the victims perish, encompassed by the flames. They regard it as more acceptable to the gods to punish those who are caught in the commission of theft, robbery, or any other crime; but in default of criminals, they actually resort to the sacrifice of the innocent.

[1] The Egyptians had similar ideas of the transmigration of souls. See page 5.

## 94. The Germans[1]

The manners and customs of the Germans differ widely from those just described. They have no Druids to preside over public worship, and care nothing for sacrifices. The only deities whom they recognize are those whom they can see, and from whose power they derive manifest benefit, namely, Sun, Moon, and Fire: the rest they have not even heard of. Their lives are passed entirely in hunting and warlike pursuits; and from infancy they are inured to toil and hardship. . . .

The Germans are not an agricultural people, and live principally upon milk, cheese, and meat. Nobody possesses any land of his own. The authorities and chieftains annually assign to the several clans and groups of kinsmen, as much land as they think proper, in whatever quarter they please, and in the following year compel them to remove to another place. . . .

The greatest distinction which a tribe can have is to be surrounded by as wide a belt as possible of waste and desert land. They regard it as a tribute to their valor that the neighboring peoples should be dispossessed and that no one should venture to settle in their vicinity. At the same time they count on gaining additional security by being relieved from the fear of sudden raids. When a tribe has to repel or make an attack, officers are chosen to conduct the campaign and are invested with powers of life and death. In time of peace there is no central magistracy. The chiefs of the various districts and cantons administer justice and settle disputes among their own people. No discredit attaches to predatory expeditions outside the tribal boundary. The people tell you that they are undertaken in order to keep the young men in training and to prevent laziness. Whenever any of the chiefs announces in the assembly his intention of leading an expedition, and calls for volunteers, those who approve the enterprise and the leader stand up and promise to help, and the whole gathering applauds them. Individuals who do not follow their leader are counted as deserters

[1] Cæsar, *Commentaries on the Gallic War*, vi, 21–23, 25–28.

and traitors, and thenceforth are no longer trusted. To ill-treat a guest is regarded as a crime: those who visit them, from whatever motive, they shield from injury and regard their persons as sacred; every man's house is open to them, and they are welcomed at meals. . . .

The Hercynian forest [1] extends over an area which a man traveling without encumbrance requires nine days to traverse. There is no other way of defining its extent, and the natives have no standards of measurement. . . . It is known to produce many kinds of wild animals which have never been seen elsewhere. The following, on account of their strongly marked characteristics, seem worthy of mention.

There is a species of ox, shaped like a stag, with a single horn standing out between its ears from the middle of its forehead, higher and straighter than horns as we know them. Tines spread out wide from the top, like hands and branches. The characteristics of the male and female are identical, and so are the shape and size of their horns. [2]

Again, there are elks, so-called, which resemble goats in shape and in having piebald coats, but are rather larger. They have blunt horns, and their legs have no knots or joints. [3] They do not lie down to sleep; and if by any chance they are knocked down, they cannot stand up again, or even raise themselves. Their resting-places are trees, against which they lean, and thus rest in a partially recumbent position. Hunters mark their usual lair from their tracks, and uproot or cut deep into all the trees in the neighborhood, so that they just look as if they were standing. The animals lean against them as usual, upset the weakened trunks by their mere weight, and fall down along with them.

There is a third species, called aurochs, [4] a little smaller than

---

[1] Extending from the Black Forest to the highlands of Bohemia.

[2] This animal was probably the reindeer, which, however, has a pair of antlers, not one only.

[3] Caesar, of course, was mistaken in saying that elks have no joints.

[4] The aurochs was the primitive ox which roamed wild in Britain and western Europe during prehistoric times.

elephants, having the appearance, color, and shape of bulls. They are very strong and swift, and attack every man and beast they catch sight of. The natives carefully trap them in pits and kill them. Young men engage in the sport, hardening their muscles by the exercise; and those who kill the largest head of game exhibit the horns as a trophy, and thereby earn high honor. These animals, even when caught young, cannot be domesticated and tamed. Their horns, in size, shape, and appearance, differ widely from those of our oxen. The natives, who are fond of collecting the horns, mount them round the rim with silver and use them as drinking-cups at grand banquets.

### 95. Vercingetorix and the Last Struggle of the Gauls [1]

Cæsar's expeditions to Britain during the years 55-54 B. C. had the result of exposing his conquests in Gaul itself to extreme peril. The strength of the Gallic resistance lay in the north and east where the Belgian tribes still proved irreconcilable foes. By a series of swift campaigns the turbulent natives were once more reduced to submission and Cæsar was left free to make another invasion of Germany for the purpose of punishing the German allies of the Gallic tribes (53 B. C.). But the insurrectionary movement was by no means crushed. The next year (52 B. C.) he had to face a grand, confederate revolt of the Gauls under the leadership of their hero, Vercingetorix. It seemed, for a time, that all of Cæsar's conquests in the previous campaigns would be lost. At length, however, Vercingetorix was shut up in the city of Alesia and there besieged by the Romans. When the defenders of the city had come to the verge of famine, an army of rescue, gathered from all parts of Gaul, suddenly appeared before Cæsar's lines. Vercingetorix now seized the opportunity for a sortie from the city against the Roman works.

[1] Cæsar, *Commentaries on the Gallic War*, vii, 84-89.

Observing his countrymen from the citadel of Alesia, Vercingetorix moved out of the town, taking from the camp the long pikes, sappers' huts, grappling-hooks, and other implements which he had prepared for the sortie. Fighting went on simultaneously at every point; and the besieged tried every expedient, concentrating their strength on the weakest points. The Roman forces, being strung out over lines of vast extent, found it hard to move to several points at once. The shouts of the combatants in their rear had a serious effect in unnerving the men, who saw that their own lives were staked upon the courage of others; for men are generally disquieted most by the unseen.

Cæsar found a good position, from which he observed all the phases of the action and reinforced those who were in difficulties. Both sides saw that now was the moment for a supreme effort. The Gauls utterly despaired of safety unless they could break the lines. The Romans, if they could but hold their ground, looked forward to the end of all their toils. The struggle was most severe at the entrenchments on the high ground, against which Vercassivelaunus[1] had been sent. . . . Some of the assailants showered in missiles, while others locked their shields above their heads and advanced to the assault; and when they were tired, fresh men took their places. The entire force shot earth against the fortifications, which at once enabled the Gauls to ascend and buried the obstacles which the Romans had hidden in the ground. And now weapons, and strength to use them, were failing our men.

On learning the state of affairs, Cæsar sent Labienus with six cohorts[2] to rescue the hard-pressed garrison, telling him, in case he could not hold out, to marshal the cohorts and charge, but only as a forlorn hope. Visiting the other divisions in person, he exhorted them not to give up. On that day, he told them, on that hour, was staked the prize of all past combats.

[1] One of the leaders of the Gauls.

[2] Cæsar's army in the field was divided into legions, and each legion into 10 cohorts or battalions.

The besieged, abandoning the hope of forcing the formidable works in the plain, took the implements which they had prepared and attempted to storm a steep ascent. With a hail of missiles they drove off the men who defended the towers, filled up the trenches with earth and hurdles, and with their grappling-hooks tore down the rampart and breastworks.

Cæsar first sent the younger Brutus with a number of cohorts and afterwards Gaius Fabius with others. Finally, as the struggle grew fiercer, he led a fresh detachment in person to the rescue. Having restored the battle and beaten off the enemy, he hastened to the point to which he had dispatched Labienus. He withdrew four cohorts from the nearest redoubt and ordered part of the cavalry to follow him and part to ride round the outer lines, and attack the enemy in the rear. Labienus, finding that neither rampart nor trench could check the enemy's onslaught, massed eleven cohorts, which he was fortunately able to withdraw from the nearest guard-posts, and sent messengers to let Cæsar know what he intended. Cæsar hastened to take part in the action.

The enemy knew that he was coming from the color of his cloak, which he generally wore in action to mark his identity. . . . Both sides raised a cheer, and the cheering was taken up along the rampart and the whole extent of the lines. Our men dropped their javelins and plied their swords. Suddenly the cavalry was seen on the enemy's rear: the fresh cohorts came up; the enemy took to flight; and the cavalry charged the fugitives. The carnage was great. . . . Few of that mighty host got safely back to camp. . . .

Next day Vercingetorix called a council. He explained that he had undertaken the war, not for private ends, but in the cause of national freedom. Since they must needs bow to fortune, he would submit to whichever alternative they preferred — either to appease the Romans by putting him to death or to surrender him alive. Envoys were sent to refer the question to Cæsar. He ordered the arms to be surrendered and the leaders brought out. The officers were conducted to the intrenchment in front of his camp, where he was seated. Vercingetorix surrendered, and all weapons were laid down. Cæsar allotted one prisoner by way of prize to every man in the army. . . .

With the decisive victory at Alesia and the surrender of Vercingetorix, Cæsar brings his narrative to an end. Six years later, when the conqueror celebrated a triumph at Rome for his victories throughout the world, the Gallic chieftain walked a captive in the splendid procession, and at its conclusion, suffered death. Such pity had Cæsar for a valiant foe.

# CHAPTER XIX

## THE MAKERS OF IMPERIAL ROME: CHARACTER SKETCHES BY SUETONIUS[1]

GAIUS SUETONIUS TRANQUILLUS (about 75–160 A. D.) was fortunate in passing a lifetime during those unclouded years of the Early Empire, when Nerva, Trajan, and Hadrian occupied the throne. Though the greater part of his voluminous writings are lost, we possess intact his *Lives of the Twelve Cæsars*. The book is one of the last productions of classic Latin prose. It begins with Julius Cæsar and ends with Domitian. The work cannot be considered a serious historical composition. It is rather a collection of personal sketches drawn with vividness and impartiality. Much of it, indeed, is gossip, but the gossip concerns the mightiest line of rulers that the world has ever known.

### 96. Julius Cæsar[2]

It is said that he was tall, of a fair complexion, round-limbed, rather full-faced, with eyes black and piercing. He enjoyed excellent health, except toward the close of his life, when he was subject to sudden fainting-fits, and disturbance in his sleep. He was likewise twice seized with the falling sickness while engaged in active service. He was so nice in the care of his person, that he not only kept the hair of his head closely cut and had his face smoothly shaved, but even caused the hair on other

---

[1] Suetonius, *The Lives of the Twelve Cæsars*. The translation of Alexander Thomson, revised by T. Forester. London, 1855. George Bell and Sons.

[2] Suetonius, *Julius Cæsar*, 45, 55–57, 60, 63–64, 74, 76.

parts of the body to be plucked out by the roots. This was a practice for which some persons rallied him. His baldness gave him much uneasiness, having often found himself upon that account exposed to the jibes of his enemies. He therefore used to bring forward the hair from the crown of his head. Of all the honors conferred upon him by the Senate and people, there was none which he either accepted or used with greater pleasure than the right of wearing constantly a laurel crown. It is said that he was particular in his dress, using the *latus clavus* [1] with fringes about the wrists, and always had it girded about him, but rather loosely. This circumstance gave origin to the expression of Sulla, who often advised the nobles to beware of "the ill-girt boy." . . .

In eloquence and warlike achievements, he equaled, at least, if he did not surpass, the greatest of men. . . . Cicero, in recounting to Brutus the famous orators, declares that he does not see that Cæsar was inferior to any one of them; and adds that "Cæsar had an elegant, splendid, noble, and magnificent vein of eloquence." . . . In his delivery Cæsar is said to have had a shrill voice. His action was animated, but not ungraceful. He has left behind him some speeches, among which are ranked a few that are not genuine. . . .

He has likewise left *Commentaries* of his own actions both in the war in Gaul and in the civil war with Pompey. . . . Of these productions Cicero, in one of his works speaks thus, "He wrote his *Commentaries* in a manner deserving of great approbation: they are plain, precise, and elegant, without any affectation of rhetorical ornament." . . .

He was perfect in the use of arms, an accomplished rider, and able to endure fatigue beyond all belief. On a march, he used to go at the head of his troops, sometimes on horseback, but oftener on foot, with his head bare in all kinds of weather. He would travel post in a light carriage without baggage, at the rate of a hundred miles a day. If he was stopped by floods in the rivers, he swam across, or floated on skins inflated with

[1] A broad strip of purple worn on the front of the toga.

wind, so that he often anticipated intelligence of his movements. . . . He not only fought pitched battles, but made
sudden attacks when an opportunity offered; often at the end
of a march, and sometimes during the most violent storms,
when nobody would imagine he could stir. Nor was he ever
backward in fighting, until toward the end of his life. . . . He
never defeated the enemy without driving them from their
camp and giving them no time to rally their forces. When
the issue of a battle was doubtful, he sent away all the horses,
and his own first, that having no means of flight, his men might
be under the greater necessity of standing their ground. . . .

The following are remarkable instances of his resolution.
After the battle of Pharsalus, having sent his troops before him
into Asia, he was passing the strait of the Hellespont in a ferry-
boat. Here he met Lucius Cassius, one of the opposite party,
with ten ships of war. So far from endeavoring to escape,
Cæsar went alongside his ship and called upon him to surrender. Cassius humbly gave him his submission. At Alexandria, in the attack of a bridge, he was forced by a sudden
sally of the enemy into a boat. Several others hurrying in
with him, he leaped into the sea, and saved himself by swimming to the next ship, which lay at the distance of two hundred
paces. In this exploit he held his left hand out of the water,
for fear of wetting some papers which he held in it; and pulled
his general's cloak after him with his teeth, lest it should fall
into the hands of the enemy. . . .

His temper was naturally averse to severity in retaliation.
After he had captured some pirates, by whom he had been taken,
having sworn that he would crucify them, he did so indeed;
but he first ordered their throats to be cut.[1] He could never
bear the thought of doing any harm to Cornelius Phagitas, who
had dogged him in the night when he was sick and a fugitive,
with the design of carrying him to Sulla, and from whose hands
he had escaped with some difficulty by giving him a bribe.
Philemon, his amanuensis, who had promised his enemies to

[1] To save them from the torture of a lingering death.

poison him, he put to death without torture. When he was summoned as a witness against Publius Clodius, who was prosecuted for the profanation of religious ceremonies, he declared he knew nothing of the affair, although his mother Aurelia and his sister Julia gave the court an exact and full account of the circumstances. And being asked why then he had divorced his wife, he said, "Because my family should not only be free from guilt, but even from the suspicion of it." . . .

His other words and actions, however, so far outweigh all his good qualities, that it is thought he abused his power and was justly cut off. For he not only obtained excessive honors, such as the consulship every year, the dictatorship for life, and the censorship, but also the title of emperor and the surname of FATHER OF HIS COUNTRY . . . . He even suffered some honors to be decreed to him, which were unbefitting the most exalted of mankind; such as a gilded chair of state in the Senate-house, a consecrated chariot, altars, statues among the gods, a bed of state in the temples, a priest, and a college of priests dedicated to himself. He also allowed one of the months to be called by his name. There were, indeed, no honors which he did not either assume himself or grant to others, at his will and pleasure. . . .

### 97. Cæsar Augustus [1]

. . . He lost his mother in his first consulship, and his sister Octavia, when he was in the fifty-fourth year of his age. He behaved toward them both with the utmost kindness while they were alive, and after their decease paid the highest honors to their memory. . . .

In bringing up his daughter and granddaughters, he accustomed them to domestic employments, even to spinning. He also obliged them to speak and act everything openly before the family, that it might be put down in the diary. He so strictly prohibited them from all converse with strangers, that he once wrote a letter to Lucius Vinicius, a handsome young man of a

[1] Suetonius, *Cæsar Augustus*, 61, 64, 66–67, 72–77, 79, 84–85, 90.

good family, in which he told him, "You have not behaved very modestly, in making a visit to my daughter at Baiæ." [1]   He usually instructed his grandsons himself in reading, swimming, and other rudiments of knowledge.   He never supped but he had them sitting at the foot of his couch.   He never traveled but with them in a chariot before him, or riding beside him. . . .

He was cautious in forming friendships, but clung to them with great constancy. . . . He expected from his friends, at their deaths as well as during their lives, some proofs of their reciprocal attachment.   Though he was far from coveting their property, and indeed would never accept any legacy left him by a stranger, yet he pondered in a melancholy mood over their last words.   He was not able to conceal his chagrin, if in their wills they made but a slight, or no very honorable, mention of him, nor his joy, on the other hand, if they expressed a grateful sense of his favors and a hearty affection for him.   Whatever legacies or shares of their property were left him by such as were parents, he used to restore with interest to their children. He did  this either immediately, or if they were under age, upon the day of their assuming the manly dress, or of their marriage.

As a patron and master, his behavior in general was mild and conciliating;  but when occasion required it, he could be severe. . . . When his slave, Cosmos, had reflected bitterly upon him, he resented the injury no further than by putting him in fetters. When his steward, Diomedes, left him to the mercy of a wild boar, which suddenly attacked them while they were walking together, he considered it rather an act of cowardice than a breach of duty; and turned an occurrence of no small hazard into a jest, because there was no knavery in his steward's conduct. . . . He broke the legs of his secretary, Thallus, for accepting a bribe of five hundred *denarii* to discover the contents of one of his letters.   And when the tutor and other attendants of his son Gaius had taken advantage of his sickness and death, to give loose to their insolence and rapacity in the province

---

[1] A Roman summer-resort.   See page 231, note 2.

Gaius governed, he caused heavy weights to be tied about their necks, and had them thrown into a river. . . .

He was moderate in his habits, and free from suspicion of any kind of vice. He lived at first near the Roman Forum. . . . He afterwards moved to the Palatine Hill, where he resided in a small house . . . not remarkable either for size or ornament. For the piazzas were but small, the pillars of Alban stone, and the rooms without anything of marble or fine paving. . . . He had a particular aversion to large and sumptuous palaces. Some residences which had been raised at a vast expense by his granddaughter, Julia, he leveled to the ground. Those of his own, which were far from being spacious, he adorned, not so much with statues and pictures, as with walks, groves, and things which were curious either for their antiquity or rarity. . . .

His frugality in the furniture of his house appears even at this day, from some beds and tables still remaining, most of which are scarcely elegant enough for a private family. It is reported that he never lay upon a bed, but such as was low and meanly furnished. He seldom wore any garment but what was made by the hands of his wife, sister, daughter, and grand-daughters. His togas were neither scanty nor full; and the *clavus* [1] was neither remarkably broad or narrow. His shoes were a little higher than common, to make him appear taller than he was. He had always clothes and shoes, fit to appear in public, ready in his bed-chamber for any sudden occasion.

At his table, which was always plentiful and elegant, he constantly entertained company; but was very scrupulous in the choice of his guests, both as to rank and character. . . . He often came late to table and withdrew early; so that the company began supper before his arrival and continued at table after his departure. His entertainments consisted of three entrées, or at most of only six. But, if his fare was moderate, his courtesy was extreme. Those who were silent or talked in whispers, he encouraged to join in the general conversation. He also often

[1] See page 219, note 1.

had buffoons and stage players, or even low performers from the circus and itinerant humorists, to enliven the company.

Festivals and holidays he usually celebrated very expensively, but sometimes only with merriment. In the Saturnalia,[1] or at any other time when the fancy took him, he distributed to his company clothes, gold, and silver; sometimes coins of all sorts, even of the ancient kings of Rome and of foreign nations. Sometimes he would give nothing but towels, sponges, rakes, and tweezers, and other things of that kind, with tickets on them which were enigmatical and had a double meaning. . . .

He ate sparingly, and commonly used a plain diet. He was particularly fond of coarse bread, small fishes, new cheese made of cow's milk, and green figs of the sort which bear fruit twice a year. He did not wait for supper, but took food at any time and in any place, when he had an appetite. The following passages relative to this subject, I have transcribed from his letters. "I ate a little bread and some small dates, in my carriage." Again. "In returning home from the palace in my litter, I ate an ounce of bread, and a few raisins." Again. "No Jew, my dear Tiberius, ever keeps such a strict fast upon the Sabbath,[2] as I have to-day. While in the bath, and after the first hour of the night, I only ate two biscuits, before I began to be rubbed with oil." From this great indifference about his diet, he sometimes supped by himself, before his company began, or after they had finished, and would not touch a morsel at table with his guests. He was by nature extremely sparing in the use of wine. Of all wines, he gave the preference to the Rætian, but scarcely ever drank any in the daytime. Instead of drinking, he used to take a piece of bread dipped in

---

[1] A festival originally held on December 17th in honor of Saturnus, an ancient Roman deity. It became a general holiday, somewhat like our Christmas, and was celebrated with sacrifices, games, and the presentation of gifts. On this occasion all classes, including the slaves, who enjoyed temporary freedom, gave themselves up to feasting and mirthful license.

[2] The Jewish Sabbath, however, was not a day of fasting.

cold water, or a slice of cucumber, or some leaves of lettuce, or a green, sharp, juicy apple. . . .

In person he was handsome and graceful, through every period of his life. But he was negligent in his dress; and so careless about arranging his hair that he usually had it done in great haste, by several barbers at a time. His beard he sometimes clipped and sometimes shaved. He read or wrote during the operation. His countenance, either when talking or when silent, was calm and serene. . . . His eyes were bright and piercing. He was willing it should be thought that there was something of a divine vigor in them. He was likewise not a little pleased to see people, upon his looking steadfastly at them, lower their countenances, as if the sun shone in their eyes. . . .

From early youth he devoted himself with great diligence and application to the study of eloquence and the other liberal arts. In one of his wars, notwithstanding the weighty affairs in which he was engaged, he is said to have read, written, and declaimed every day. He never addressed the Senate, the people, or the army, except in a premeditated speech, though he did not lack the talent of speaking on the spur of the occasion. And lest his memory should fail him, as well as to prevent the loss of time in getting up his speeches, it was his general practice to recite them. . . .

He composed many tracts in prose on various subjects, some of which he read occasionally in the circle of his friends. . . . He likewise made some attempts at poetry. There is extant one book written by him in hexameter verse, of which both the subject and title is *Sicily*. There is also a book of *Epigrams*, no larger than the last, which he composed almost entirely while he was in the bath. These are all his poetical compositions. Though he began a tragedy with great zest, becoming dissatisfied with the style, he obliterated the whole. Upon his friends saying to him, "What is your *Ajax* doing?" he answered, "My *Ajax* has met with a sponge." . . .

We have the following account of him respecting his belief

in omens and other superstitions.  He had so great a dread of thunder and lightning that he always carried about him a seal's skin, by way of preservation.  And upon any apprehension of a violent storm, he would retire to some place of concealment in an under-ground vault; having formerly been terrified by a flash of lightning, while traveling in the night.

# CHAPTER XX

## NERO: A ROMAN EMPEROR[1]

AFTER Livy, the greatest of Roman historians is Cornelius Tacitus (about 55–117 A. D.). One of his earlier works was a charming biography of his father-in-law, Agricola, the conqueror of Britain. It contains an interesting sketch of the history of the island under Roman rule. Tacitus also published a brief treatise on Germany, its geography, and its peoples. But the crowning work of his life was a history of Rome from Tiberius to Domitian. Of this narrative, issued under the two titles of *Histories* and *Annals*, only about one half is extant. The loss of so much of it is one of the great calamities of literature. In reading Tacitus we must always remember that he belonged to the aristocratic circle of nobles who regarded the empire with the bitterest hatred and who found little but evil in the emperors themselves. Tacitus is a powerful writer, but he is as much a satirist as a historian. Even his account of Nero, that half-crazed wretch who for fourteen years sullied the imperial purple by his crimes, has probably been colored by the author's deep-seated prejudices. Few pages of Roman history, however, present greater interest and fascination.

### 98. Murder of Britannicus[2]

When a youth of seventeen, Nero obtained the throne through the influence of his mother, Agrippina. People,

[1] *The Annals of Tacitus*, translated by A. J. Church and W. J. Brodribb. London, 1882. Macmillan and Co.    [2] Tacitus, *Annals*, xiii, 15–17.

indeed, suspected that she had poisoned her husband, the emperor Claudius, in order to obtain the succession for Nero, who was her son by a former marriage. Agrippina meant to be the real ruler of the Roman world, but she soon discovered that Nero had a will and mind of his own. It was not long before mother and son were bitter enemies. Then Agrippina declared that she would espouse the cause of the young Britannicus, who, as the child of the emperor Claudius, had a better right to the throne than Nero himself.

Nero was confounded at this threat, and as the day was near on which Britannicus would complete his fourteenth year, he reflected, now on the domineering temper of his mother, and now again on the character of the young prince, which a trifling circumstance had lately tested. It was sufficient, however, to gain for Britannicus wide popularity. During the feast of Saturn,[1] amid other pastimes of his playmates, at a game of lot drawing for king, the lot fell to Nero, upon which he gave all his other companions different orders, and such as would not put them to the blush. When, however, he told Britannicus to step forward and begin a song, hoping for a laugh at the expense of a boy who knew nothing of sober, much less of riotous, society, the lad with perfect coolness commenced some verses which hinted at Nero's expulsion from his father's house and from supreme power. This procured him pity, which was the more conspicuous, as night with its merriment had stripped off all disguise. Nero saw the reproach and redoubled his hate.

Pressed by Agrippina's menaces, having no charge against his brother[2] and not daring openly to order his murder, Nero meditated a secret device. He directed poison to be prepared through the agency of Julius Pollio, tribune of one of the prætorian cohorts, who had in his custody a woman under sentence for poisoning, Locusta by name, with a great reputation for

[1] The Saturnalia. See page 224, note 1.
[2] More properly, stepbrother.

crime. That every one about the person of Britannicus should care nothing for right or honor, had long ago been provided for. He actually received his first dose of poison from his tutors, but it had no effect, as it was either rather weak or so qualified as not at once to prove deadly. But Nero, impatient at such slow progress in crime, threatened the tribune and ordered the poisoner to execution for prolonging his anxiety. . . . Then they promised that death should be as sudden as if it was the hurried work of the dagger, and a rapid poison of previously tested ingredients was prepared close to the emperor's chamber.

It was customary for the imperial princes to sit during their meals with other nobles of the same age, in the sight of their kinsfolk but at a table of their own. . . . There Britannicus was dining. As what he ate and drank was always tested by the taste of a select attendant, the following device was contrived. . . . A cup as yet harmless, but extremely hot and already tasted, was handed to Britannicus. Then, on his refusing it because of its warmth, poison was poured in with some cold water, and this so penetrated his entire frame that he lost both voice and breath. There was a stir among the company; some, taken by surprise, ran hither and thither, while those whose discernment was keener, remained motionless, with their eyes fixed on Nero. The emperor, who still reclined in seeming unconsciousness, said that this was a common occurrence, because of a periodical epilepsy with which Britannicus had been afflicted from his earliest infancy, and that his sight and senses would gradually return. As for Agrippina, her terror and confusion, though her countenance struggled to hide it, visibly showed that she was clearly just as innocent as was Octavia,[1] Britannicus' own sister. She saw, in fact, that she was robbed of her only remaining refuge, and that here was a precedent for parricide. Even Octavia, notwithstanding her youthful inexperience, had learned to hide her grief, her affection, and indeed every emotion. And so after a brief pause the company resumed its mirth.

[1] At this time she was already married to Nero.

One and the same night witnessed Britannicus' death and funeral, preparations having been already made for his obsequies, which were on a humble scale. . . .

## 99. Murder of Agrippina [1]

Britannicus was murdered in 55 A. D.   Four years later, Agrippina herself, stained by many crimes, fell a victim to her son.

. . . At last convinced that she would become too formidable Nero resolved to destroy her, merely deliberating whether it was to be accomplished by poison, or by the sword, or by any other violent means.   Poison at first seemed best, but, were it to be administered at the imperial table, the result could not be referred to chance after the recent circumstances of the death of Britannicus.   Again, to tamper with the servants of a woman who, from her familiarity with crime, was on her guard against treachery, appeared to be extremely difficult.   Then, too, she had fortified her constitution by the use of antidotes.   How, again, the dagger and its work were to be kept secret, no one could suggest, and it was feared, too, that whoever might be chosen to execute such a crime would spurn the order.

An ingenious suggestion was offered by Anicetus, a freedman, commander of the fleet at Misenum,[2] who had been tutor to Nero in boyhood and had a hatred of Agrippina which she reciprocated.   He explained that a vessel could be constructed, from which a part might by a contrivance be detached when out at sea, so as to plunge her unawares into the water. "Nothing," he said, "permitted accidents so much as the sea, and should she be overtaken by shipwreck, who would be so unfair as to impute to crime an offense committed by the winds and waves?   The emperor would add the honor of a temple and of shrines to the deceased lady, with every other display of filial affection."

[1] Tacitus, *Annals*, xiv, 3–5, 8–9.
[2] A promontory on the coast of Campania.

Nero liked the device, favored as it was, also, by the particular time, for he was celebrating Minerva's five days' festival [1] at Baiæ.[2] Thither he enticed his mother by repeated assurances that children ought to bear with the irritability of parents and to soothe their tempers. Nero wished thus to spread a rumor of reconciliation and to secure Agrippina's acceptance through feminine credulity, which easily believes what gives joy. As she approached, he went to the shore to meet her (she was coming from Antium [3]), welcomed her with outstretched hands, and conducted her to Bauli. This was the name of a country house, washed by a bay of the sea, between the promontory of Misenum and the Lucrine Lake. Here was a vessel distinguished from others by its equipment and seemingly meant to do honor to his mother. . . .

It was a night of brilliant starlight with the calm of a tranquil sea. . . . Agrippina had with her two of her intimate attendants, one of whom, Crepereius, stood near the helm, while Acerronia, reclining at Agrippina's feet as she reposed herself, spoke joyfully of Nero's full repentance and of the recovery of the mother's influence. The vessel had not gone far when at a given signal the ceiling of the place, which was loaded with a quantity of lead, fell in, and Crepereius was crushed and instantly killed. Agrippina and Acerronia were protected by the projecting sides of the couch, which happened to be too strong to yield under the weight. But this was not followed by the breaking up of the vessel; for all were bewildered, and those too, who were in the plot, were hindered by the unconscious majority. The crew then thought it best to throw the vessel on one side and so sink it, but they could not themselves promptly unite to face the emergency, and others, by counteracting the attempt, gave an opportunity of a gentler fall into the sea. Acerronia, however, who thoughtlessly exclaimed that she was Agrippina and implored help for the emperor's mother, was killed with

[1] On the 19th of March and the four following days.
[2] A celebrated bathing resort of the Romans, located on the promontory of Misenum.   [3] On the coast of Latium.

poles and oars, and such naval implements as chance offered. Agrippina was silent and was thus the less recognized; still, she received a wound in her shoulder. She swam away, then met some small boats which conveyed her to the Lucrine Lake, and so entered her house. . . .

The failure of the plot merely postponed the death of the intended victim. Anicetus, with a body of soldiers, was now dispatched to finish the bloody work.

Anicetus surrounded the house with a guard, and having burst open the gates, dragged off the slaves who met him, till he came to the door of her chamber. . . . A small lamp was in the room, and one slave-girl with Agrippina, who grew more and more anxious, as no messenger came from her son. . . . When the girl rose to depart, Agrippina exclaimed, "Do you also forsake me?" Looking around she saw Anicetus, who had with him the captain of the trireme, Herculeius, and Obaritus, a centurion of marines. "If," said she, "you have come to see me, take back word that I have recovered, but if you are here to do a crime, I believe nothing about my son; he has not ordered his mother's murder." The assassins closed in round her couch, and the captain of the trireme first struck her head violently with a club. Then with numerous wounds she was slain. . . .

Many years before Agrippina had anticipated this end for herself and had spurned the thought. For, when she consulted the astrologers about Nero, they replied that he would be emperor and kill his mother. "Let him kill her," she said, "provided he is emperor."

### 100. The Great Fire at Rome [1]

The disaster, whether accidental, or treacherously contrived by the emperor [2] . . . was, however, more dreadful than any other which has ever happened to Rome by the violence of fire.

---

[1] Tacitus, *Annals*, xv, 38–39, 43–44.

[2] The degree of Nero's responsibility for the fire of 64 A. D. will never be known. Assuming that the conflagration was caused by Nero, he could hardly have chosen a worse time than that at which it actually occurred

It had its beginning in that part of the Circus which adjoins the Palatine and Cælian hills, where, amid the shops containing inflammable wares, the conflagration broke out. It instantly became so fierce and so rapid from the wind that it seized in its grasp the entire length of the Circus. For here there were no houses fenced in by solid masonry, or temples surrounded by walls, or any other obstacle to interpose delay. The blaze in its fury ran first through the level portions of the city. Then, rising to the hills, while it again devastated every place below them, it outstripped all preventive measures; so rapid was the mischief and so completely at its mercy the city, with those narrow winding passages and irregular streets, which characterized old Rome. . . .

Nero at this time was at Antium, and did not return to Rome until the fire approached his house, which he had built to connect the palace with the gardens of Mæcenas. It could not, however, be stopped from devouring the palace, the house, and everything around it. However, to relieve the people, driven out homeless as they were, he threw open to them the Campus Martius and the public buildings of Agrippa, and even his own gardens, and raised temporary structures to receive the destitute multitude. Supplies of food were brought up from the neighboring towns, and the price of wheat was reduced to three sesterces [1] a peck. These acts, though popular, produced no effect, since a rumor had gone forth that, at the very time when the city was in flames, the emperor appeared on a private stage and sang of the destruction of Troy, comparing present misfortunes with the calamities of antiquity. . . .

Rome, meanwhile . . . was not built up, as it had been after its burning by the Gauls [2] without any regularity, but with rows of streets according to measurement, with broad thoroughfares, with a restriction on the height of houses, with open

(the night of July 18–19). There was a full moon on the previous night, and consequently Nero's agents would have run great risk of detection. From this circumstance it has been argued that the fire was accidental.

[1] About fifteen cents.          [2] See page 169.

spaces, and the further addition of colonnades as a protection to the frontage of the blocks of tenements. These colonnades Nero promised to erect at his own expense. . . . Such changes, which were liked for their utility, also added beauty to the new city. Some thought, however, that its old arrangement had been more conducive to health, inasmuch as the narrow streets, with the elevation of the roofs, were not equally penetrated by the sun's heat, while now the open space, unsheltered by any shade, was scorched by a fiercer glow.

Such, indeed, were the precautions of human wisdom. The next thing was to seek means of propitiating the gods, and recourse was had to the Sibylline books,[1] by the direction of which prayers were offered to Vulcan, Ceres, and Proserpine. Juno, too, was entreated by the matrons, first, in the Capitol, then on the nearest part of the coast, whence water was procured to sprinkle the fane and image of the goddess. And there were sacred banquets and nightly vigils celebrated by married women. . . .

But all human efforts, all the lavish gifts of the emperor, and the propitiations of the gods, did not banish the sinister belief that the conflagration was the result of an order. Consequently, to get rid of the report, Nero fastened the guilt and inflicted the most exquisite tortures on a class hated for their abominations, called Christians by the populace. Christus, from whom the name had its origin, suffered the extreme penalty during the reign of Tiberius, at the hands of one of our procurators, Pontius Pilatus.[2] A most mischievous superstition, thus checked for the moment, again broke out, not only in Judea, the first source of the evil, but even in Rome, where all things hideous and shameful from every part of the world find their center.[3] Accordingly, an arrest was first made of all who

---

[1] See page 178, note 1.      [2] Procurator of Syria, 26–36 A. D.

[3] The ignorance which Tacitus exhibits in regard to the Christians is the more remarkable because his friend, the Younger Pliny, had learned something about this new sect while a Roman governor in Asia Minor. See pages 250–252.

pleaded guilty. Then, upon their information, an immense multitude was convicted, not so much of the crime of firing the city, as of hatred against mankind. Mockery of every sort was added to their deaths. Covered with the skins of beasts, they were torn by dogs and perished, or were nailed to crosses, or were doomed to the flames and burnt, to serve as a nightly illumination when daylight had expired.

Nero offered his gardens for the spectacle, and was exhibiting a show in the Circus, while he mingled with the people in the dress of a charioteer or stood aloft on a car. Hence, even for criminals who deserve extreme and exemplary punishment, there arose a feeling of compassion; for it was not, as it seemed, for the public good, but to glut one man's cruelty, that they were being destroyed.

### 101. Death of Seneca [1]

Seneca, the famous Stoic philosopher, had been Nero's tutor and adviser from the emperor's earliest years. But the friendship of Nero was a dangerous possession. At last even Seneca had to face the doom which had already overtaken so many other noble Romans during those troubled times. He was accused of participation in a conspiracy against the emperor's life. The accusation was equivalent to condemnation. Nero sent him the imperial mandate to commit suicide.

Seneca, quite unmoved, asked for tablets on which to inscribe his will. On the centurion's refusal, Seneca turned to his friends, protesting that, as he was forbidden to reward them, he bequeathed to them the only, but still the noblest, possession yet remaining to him, the pattern of his life. If they remembered this, they would win a name for moral worth and steadfast friendship. At the same time he called them back from their tears to manly resolution, now with friendly talk, and now with the sterner language of rebuke. "Where," he asked again and

[1] Tacitus, *Annals*, xv, 62–64.

again, "are your maxims of philosophy, or the preparation of so many years' study against evils to come? Who knew not Nero's cruelty? After a mother's and a brother's murder, nothing remains but to add the destruction of a guardian and a tutor."

Having spoken these and like words, he embraced his wife. Then, softening awhile from the stern resolution of the hour, he begged and implored her to spare herself the burden of perpetual sorrow, and, in the contemplation of a life virtuously spent, to endure a husband's loss with honorable consolations. She declared, in answer, that she too had decided to die, and claimed for herself the blow of the executioner. Thereupon Seneca, not to thwart her noble ambition, from an affection which would not leave behind him for insult one whom he dearly loved, replied, "I have shown you ways of smoothing life; you prefer the glory of dying. I will not grudge you such a noble example. Let the fortitude of so courageous an end be alike in both of us, but let there be more in your decease to win fame." Then by one and the same stroke they sundered with a dagger the arteries of their arms. . . .

Nero, meanwhile, having no personal hatred against Paulina and not wishing to heighten the odium of his cruelty, forbade her death. At the soldiers' prompting, her slaves and freedmen bound up her arms and stanched the bleeding, but whether with her knowledge is doubtful. . . .

Seneca, meantime, as the tedious process of death still lingered on, begged Statius Annæus, whom he had long esteemed for his faithful friendship and medical skill, to produce a poison with which he had some time before provided himself. It was the same drug[1] which extinguished the life of those who were condemned by a public sentence of the people of Athens. It was brought to him and he drank it in vain, chilled as he was throughout his limbs, and his frame closed against the efficacy of the poison. At last he entered a pool of heated water, from which he sprinkled the nearest of his slaves, adding the exclama-

[1] The poison hemlock. See page 127.

tion, "I offer this liquid as a libation to Jupiter the Deliverer." [1]
He was then carried into a bath, with the steam of which he was
suffocated, and he was burnt without any of the usual funeral
rites. So he had directed in a codicil of his will, when even in
the height of his wealth and power he was thinking of his life's
close.

## 102. Death of Petronius [2]

The compulsory suicide of another victim of the emperor's hatred is thus described.

With regard to Gaius Petronius, I ought to dwell a little on
his character. His days he passed in sleep, his nights in the
business and pleasures of life. Indolence had raised him to
fame, as energy raises others, and he was reckoned not a de-
bauchee and spendthrift, like most of those who squandered
their substance, but a man of refined luxury. . . .

It happened at the time that the emperor was on his way to
Campania and that Petronius, after going as far as Cumæ,
was there detained. He bore no longer the suspense of fear or
of hope. Yet he did not fling away life with precipitate haste,
but having made an incision in his veins and then, according to
his humor, bound them up, he again opened them, while he
conversed with his friends, not in a serious strain or on topics
that might win for him the glory of courage. And he listened
to them as they repeated, not thoughts on the immortality of the
soul or on the theories of philosophers, but light poetry and
playful verses. To some of his slaves he gave liberal presents,
a flogging to others. He dined, indulged himself in sleep, that
death, though forced on him, might have a natural appearance.
Even in his will he did not, as did many in their last moments,
flatter Nero or Tigellinus or any other of the men in power.
On the contrary, he described fully the prince's shameful

---

[1] It was usual with Greeks, when a party broke up, to drink to Zeus the
Savior. Seneca, with gentle irony, imitates this custom in the hour of
death.

[2] *Tacitus, Annals*, xvi, 18–19.

excesses . . . and sent the account under seal to Nero. Then he broke his signet-ring, that it might not be subsequently available for imperiling others.

The history of Nero's reign by Tacitus, as it has come down to us, breaks off abruptly with the last two years unchronicled. From other historians we learn that at length the unbridled license and tyranny of Nero's career stirred up rebellion. The legions proclaimed a new emperor (Galba), and the Roman Senate, so long subservient to Nero, declared him an outlaw. He fled from Rome and took refuge in a house outside the city, belonging to his freedman, Phaon. Nero's flight was known and soldiers were sent in search for him. "All who surrounded him pressed him to save himself from the indignities which were ready to befall him. Nero then ordered a pit to be sunk before his eyes, of the size of his body, and the bottom to be covered with pieces of marble put together, if any could be found about the house; and water and wood to be got ready for immediate use about his corpse. He kept weeping and frequently saying, 'What an artist is now about to perish!' Meanwhile, when letters were brought in by a servant belonging to Phaon, he snatched them out of his hand, and there read, 'That he had been declared an enemy by the Senate, and that search was making for him, that he might be punished according to the ancient custom of the Romans.' He then inquired what kind of punishment that was; and learned that the practice was to strip the criminal naked, and scourge him to death, while his neck was fastened within a forked stake. At this Nero was so terrified that he took up two daggers which he had brought with him, and after feeling the points of both, put them up again, saying, 'The fatal hour is not yet come.' At one time he begged Sporus to begin to wail and lament; at another time he asked that one of them would set him an example by killing himself; and then again, he condemned his own want of resolution in these words, 'I yet live to my shame and disgrace: this is not becoming for Nero: it is not becoming. Thou oughtest in such circumstances to have a good heart. Come, then: courage, man!' The horsemen who had received orders to bring him away alive, were now approaching the house. As soon as he heard them coming, he uttered with a trembling voice the following verse,

'The noise of swift-heeled steeds assails my ears'[1]

and then drove a dagger into his throat, being assisted in the act by Epaphroditus, his secretary. A centurion burst in just as he was half-dead, and applied his cloak to the wound, pretending that he had come to his assistance. Nero made no other reply but this, 'It is too late': and 'Is this your loyalty?' Immediately after pronouncing these words, he expired. . . . He had requested of his attendants as the most essential favor, that they would let no one have his head, but that by all means his body might be burnt entire. And this, Icelus, Galba's freedman, granted." [2] . . .

[1] *Iliad*, x, 535.          [2] Suetonius, *Nero*, 49.

# CHAPTER XXI

## ROMAN LIFE AS SEEN IN PLINY'S LETTERS [1]

PLINY (about 61–113 A. D.), called the Younger, to distinguish him from his famous uncle, the Elder Pliny,[2] was a Roman gentleman fitted by birth and education for a brilliant public career. He filled many offices of state, traveled extensively, knew everybody worth knowing, and lived a happy, useful life, surrounded by his books and his friends. Of his letters more than three hundred have been preserved. They do not rise to a very high level as literature; Pliny's letters seem stilted and artificial when compared with the animated correspondence of Cicero. But there are few works by ancient authors which make pleasanter reading. Moreover, they afford us an attractive picture of Roman society during the most interesting period of the Early Empire.

### 103. Pliny's Wife [3]

As you [4] yourself are a model of the family virtues, as you returned the affection of your brother, who was the best of men and devoted to you, and as you love his daughter as though she was your own child, and show her not only the affection of an aunt, but even that of the father she has lost, I feel sure you will

[1] *The Letters of the Younger Pliny*, translated by J. B. Firth. 2 vols. London, 1900. Walter Scott.

[2] See page 243, note 2.

[3] Pliny, *Letters*, iv, 19.

[4] This letter was written to a lady named Hispulla, the aunt of Pliny's third wife, Calpurnia.

be delighted to know that she is proving herself worthy of her father, worthy of you, and worthy of her grandfather. She has a sharp wit, she is wonderfully economical, and she loves me dearly. . . . Moreover, owing to her fondness for me, she has developed a taste for study. She collects all my speeches, she reads them, and learns them by heart. When I am about to plead, what anxiety she shows; when the pleading is over, how pleased she is! She has relays of people to bring her news as to the reception I get, the applause I excite, and the verdicts I win from the judges. Whenever I recite, she sits near me, screened from the audience by a curtain, and her ears greedily drink in what people say to my credit. She even sings my verses and sets them to music, though she has no master to teach her but love, which is the best instructor of all. Hence, I feel perfectly assured that our mutual happiness will be lasting, and will continue to grow day by day. For she loves in me not my youth or my person — both of which are subject to gradual decay and age — but my reputation. . . .

### 104. Pliny to his Wife Calpurnia [1]

You say that you are quite distressed at my absence, and that your only solace is to embrace my writings instead of me, and constantly to put them in the place I am wont to occupy. I am glad you miss me, and glad, too, that you find comfort in such consolations. I, in my turn, continually read over your letters, and take them up again and again as though they were new ones. Yet this only makes me feel your absence the more keenly, for if your letters have such a charm for me, you can imagine how sweet I find your conversation. However, do not fail to write as often as you can, even though your letters torture as well as delight me.

### 105. A Visit to Spurinna [2]

I don't think I ever spent a more delightful time than during my recent visit at Spurinna's house. Indeed, I enjoyed myself

[1] Pliny, *Letters*, vi, 7.  [2] *Ibid.*, iii, 1.

so much that, if it is my fortune to grow old, there is no one more than Spurinna whom I should prefer to take as my model in old age, as there is nothing more methodical than that time of life.   Personally, I like to see men map out their lives with the regularity of the fixed courses of the stars, and especially old men.   While one is young, a little disorder and rush, so to speak, is not unbecoming.   But for old folks, whose days of exertion are past and in whom personal ambition is disgraceful, a placid and well-ordered life is highly suitable.   That is the principle upon which Spurinna acts most religiously.   Even trifles, or what would be trifles were they not of daily occurrence, he goes through in a fixed and regular order.

In the morning he keeps his couch; at the second hour he calls for his shoes and walks three miles, exercising mind as well as body.   If he has friends with him, the time is passed in conversation on the noblest of themes, otherwise a book is read aloud, and sometimes this is done even when his friends are present, but never in such a way as to bore them. . . . Then he sits down, and there is more reading aloud or more conversation. Afterwards he enters his carriage, taking with him either his wife or one of his friends. . . . After riding seven miles he walks another mile, then he again resumes his seat or betakes himself to his room and his pen.   For he composes, both in Latin and Greek, the most scholarly poems. . . . When he is told that the bathing hour has come—which is the ninth hour in winter and the eighth in summer — he takes a walk naked in the sun, if there is no wind.   Then he plays at ball for a long spell, throwing himself heartily into the game, for it is by means of this kind of exercise that he battles with old age.   After his bath he lies down and waits a short time before taking food, meanwhile listening to the reading of some light and pleasant book.   All this time his friends are at perfect liberty to imitate his example or do anything else they prefer.   Then dinner is served, the table being as bright as it is modest, and the silver plain and old-fashioned. . . . The dinner is often relieved by actors of comedy, so that the pleasures of the table may have a seasoning of letters. Even in the summer the meal lasts well into the night, but no one finds it long, for it is kept up with such good humor and charm.

The consequence of this mode of living is that, though Spurinna has passed his seventy-seventh year, his hearing and eyesight are as good as ever, his body is still active and alert, and the only symptom of his age is his wisdom. This is the sort of life that I have vowed and determined to forestall, and I shall enter upon it with zest as soon as my age justifies me in beating a retreat. . . .

## 106. Pliny the Elder[1]

. . . Does it surprise you that a busy man like my uncle[2] found time to finish so many volumes, many of which deal with such minute details? You will wonder the more when I tell you that for many years he pleaded in the law courts, that he died in his fifty-seventh year, and that in the interval his time was taken up and his studies were hindered by the important offices he held and the duties arising out of his friendship with the emperors. But he possessed a keen intellect; he had a marvelous capacity for work, and his powers of application were enormous. . . . He could sleep at call, and sleep would come upon him and leave him in the middle of his work. Before daybreak he would go to Vespasian[3] — for he too was a night-worker — and then set about his official duties. On his return home he would again give to study any time that he had free. Often in summer, after taking a meal, which with him was always a simple and light one, he would lie in the sun if he had any time to spare, and a book would be read aloud, from which he would take notes and extracts. He never read without taking extracts, and used to say that there never was a book so bad that was not good in some passage or

[1] Pliny, *Letters*, iii, 5.

[2] Pliny the Elder (23–79 A. D.) was the greatest scholar of his time. Among other works he published a *Natural History*, really a colossal encyclopedia of all knowledge. He perished in the eruption of Vesuvius.

[3] Emperor, 69–79 A. D.

another. After his sun bath he usually bathed in cold water, then he took a bite and a brief nap, and subsequently, as though another day had begun, he would study till dinner-time. After dinner a book would be read aloud, and he would take notes in a cursory way. I remember that one of his friends, when the reader pronounced a word wrongly, checked him and made him read it again, and my uncle said to him, "Did you not catch the meaning?" When his friend said "Yes," he remarked, "Why then did you make him turn back? We have lost more than ten lines through your interruption." So jealous was he of every moment lost. . . .

Such was the application which enabled him to compile a great number of literary works. He left me, besides, one hundred and sixty commonplace books, written on both sides of the scrolls, and in a very small handwriting, which really makes the number of the volumes considerably more. . . . So I often smile, when some of my friends call me a book-worm, for if I compare myself with him I am but a shocking idler. . . .

### 107. Treatment of Children[1]

A friend of mine was thrashing his son for spending money too lavishly in buying horses and dogs. When the youth had gone, I said to the father, "Come now, did you never commit a fault, for which your father might have reproved you? Why, of course you have. Do you not now and then still commit actions for which your son would also severely reprimand you, if your positions were suddenly changed, and he became the father and you the son? Are not all men liable to make mistakes? Does not one man indulge himself in one way and another in another?" I was so struck with this man's undue severity that I have written and told you about it, out of the affection we bear one another, so that you may never act with undue bitterness and harshness toward your son. Remember that he is a boy and that you have been a boy yourself. And in

[1] Pliny, *Letters*, ix, 12.

exercising your parental authority, do not forget that you are a man and the father of a man.

## 108. Slaves' Vengeance [1]

A shocking affair, worthy of more publicity than a letter can bestow, has befallen Largius Macedo, a man of prætorian rank, at the hands of his own slaves. He was known to be an over-bearing and cruel master, and one who forgot — or rather re-membered too keenly — that his own father had been a slave. He was bathing at his villa near Formiæ,[2] when he was sud-denly surrounded by his slaves. One seized him by the throat, another struck him on the forehead, and others smote him in the chest. . . . When they thought the breath had left his body they flung him on to the hot tiled floor to see if he was still alive. Whether he was insensible, or merely pretended to be so, he certainly did not move, and lying there at full length, he made them think that he was actually dead. At length they carried him out, as though he had been overcome by the heat, and handed him over to his more trusty servants, while his women ran shrieking and wailing to his side. Aroused by their cries and restored by the coolness of the room where he lay, he opened his eyes and moved his limbs, betraying thereby that he was still alive, as it was then safe to do so. His slaves took to flight; most of them have been captured, but some are still being hunted for. Thanks to the attentions he received, Macedo was kept alive for a few days and had the satisfaction of full vengeance before he died, for he exacted the same punishment while he still lived as is usually taken when the victim of a murder dies. You see the dangers, the affronts and insults we are exposed to, and no one can feel at all secure because he is an easy and mild-tempered master. . . .

## 109. On the Treatment of Slaves [3]

I have been greatly upset by illness in my household, some of my servants having died, and at an early age. I have two

[1] Pliny, *Letters*, iii, 14.     [2] See page 259.     [3] Pliny, *Letters*, viii, 16.

consolations, which, though they are by no means equivalent to my grief, do certainly afford me comfort. One is, that I have been generous in giving them their freedom. . . . The other is, that I allow my slaves to make, as it were, valid wills, and I preserve them as if they were strictly legal documents. My slaves lay their commissions and requests before me just as they please, and I carry them out as though I were obeying an order. They have full power to divide their property and leave donations and bequests as they will, provided that the beneficiaries are members of my household, for with slaves their master's house takes the place of commonwealth and state.

Though I have these consolations to make my mind easier, I feel shattered and broken by just that same sense of common humanity which led me to grant them these indulgences. Not that I wish I was harder of heart. I am quite aware that there are other people who call misfortunes of this kind a mere pecuniary loss, and plume themselves thereon as great men and wise. Whether they are great and wise I do not know, but they certainly are not men. The true man is sensible to pain and feeling. . . .

### 110. A Gladiatorial Show at Verona[1]

You did quite right in promising a gladiatorial display to my clients at Verona,[2] for they have long loved you, looked up to you, and honored you. You took from that city your dearly loved and most estimable wife, and you owe to her memory some public work or festival, and a gladiatorial show is most suitable for a funeral honor. Besides, as the people were so unanimous in asking for that form of entertainment, you would have appeared boorish rather than consistent had you refused. . . . I wish that the numerous African panthers you had bought had turned up by the appointed day, but it may be that they were detained by stress of weather. At any rate you have deserved the fullest credit for them, for it was not your fault that the exhibition was incomplete.

[1] Pliny, *Letters*, vi, 34.      [2] A city of Gallia Cisalpina.

### 111. The Games of the Circus[1]

I have been spending all my time here among my tablets and books, as quietly as I could wish. "How is that possible," you ask, "in Rome?" Well, the Circensian [2] games have been on, and that is a kind of spectacle which has not the slightest attraction for me. There is no novelty, no variety in it, nothing which one wants to see twice. Hence I am the more amazed that so many thousands of men should be eager, like a pack of children, to see horses running time after time, and the charioteers bending over their cars. There might be some reason for their enthusiasm if it was the speed of the horses or the skill of the drivers that was the attraction, but it is the racing-colors [3] which they favor, and the racing-colors which fire their love. . . . I really feel a sort of pleasure in the thought that what they take delight in has no charm for me. Thus it is that I have been only too glad to pass my leisure time among my books during the race-meeting, while others have been wasting their days in the most idle occupations.

### 112. Entertainments at Banquets [4]

I have received your letter in which you complain how offensive to you a really magnificent banquet was, owing to the fact that there were buffoons, dancers, and jesters going round from table to table. Ah! will you never relax that severe frown of yours, even a little? For my own part, I do not provide any such entertainments as those, but I can put up with people who do. Why then do I not provide them myself? For this reason, that if any dancer makes an improper movement, if a buffoon is impudent, or a jester makes a senseless fool of himself, it does not amuse me at all, for I see no novelty or fun in it. I am

[1] Pliny, *Letters*, ix, 6.

[2] The chariot races were held in the Circus Maximus.

[3] The chariots and horses were supplied by rival companies, each indicating its drivers by a distinguishing color. The spectators supported one or other of these colors.

[4] Pliny, *Letters*, ix, 17.

not giving you a high moral reason, but am only telling you my individual taste. Yet think how many people there are who would regard with disfavor, as partly insipid and partly wearisome, the entertainments which charm and attract you and me. When a reader, or a musician, or a comic actor enters the banqueting-room, how many there are who call for their shoes or lie back on their couches just as completely bored as you were, when you endured what you describe as those monstrosities. Let us then make allowances for what pleases other people, so that we may induce others to make allowances for us.

### 113. The Eruption of Vesuvius, 79 A.D.[1]

You say that the letter [2] which I wrote to you at your request, describing the death of my uncle,[3] has made you anxious to know not only the terrors, but also the distress I suffered while I remained behind at Misenum. I had, indeed, started to tell you of these, but then broke off. Well, though my mind shudders at the recollection, I will essay the task. . . .

For many days previous there had been slight shocks of earthquake, which were not particularly alarming, because they are common enough in Campania. But on that night the shocks were so intense that everything round us seemed not only to be disturbed, but to be tottering to its fall. My mother rushed into my bedchamber, just as I myself was getting up in order to arouse her, if she was still sleeping. We sat down in the courtyard of the house, which was of small size and lay between the sea and the buildings. . . .

It was now the first hour of the day, but the light was still faint and weak. . . . Soon a black, fearful cloud of fiery vapor descended upon the earth and . . . covered the whole

[1] Pliny, *Letters*, vi, 20.

[2] This refers to a previous letter addressed to Pliny's friend, the famous historian Tacitus.

[3] In his anxiety to study more closely the extraordinary spectacle of the eruption, Pliny the Elder ventured too near the zone of danger and perished.

bay. It encircled Capreæ[1] and hid it from sight, and we could no longer see the promontory of Misenum. Then my mother prayed, entreated, and commanded me to fly as best I could, saying that I was young and could escape, while she was old and infirm, and would not fear to die, if only she knew that she had not been the cause of my death. I replied that I would not save myself unless I could save her too, and so, after taking tight hold of her hand, I forced her to quicken her steps. She reluctantly obeyed, accusing herself for retarding my flight. Then the ashes began to fall, but not thickly. I looked back, and a dense blackness was rolling up behind us, which spread itself over the ground and followed like a torrent. "Let us turn aside," I said, "while we can still see, lest we be thrown down in the road and trampled on in the darkness by the thronging crowd."

We were considering what to do, when the blackness of night overtook us, not that of a moonless or cloudy night, but the blackness of pent-up places which never see the light. You could hear the wailing of women, the screams of little children, and the shouts of men. Some were trying to find their parents, others their children, others their wives, by calling for them and recognizing them by their voices alone. Some were commiserating their own lot, others that of their relatives, while some again prayed for death in sheer terror of dying. Many were lifting up their hands to the gods, but more were declaring that now there were no longer any gods, and that this night would last forever, and be the end of all the world. Nor were there wanting those who added to the real perils by inventing new and false terrors, for some said that part of Misenum was in ruins and the rest in flames, and though the tale was untrue, it found ready believers.

A gleam of light now appeared, which seemed to us not so much daylight as a token of the approaching fire. The latter remained at a distance, but the darkness came on again, and the ashes once more fell thickly and heavily. We had to keep rising

[1] A small island off the Bay of Naples (the modern Capri).

and shaking the latter off us, or we should have been buried by them and crushed by their weight. I might boast that not one groan or cowardly exclamation escaped my lips, despite these perils, had I not believed that I and the world were perishing together — a miserable consolation, indeed, yet one which a mortal creature finds very soothing.

At length the blackness became less dense, and dissipated, as it were, into smoke and cloud. Then came the real light of day, and the sun shone out, but as blood-red as it is wont to be at its setting. Our still trembling eyes saw that everything had been transformed, and covered with a deep layer of ashes, like snow. Making our way back to Misenum, we refreshed our bodies as best we could, and passed an anxious, troubled night, hovering between hope and fear. . . .

### 114. Pliny to Trajan regarding the Christians [1]

It is my custom, Sir, to refer to you in all cases where I do not feel sure, for who can better direct my doubts or inform my ignorance? [2] I have never been present at any legal examination of the Christians, and I do not know, therefore, what are the usual penalties passed upon them or the limits of those penalties, or how searching an inquiry should be made. . . . In the meantime, this is the plan which I have adopted in the case of those Christians who have been brought before me. I ask them if they are Christians. If they say they are, then I repeat the question a second and a third time, warning them of the penalties it entails, and if they still persist, I order them to be taken away to prison. For I do not doubt that, whatever the character of the crime may be which they confess, their pertinacity and inflexible obstinacy certainly ought to be punished. There were others who showed similar mad folly whom I reserved to be sent to Rome, as they were Roman citizens.

[1] Pliny, *Letters*, x, 98.

[2] This letter was written to the emperor Trajan, when Pliny was acting as governor of the province of Pontus and Bithynia in Asia Minor. The year was probably 111 A. D.

As is usually the way, the very fact of my taking up this question led subsequently to a great increase of accusations, and a variety of cases were brought before me. A pamphlet was issued anonymously, containing the names of a number of people. Those who denied that they were or had been Christians and called upon the gods in the usual formula, reciting the words after me, those who offered incense and wine before your image . . . all such I considered should be discharged, especially as they cursed the name of Christ. This is something, it is said, which those who are really Christians cannot be induced to do. Others, whose names were given me by an informer, first said that they were Christians and afterwards denied it, declaring that they had been but were so no longer, some of them having recanted many years before, and more than one as long as twenty years back. They all worshiped your image and the statues of the deities, and cursed the name of Christ.

But they declared that the sum of their guilt or their error only amounted to this, that on a stated day they had been accustomed to meet before daybreak and to recite a hymn among themselves to Christ, as though he was a god. They added, that so far from binding themselves by oath to commit any crime, their oath was to abstain from theft, robbery, adultery, and from breach of faith, and not to deny trust money placed in their keeping when called upon to deliver it. When this ceremony was concluded, it had been their custom to depart and meet again to take food, but it was of no special character and quite harmless, and they had ceased this practice after the edict in which, in accordance with your orders, I had forbidden all secret societies. I thought it the more necessary, therefore, to find out what truth there was in these statements by submitting two women, who were called deaconesses, to the torture, but I found nothing but a debased superstition carried to great lengths. So I postponed my examination, and immediately consulted you.

The matter seems to me worthy of your consideration, especially as there are so many people involved in the danger.

Many persons of all ages, and of both sexes alike, are being brought into peril of their lives by their accusers, and the process will go on. For the contagion of this superstition has spread, not only through the free cities, but into the villages and the rural districts, and yet it seems to me that it can be checked and set right. It is beyond doubt that the temples, which have been almost deserted, are beginning again to be thronged with worshipers, that the sacred rites which have for a long time been allowed to lapse are now being renewed, and that the food for the sacrificial victims is once more finding a sale, whereas, up to recently, a buyer was hardly to be found. From this it is easy to infer what vast numbers of people might be reclaimed, if only they were given an opportunity of repentance.

### 115. Trajan in Answer to Pliny [1]

You have adopted the proper course, my dear Pliny, in examining into the cases of those who have been denounced to you as Christians, for no hard and fast rule can be laid down to meet a question of such wide extent. The Christians are not to be hunted out. If they are brought before you and the offense is proved, they are to be punished, but with this reservation — that if anyone denies that he is a Christian and makes it clear that he is not, by offering prayers to our deities, then he is to be pardoned because of his recantation, however suspicious his past conduct may have been. But pamphlets published anonymously must not carry any weight whatever, no matter what the charge may be, for they are not only a precedent of the very worst type, but they are not in consonance with the spirit of our age.

[1] Pliny, *Letters*, x, 99.

# CHAPTER XXII

## A SATIRIST OF ROMAN SOCIETY[1]

MARTIAL (about 40–104 A. D.), the friend and contemporary of Pliny the Younger, was a satiric poet whose business it was to see only the unpleasant and evil side of Roman life. In a letter composed shortly after Martial's death, Pliny says very aptly of him, "He was a man of genius, witty and caustic, yet one who in his writings showed as much candor as he did biting wit and ability to sting."[2] Martial was the author of more than twelve hundred epigrams, each a brief poem, the concentration of satire and pointed invective. From Martial, as well as from Pliny, we can learn a great deal about Roman society during the first century of the empire.

### 116. Some "Characters" of the Capital City[3]

But a short time since, Calenus, you had not quite two millions of sesterces;[4] but you were so prodigal and open-handed and hospitable, that all your friends wished you ten millions. Heaven heard the wish and our prayers; and within, I think, six months, four deaths gave you the desired fortune. But you, as if ten millions had not been left to you, but taken from you, condemned yourself to such abstinence, wretched man, that you prepare even your most sumptuous feasts . . . at the cost of but a few dirty pieces of black coin. So we, seven of your old

---

[1] *The Epigrams of Martial translated into English Prose.* London, 1860. George Bell and Sons.

[2] *Letters*, iii, 21.

[3] Martial, *Epigrams*, i, 99; iii, 62; vi, 59; x, 31; iii, 44; xi, 56.

[4] About $100,000.

companions, stand you in just half a pound of leaden money. What blessing are we to invoke upon you worthy of such merits? We wish you, Calenus, a fortune of a hundred millions. If this falls to your lot, you will die of hunger.

Because you purchase slaves at a hundred and often two hundred thousand sesterces; because you drink wines stored in the reign of Numa;[1] because your not over-large stock of furniture cost you a million; because a pound weight of wrought silver costs you five thousand; because a golden chariot becomes yours at the price of a whole farm; because your mule cost you more than the value of a house — do you imagine that such expenses are the proof of a great mind, Quintus? You are mistaken, Quintus; they are the extravagances of a small mind.

Baccara, desirous of exhibiting his six hundred fur mantles, grieves and complains that the cold does not attack him. He prays for dark days, and wind, and snow; and hates wintry days which are at all warm. What ill, cruel mortal, have our light cloaks, which the least breath of wind may carry off our shoulders, done you? How much simpler would it be for you to wear your fur cloaks even in the month of August.

You sold a slave yesterday for the sum of thirteen hundred sesterces, in order, Calliodorus, that you might dine well once in your life. Nevertheless you did not dine well; a mullet of four pounds' weight, which you purchased, was the chief dish, the very crown of your repast. I feel inclined to exclaim, "It was not a fish, shameless fellow, it was a man, a veritable man, Calliodorus, that you ate."

Do you wish to know the reason, Ligurinus, why no one willingly meets you; why, wherever you come, everybody takes flight, and a vast solitude is left around you? You are too much of a poet. This is an extremely dangerous fault. The tigress aroused by the loss of her whelps, the viper scorched by the midday sun, or the ruthless scorpion, are objects of less terror than you. For who, I ask, could undergo such calls upon his patience as you make? You read your verses to me, whether I

[1] A legendary king of Rome, the successor of Romulus.

am standing, or sitting, or running, or about private business. I fly to the hot baths, there you din my ears. I seek the cold bath, there I cannot swim for your noise. I hasten to dinner, you stop me on my way. I sit down to dinner, you drive me from my seat. Wearied, I fall asleep, you rouse me from my couch. Do you wish to see how much evil you occasion? You, a man just, upright, and innocent, are an object of fear.

When you extol death in such extravagant terms, Stoic[1] Chæremon, you wish me to admire and respect your spirit. Such magnanimity arises from your possession of only a pitcher with a broken handle, a cheerless hearth warmed with no fire, a mat, plenty of fleas, a bare bedstead, and a short toga that serves you both night and day. How great a man you are, that can think of abandoning dregs of red vinegar, and straw, and black bread! But let your cushions swell with precious wool, and soft purple covers adorn your couches; and let a favorite share your couch, who, when mixing the wine for your guests, tortures them with the ruddiest of lips, how earnestly then will you desire to live thrice as long as Nestor[2] and study to lose no part of a single day. In adversity it is easy to despise life; the truly brave man is he who can endure to be miserable.

### 117. Some Good Advice[3]

What cause or what presumption, Sextus, brings you to Rome? What do you expect or seek here? Tell me. "I will plead causes," you say, "more eloquently than Cicero himself, and in the three forums[4] there shall be no one to equal me." Atestinus pleaded causes, and Civis; you knew both of them; but neither made enough to pay for his lodging. "If nothing is to be gained from this pursuit, I will write verses: when one has heard them, one will say they are Vergil's own." You are

[1] During the first century of the empire the Greek philosophy of Stoicism gained many adherents at Rome.

[2] An old Greek chieftain at the siege of Troy.

[3] Martial, *Epigrams*, iii, 38; x, 62; xi, 70.

[4] The old Roman Forum, that of Julius Cæsar, and that of Augustus.

mad; all that you see here shivering in threadbare cloaks are
Vergils. "I will push my way among the great." That trick
has found support for but two or three that have attempted
it, while all the rest are pale with hunger. "What shall I do?
Advise me: for I am determined to live at Rome." If you
are a good man, Sextus, you will have to live by chance.[1]

Schoolmaster, be indulgent to your simple scholars, if you
would have many a long-haired youth resort to your lectures,
and the class seated round your critical table love you. So
may no teacher of arithmetic, or of swift writing, be surrounded
by a greater ring of pupils. The days are bright and glow
under the flaming constellation of the Lion, and fervid July is
ripening the teeming harvest. Let the Scythian scourge with
its formidable thongs, such as flogged Marsyas,[2] and the
terrible cane, the schoolmaster's scepter, be laid aside, and
sleep until the Ides of October.[3] In summer, if boys preserve
their health, they do enough.

Can you, Tucca, sell these slaves whom you bought for a
hundred thousand sesterces apiece? Can you sell the weeping
despots of your affection, Tucca? Do neither their caresses
nor their words and untutored lamentations move you? If a
quantity of hard cash is your object, sell your plate, your tables,
your myrrhine vases, your estate, your house. Sell your old
slaves, sell even your hereditary lands. Sell everything, wretched
man, to avoid selling your young favorites. It was extravagance
to buy them; who denies or doubts it? But it is far greater
extravagance to sell them.

### 118. Aspects of Life at Rome and in Italy [4]

You may have a good dinner, Julius Cerealis, with me. If you
have no better engagement, come. You may keep your own

---

[1] Since only the bad man can make sure of a living at Rome.

[2] Referring to the legend that Marsyas, the satyr, having challenged
Apollo to a musical contest on the flute, and having been defeated, was
flayed alive by the god for his presumption. See page 100.

[3] Until October 15.

[4] Martial, *Epigrams*, xi, 52; i, 104; iv, 8; xii, 57; x, 30; v, 20.

hour, the eighth; we will go to the bath together; you know how near the baths of Stephanus are to my house. Lettuce will first be set before you . . . and leeks cut into shreds; next tunny-fish, full grown, and larger than the slender eel, which will be garnished with egg and leaves of rue. Nor will there be wanting eggs lightly poached, or cheese hardened on a Velabrian hearth; or olives which have experienced the cold of a Picenian winter. These ought to be sufficient to whet the appetite. Do you want to know what is to follow? I will play the braggart, to tempt you to come. There will be fish, oysters . . . well-fattened fowl; dainties which not even Stella, except on rare occasions, is used to place before his guests. I promise you still more: I will recite no verses to you; while you shall be at liberty to read to me again your *War of the Giants*, or your *Georgics*, second only to those of the immortal Vergil.

When we see the leopard wear upon his spotted neck a light and easy yoke, and the furious tigers endure with patience the blows of the whip; the stags champ the golden curbs; the African bears tamed by the bit; a boar, huge as that which Calydon[1] is said to have produced, obey the purple muzzle; the ugly buffaloes drag chariots, and the elephant, when ordered to dance nimbly, pay prompt obedience to his swarthy leader — who would not imagine such things a spectacle given by the gods? These, however, anyone who sees the condescension of the lions, which the swift-footed timorous hares fatigue in the chase, disregards as an inferior attraction. They let go the little animals, catch them again, and caress them when caught. The latter are safer in their captors' mouths than elsewhere; since the lions delight in granting them free passage through their open jaws, and in holding their teeth as with fear. They are ashamed to crush the tender prey, after having just come from slaying bulls. This clemency does not proceed from art; the lions know whom they serve.

---

[1] According to a Greek legend, the neighborhood of Calydon, in Ætolia, was once ravaged by a monstrous boar. It was finally slain by Meleager, aided by other heroes from all parts of Greece.

The first and second hours of the day exhaust the clients who pay their respects to their patrons; the third exercises the lungs of the noisy pleaders; until the fifth, Rome employs herself in various occupations; the sixth brings rest to the fatigued; the seventh closes the day's labors. The eighth suffices for the games of the oily palestra; the ninth bids us press the piled-up couches at table. The tenth is the hour for my effusions, Euphemus, when your skill is preparing ambrosial delicacies, and our excellent Cæsar [1] relaxes his cares with celestial nectar, and holds the little cups in his powerful hand. At that time give my pleasantries access to him; my muse with her free step fears to approach Jupiter in the morning.

You ask why I so often go to my small domain at arid Nomentum [2] and the humble household at my farm? There is no place in town, Sparsus, where a poor man can either think or rest. One cannot live for schoolmasters in the morning, corn grinders at night, and braziers' hammers all day and night. Here the money-changer indolently rattles piles of Nero's rough coins on his dirty counter; there a beater of Spanish gold belabors his worn stone with shining mallet. Nor does the fanatic rabble of Bellona [3] cease from its clamor, or the gabbling sailor with his piece of wreck hung over his shoulder; or the Jew boy, brought up to begging by his mother, or the blear-eyed huckster of sulphur. Who can enumerate the various interruptions to sleep at Rome? . . . You, Sparsus, are ignorant of such things, living, as you do, in luxurious ease on your Petilian domain. [4] Your mansion, though on a level plain, overlooks the lofty hills which surround it. You enjoy the country in the city, with a Roman vine-dresser, and a vintage not to be surpassed on the Falernian [5] mount. Within your own premises is a retired carriage drive; in your deep recesses sleep and repose are

---

[1] The emperor Domitian.

[2] A Sabine town, fourteen miles from Rome.

[3] Goddess of war.     [4] A villa on the Janiculum Hill.

[5] Falernian wine, from a district of northern Campania, was much prized by the Romans.

unbroken by the noise of tongues: and no daylight penetrates unless purposely admitted. But I am awakened by the laughter of the passing crowd; and all Rome is at my bedside. Whenever, overcome with weariness, I long for repose, I repair to my country-house.

O delightful shore of salubrious Formiæ![1] Apollinaris, when he flees from the city of stern Mars, and wearied lays aside his anxious cares, prefers thee to every other spot. . . . At Formiæ the surface of the ocean is but lightly crisped by the breeze; and though tranquil, is ever in motion, and bears along the painted skiff under the influence of a gale as gentle as that wafted by a maiden's fan when she is distressed by heat. Nor has the fishing-line to seek its victim far out at sea; but the fish may be seen beneath the pellucid waters, seizing the line as it drops from the chamber or the couch. Were Æolus[2] ever to send a storm, the table, still sure of its provision, might laugh at his railings. For the fish-pool protects the turbot and the pike; delicate lampreys swim up to their master; delicious mullet obey the call of the keeper, and the old carp come forth at the sound of his voice. But when does Rome permit him to partake of these enjoyments? How many days at Formiæ does the year allot to him, closely chained as he is to the pursuits of the city? Happy gate-keepers and bailiffs! These gratifications, provided for your masters, are enjoyed by you.

If you and I, dear Martialis,[3] might enjoy our days together free from care — if it rested with us to dispose of our leisure time and to spend in each other's company a life of true ease — we should know no halls or mansions of lordly patrons, or vexatious lawsuits and troubles of courts, or proud family busts. We should enjoy, instead, carriage airings, conversation, reading, the Campus Martius,[4] the shady porticoes, the Virgin water,[5]

---

[1] A famous seaside resort in Latium, south of Rome.
[2] God of the winds.    [3] Julius Martialis, a friend of the poet.
[4] The great athletic field of Rome.
[5] Water brought by an aqueduct from Præneste, twenty-three miles southeast of Rome.

the warm baths. Such places would be our constant resorts, and such our daily occupation. As it is, neither of us lives for himself, but sees his good days flee from him and vanish; days which are ever being lost to us, and set down to our account. Should anyone, then, delay to live, when he knows how?

# CHAPTER XXIII

## THE GERMANS AS DESCRIBED BY TACITUS[1]

THE historian Tacitus, a contemporary of Martial and the Younger Pliny, was the author of a valuable treatise on the Germans. His little book, published in 98 A. D., gives us the first connected account of those blue-eyed, fair-haired barbarians whose inroads three hundred years after Tacitus were to break up the Roman Empire. The student should not forget, however, that during this time the German tribes along the Roman frontier had made considerable progress towards civilization. The statements of Tacitus do not quite accurately describe their condition at the close of the fourth century A. D. Moreover, there is no evidence that Tacitus had ever traveled in Germany and had observed the Germans at first-hand. His work is compiled from earlier Roman writings which have not come down to us.

### 119. Land and People[2]

For my own part, I agree with those who think that the tribes of Germany are free from all taint of intermarriages with foreign nations, and that they appear as a distinct, unmixed race, like none but themselves. Hence, too, the same physical peculiarities throughout so vast a population. All have fierce blue eyes, red hair, and huge frames, fit only for a sudden exertion. They are less able to bear laborious work. Heat and

---

[1] *The Agricola and Germany of Tacitus and the Dialogue on Oratory*, translated by A. J. Church and W. J. Brodribb. 2d edition. London, 1877. Macmillan and Co.     [2] Tacitus, *Germany*, 4–5, 16, 26.

thirst they cannot in the least endure; to cold and hunger their climate and their soil inure them.

Their country, though somewhat varied in appearance, yet generally either bristles with forests or reeks with swamps. . . . It is productive of grain, but unfavorable to fruit-bearing trees. It is rich in flocks and herds, but these are for the most part undersized, and even the cattle have not their usual beauty or noble head. Their number is chiefly regarded; they are the most highly prized, indeed the only, riches of the people. Silver and gold the gods have refused to them, whether in kindness or in anger I cannot say. . . . They care but little to possess or use them. You may see among them vessels of silver, which have been presented to their envoys and chieftains, held as cheap as those of clay. The border population, however, value gold and silver for their commercial utility, and are familiar with, and show a preference for, some of our coins. The tribes of the interior use the simpler and more ancient practice of the barter of commodities. . . .

It is well known that the nations of Germany have no cities, and that they do not even tolerate closely contiguous dwellings. They live scattered and apart, just as a spring, a meadow, or a wood has attracted them. Their villages they do not arrange in our fashion, with the buildings connected and joined together. Every person surrounds his dwelling with an open space, either as a precaution against the disasters of fire, or because they do not know how to build. No use is made by them of stone or tile; they employ timber for all purposes, rude masses without ornament or attractiveness. Some parts of their buildings they stain more carefully with a clay so clear and bright that it resembles painting. They are wont also to dig out subterranean caves, and pile on them great heaps of dung, as a shelter from winter and as a receptacle for the year's produce. By such means they lessen the rigor of the cold. And should an enemy approach, he lays waste the open country, while what is hidden and buried is either not known to exist, or else escapes him from the very fact that it has to be searched for. . . .

Land proportioned to the number of inhabitants is occupied by the whole community in turn, and afterwards divided among them according to rank. A wide expanse of plains makes the partition easy. They till fresh fields every year, and yet have more than enough land. Because of the richness and extent of their soil, they do not laboriously exert themselves in planting orchards, inclosing meadows, and watering gardens. Grain is the only produce required from the earth; hence even the year itself is not divided by them into as many seasons as with us. Winter, spring, and summer have both a meaning and a name; the name and blessings of autumn are alike unknown.

## 120. Government [1]

They choose their kings by birth, their generals for merit. These kings have not unlimited or arbitrary power, and the generals do more by example than by authority. If they are energetic, if they are conspicuous, if they fight in the front, they lead because they are admired. . . . They also carry with them into battle certain figures and images taken from their sacred groves. And what most stimulates their courage is that their squadrons or battalions, instead of being formed by chance or by a fortuitous gathering, are composed of families and clans.[2] Close by them, too, are those dearest to them, so that they hear the shrieks of women, the cries of infants. *They* are to every man the most sacred witnesses of his bravery — *they* are his most generous applauders. The soldier brings his wounds to mother and wife, who shrink not from counting or even demanding them, and who administer both food and encouragement to the combatants. . . .

About minor matters the chiefs deliberate, about the more important the whole tribe. Yet even when the final decision rests with the people, the affair is always thoroughly discussed by the chiefs. They assemble, except in the case of a sudden emergency, on certain fixed days, either at new or at full moon;

---

[1] Tacitus, *Germany*, 7, 11–12.     [2] Groups of related families.

for this they consider the most auspicious season for the trans-action of business. . . . When the multitude think proper, they sit down armed.  Silence is proclaimed by the priests, who have on these occasions the right of keeping order.  Then the king or the chief, according to age, birth, distinction in war, or elo-quence, is heard, more because he has influence to persuade than because he has power to command.  If his sentiments displease them, they reject them with murmurs; if they are satisfied, they brandish their spears.  The most complimentary form of assent is to express approbation with their weapons. . . .

Penalties are distinguished according to the offense.  Traitors and deserters are hanged on trees, the coward, the unwarlike, the man stained with abominable vices, is plunged into the mire of the morass, with a hurdle put over him.[1]  This distinction in punishment means that crime, they think, ought to be pub-licly exposed, while infamy ought to be buried out of sight. Lighter offenses, too, have penalties proportioned to them; he who is convicted is fined a certain number of horses or of cattle. Half of the fine is paid to the king or to the state, half to the man whose wrongs are avenged and to his relatives. . . .

### 121. Religion [2]

. . . The Germans do not consider it consistent with the grandeur of celestial beings to confine the gods within walls, or to liken them to the form of any human countenance.  They consecrate woods and groves, and they apply the names of deities to the abstractions which they see only in spiritual worship.

Augury and divination by lot no people cultivate more dili-gently. . . . They are also familiar with the practice of consulting the notes and the flight of birds.  It is peculiar to this people to seek omens and monitions from horses. . . . White horses, pure from the taint of earthly labor, are yoked to a sacred car, and accompanied by the priest and the king, or chief of the tribe,

[1] The hurdle, filled with stones to cause it to sink, was placed over the head of the offender.          [2] Tacitus, *Germany*, 9-10.

who note their neighings and snortings. . . . They have also another method of observing auspices, by which they seek to learn the result of an important war. Having taken a prisoner from the tribe with whom they are at enmity, they pit him against a picked man of their own tribe, each combatant using the weapons of his country. The victory of the one or the other is accepted as an indication of the issue.

## 122. Military Customs [1]

. . . Their line of battle is drawn up in a wedge-like formation. To give ground, provided you return to the attack, is considered prudence rather than cowardice. The bodies of their slain they carry off even in indecisive engagements. To abandon your shield is the basest of crimes; nor may a man thus disgraced be present at the sacred rites, or enter their council. Many, indeed, after escaping from battle, have ended their infamy with the halter. . . .

Young men attach themselves to warriors of mature strength and of long approved valor and become their followers. These followers vie keenly with each other as to who shall rank first with his chiefs; the chiefs vie with each other as to who shall have the most numerous and the bravest followers. It is an honor as well as a source of strength to be thus always surrounded by a large body of picked youths; it is an ornament in peace and a defense in war. . . .

When they go into battle, it is a disgrace for the chief to be surpassed in valor, a disgrace for his followers not to equal the valor of the chief. It is an infamy and a reproach for life to have survived the chief. To defend him, to protect him, to ascribe one's own brave deeds to his renown, is the height of loyalty. The chief fights for victory; his vassals fight for their chief. . . . Feasts and entertainments, which, though inelegant, are plentifully furnished, are their only pay. The means of this bounty come from war and rapine. Nor are they as easily persuaded to plough the earth and to wait for the year's produce as to

[1] Tacitus, *Germany*, 6, 13-14.

challenge an enemy and earn the honor of wounds. Nay, they actually think it tame and stupid to acquire by the sweat of toil what they might win by their blood.

### 123. Domestic Relations [1]

Their marriage code is strict, and indeed no part of their manners is more praiseworthy. Almost alone among barbarians they are content with one wife. . . . The wife does not bring a dower to the husband, but the husband to the wife. . . .

With their virtue protected they live uncorrupted by the allurements of public shows or the stimulant of feastings. . . . No one in Germany laughs at vice, or do they call it the fashion to corrupt and to be corrupted. . . . To limit the number of their children or to destroy any of their subsequent offspring is accounted infamous, and good habits are here more effectual than good laws elsewhere.[2]

In every household the children, naked and filthy, grow up with those stout frames and limbs which we so much admire. Every mother suckles her own offspring, and never intrusts it to servants and nurses. The master is not distinguished from the slave by being brought up with greater delicacy. Both live amid the same flocks and lie on the same ground, till the freeborn are distinguished by age and recognized by merit. The young men marry late, and their vigor is thus unimpaired. Nor are the maidens hurried into marriage; the same age and a similar stature is required. Well-matched and vigorous they wed, and the offspring reproduce the strength of the parents. . . .

### 124. Private and Social Life [3]

Whenever they are not fighting, they pass much of their time in the chase, and still more in idleness, giving themselves up to

---

[1] Tacitus, *Germany*, 18–20.

[2] It is probable that in this description Tacitus presents a somewhat idealized picture of the family life and domestic virtues of the early Germans, to heighten the contrast with the deplorable state of social morality at Rome.     [3] Tacitus, *Germany*, 15, 17, 21–24, 27.

sleep and to feasting. Thus the bravest and the most warlike do nothing. They surrender the management of the household, of the home, and of the land, to the women, the old men, and all the weakest members of the family. . . .

They all wrap themselves in a cloak which is fastened with a clasp, or, if this is not forthcoming, with a thorn, leaving the rest of their persons bare. . . .

No nation indulges more profusely in entertainments and hospitality. To exclude any human being from their roof is thought impious; every German, according to his means, receives his guest with a well-furnished table. When his supplies are exhausted, he who was just now the host becomes the guide and companion to further hospitality, and without invitation they go to the next house. It matters not; they are entertained with like cordiality. . . .

On waking from sleep, which they generally prolong to a late hour of the day, they have a bath, oftenest of warm water, which suits a country where winter is the longest of the seasons. After their bath they take their meal, each having a separate seat and table of his own. Then they go armed to business, or no less often to their festal meetings. To pass an entire day and night in drinking disgraces no one. . . .

A liquor for drinking is made out of barley or other grain, and fermented into a certain resemblance to wine.[2] The dwellers on the river-bank also buy wine. Their food is of a simple kind, consisting of wild fruit, fresh game, and curdled milk. They satisfy their hunger without elaborate preparation and without delicacies. In quenching their thirst they are not equally moderate. If you indulge their love of drinking by supplying them with as much as they desire, they will be overcome by their own vices as easily as by the arms of an enemy.

One and the same kind of spectacle is always exhibited at every gathering. Naked youths who practice the sport bound in the dance amid swords and lances that threaten their lives. Experience gives them skill, and skill again gives grace. Profit

[1] The liquor referred to is beer.

or pay is out of the question; however reckless their pastime, the reward is the pleasure of the spectators. Strangely enough, they make games of hazard a serious occupation even when sober. So venturesome are they about gaining or losing, that, when every other resource has failed, on the last and final throw they stake the freedom of their own persons. The loser goes into voluntary slavery; though the younger and stronger, he suffers himself to be bound and sold. Such is their stubborn persistency in a bad custom; they themselves call it honor. Slaves of this kind the owners part with in the way of commerce, to relieve themselves also from the scandal of such a victory. . . .

In their funerals there is no pomp; they simply observe the custom of burning the bodies of illustrious men with certain kinds of wood. They do not heap garments or spices on the funeral pile. The arms of the dead man, and in some cases his horse, are consigned to the fire. A turf mound forms the tomb. Monuments with their lofty and elaborate splendor they reject as oppressive to the dead. Tears and lamentations they soon dismiss; grief and sorrow but slowly. It is thought becoming for women to bewail, for men to remember, the dead. . . .

# INDEX AND PRONOUNCING VOCABULARY

NOTE. — The pronunciation of all proper names is indicated either by a simplified spelling or by their accentuation and division into syllables. The diacritical marks employed are those found in Webster's *New International Dictionary* and are the following:

ā as in āle.
ă " " senăte.
â " " câre.
ă " " ăm.
ȧ " " ȧccount.
ä " " ärm.
å " " åsk.
ȧ " " sofȧ.
ē " " ēve.
ê " " êvent.
ĕ " " ĕnd.
ĕ " " recĕnt.
ẽ " " makẽr.
ī " " īce.
ĭ " " ĭll.

ō as in ōld.
ŏ " " ŏbey.
ô " " ôrb.
ŏ " " ŏdd.
ŏ " " sŏft.
ŏ " " cŏnnect.
ū " " ūse.
ū " " ūnite.
û " " ûrn.
ŭ " " ŭp.
ŭ " " circŭs.
ü " " menü.
ōō as in fōōd.
ŏŏ " " fŏŏt.
ou " " out.

oi as in oil.
ch " " chair.
g " " go.
ng " " sing.
ŋ " " iŋk.
t̶h̶ " " t̶h̶en.
th " " thin.
tu " " natu̱re.
du " " verdu̱re.
ᴋ for ch as in Ger. ich, ach.
ɴ as in Fr. bon.
y " " yet.
zh for z as in azure.

---